I0015057

SAP® ABAP
List Viewer (ALV) —
A Practical Guide for
ABAP Developers

Kathi Kones

Thank you for purchasing this book from Espresso Tutorials!

Like a cup of espresso coffee, Espresso Tutorials SAP books are concise and effective. We know that your time is valuable and we deliver information in a succinct and straightforward manner. It only takes our readers a short amount of time to consume SAP concepts. Our books are well recognized in the industry for leveraging tutorial-style instruction and videos to show you step by step how to successfully work with SAP.

Check out our YouTube channel to watch our videos at *https://www.youtube.com/user/EspressoTutorials*.

If you are interested in SAP Finance and Controlling, join us at *http://www.fico-forum.com/forum2/* to get your SAP questions answered and contribute to discussions.

Related titles from Espresso Tutorials:

- ▶ Boris Rubarth: First Steps in ABAP®
  http://5015.espresso-tutorials.com

- ▶ Antje Kunz: SAP® Legacy System Migration Workbench (LSMW)
  http://5051.espresso-tutorials.com

- ▶ Darren Hague: Universal Worklist with SAP NetWeaver® Portal
  http://5076.espresso-tutorials.com/

- ▶ Michal Krawczyk: SAP® SOA Integration
  http://5077.espresso-tutorials.com

- ▶ Shreekant Shiralkar & Deepak Sawant: SAP® BW Performance Optimization
  http://5102.espresso-tutorials.com

- ▶ Dominique Alfermann, Stefan Hartmann, Benedikt Engel: SAP® HANA Advanced Modeling
  http://4110.espresso-tutorials.com

LEARN SAP ANYTIME,
ANYWHERE, AND ON ANY
DEVICE

The SAP eBook Library
for companies

Provide effective SAP training for your team
without travel costs and external trainers

▸ 150+ eBooks and video tutorials

▸ Regularly updated with
  new content

▸ Access via web browser or app
  (iOS/Android)

▸ Pricing based on number of users

Try a free 7-day, no obligation trial:
http://free.espresso-tutorials.com

Get a quote for your team today:
http://company.espresso-tutorials.com

Kathi Kones
SAP ABAP List Viewer (ALV)—A Practical Guide for ABAP Developers

ISBN: 978-1-5334-3846-1

Editor: Lisa Jackson

Cover Design: Philip Esch, Martin Munzel

Cover Photo: Fotolia #71513853 © polygraphus

Interior Design: Johann-Christian Hanke

All rights reserved.

2nd Edition 2016, 2nd print 2019, Gleichen

© 2019 by Espresso Tutorials GmbH

URL: *www.espresso-tutorials.com*

All rights reserved. Neither this publication nor any part of it may be copied or reproduced in any form or by any means or translated into another language without the prior consent of Espresso Tutorials GmbH, Zum Gelenberg 11, 37130 Gleichen, Germany.

Espresso Tutorials makes no warranties or representations with respect to the content hereof and specifically disclaims any implied warranties of merchantability or fitness for any particular purpose. Espresso Tutorials assumes no responsibility for any errors that may appear in this publication.

Feedback
We greatly appreciate any kind of feedback you have concerning this book. Please e-mail us at *info@espresso-tutorials.com*.

Table of Contents

Preface

SAP List Viewer (ALV) for ABAP Developers provides examples of two techniques used to display business data with an interface that lets users rearrange, sort, total, and download the data. The techniques are:

- ▶ A newer object-oriented ALV control framework
- ▶ An older ALV function module (FM) REUSE_ALV_GRID_DISPLAY.

(ALV is an acronym for **SAP List Viewer**, carried over from the former name, **ABAP List Viewer**.)

Both of these techniques can be found in custom ALV programs, especially at companies that have run SAP software for many years.

As a developer, you should use object-oriented techniques for new programs, but you sometimes find yourself tasked with modifying legacy ALV programs that use function module techniques. The function module examples are provided here to help you quickly modify legacy ALV programs when work prioritization, time, or cost prevents a re-write.

The alternating presentation of the two techniques in chapters 4, 5, 6, and 8 facilitates comparison. Information common to both techniques is found at the beginning of sub-chapters or is repeated, in context, in both technique sections. Figures relevant to the ALV control framework are denoted by **CF**. Figures relevant to the function module technique are denoted by **FM**.

You should focus on the ALV control framework examples when working through the training scenario.

- ▶ Chapter 3 covers writing a basic ALV program
- ▶ Chapter 4 shows how to add layout features
- ▶ Chapter 5 covers adding sorting and grouping features
- ▶ Chapter 6 highlights adding more features, such as events and layout variant handling
- ▶ Chapter 8 covers adding editable fields

Coding style varies from person to person, and personal experience influences the inevitable tradeoff decisions you make when you write a program. The examples in this book will guide you, but should not limit you to a single solution. (The training scenario requirements will not match your own, but provide options that can be adapted.)

Developers who wish to code and run the programs shown in this book will need developer access to an SAP ECC environment that contains the SAP Flight Application sample data. Those who don't have access at work or school can research other options available from the SAP Store (*https://www.store.sap.com*) or from a provider of SAP Internet Demonstration and Evaluation Systems (IDES). If the SAP Flight Application is not loaded, contact your Basis or IDES support personnel.

Familiarity with SAP navigation and ABAP development tools such as the editor and debugger is assumed, but developers without ABAP experience or access will most likely be able to follow the examples in the book to learn the concepts.

The naming convention for the ABAPs used in this book begin with this pattern:

1. Z (SAP standard for custom ABAP programs)

2. KK (my initials, some companies use a mnemonic for the application area such as FI or SD or follow another convention)

3. _CTRLFW or _FM (to differentiate the ALV control framework program examples from the function module program examples)

System variables are denoted SYST- and SY-. Both versions are acceptable and interchangeable in the exercises.

We have added a few icons to highlight important information. These include:

Tips	
	Tips highlight information concerning more details about the subject being described and/or additional background information.

Attention

Attention notices draw attention to information that you should be aware of when you go through the examples from this book on your own.

Finally, a note concerning the copyright: all screenshots printed in this book are the copyright of SAP SE. All rights are reserved by SAP SE. Copyright pertains to all SAP images in this publication. For simplification, we will not mention this specifically underneath every screenshot.

1 SAP List Viewer (ALV) types

The SAP List Viewer, also known as ALV, allows developers to display business data together with a set of functions that are presented in an easy-to-use interface. It has evolved over time, reflecting changes in software engineering design theory.

In 1972, German company SAP was formed. Over time, the SAP development environment changed to the mainframe-based R/2 platform (keyboard centric and text based), then to the client-server R/3 platform (graphical displays and mouse-aware screens). New development tools and techniques arrived with the introduction of SAP NetWeaver. Today, companies are looking closely at SAP S/4HANA, a revolutionary software platform for in-memory computing.

An SAP developer is exposed to much change during a career, but much remains familiar. Older techniques remain functional in many cases, even when new techniques are introduced.

New developers may be confused by the variety of options, not realizing that they are viewing decades of progress. The appearance of the output has changed little over time, but the code and the structures used by developers have changed. Let's take a look at the evolution of ALV.

1.1 ALV predecessors

1.1.1 Standard lists

Standard lists were the norm for reporting for many years (Figure 1.1). Developers used WRITE statements to output the data to screen and/or paper. They could add logic to sum amounts at control breaks and to print page headers or footers. Line-processing and hotspot-branching logic could be added for online users, if needed.

Developers had to consider page width limitations and take care to provide enough space so that truncation of large numbers did not occur. Standard lists were particularly well-suited for audit reports and for reports distributed via a third-party output management system that needed predefined header regions to determine printer destinations.

Standard List

Nbr	Agency	ID	Conn	Date	BookNbr	Amount	Curr
00000102	Hot Socks Travel	AZ	0789	02/01/2012	00009659	1,469.88	AUD
00000102	Hot Socks Travel	AZ	0789	02/01/2012	00009699	696.26	AUD
00000102	Hot Socks Travel	AZ	0789	02/01/2012	00009729	696.26	AUD
00000102	Hot Socks Travel	AZ	0789	02/01/2012	00009751	750.41	AUD
00000107	Ben McCloskey Ltd.	AZ	0789	02/01/2012	00009653	1,277.92	GBP
00000107	Ben McCloskey Ltd.	AZ	0789	02/01/2012	00009757	575.06	GBP
00000109	Kangeroos	AZ	0789	02/01/2012	00009656	1,214.02	GBP
00000109	Kangeroos	AZ	0789	02/01/2012	00009684	638.96	GBP
00000112	Super Agency	AZ	0789	02/01/2012	00009702	607.01	GBP
00000123	Aussie Travel	AZ	0789	02/01/2012	00009760	638.96	GBP
00000295	The Ultimate Answer	AZ	0789	02/01/2012	00009671	638.96	GBP
00000295	The Ultimate Answer	AZ	0789	02/01/2012	00009730	607.01	GBP
00000295	The Ultimate Answer	AZ	0789	02/01/2012	00009771	638.96	GBP

Figure 1.1: Standard list

1.1.2 Dialog-oriented programs

Dialog-oriented programs may use module pools, table control functionality, and screen flow logic to provide interactive data displays (Figure 1.2). The developer writes the logic for each toolbar button and screen transfer and keeps the internal table content synchronized with the screen view.

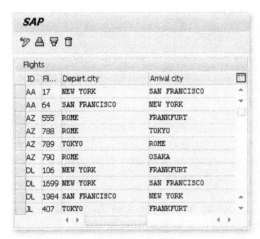

Figure 1.2: Dialog output using table control

1.2   Function module techniques

1.2.1   ALV list display function modules

Developers began using the REUSE_ALV_LIST_DISPLAY function module to simplify the coding of interactive reports (Figure 1.3). The report itself was similar to a standard list, but the buttons were backed with pre-programmed logic and gave users more opportunity to customize and extract the output. Though released only for internal use by SAP, some developers wrote programs that called the REUSE_ALV_LIST* function modules.

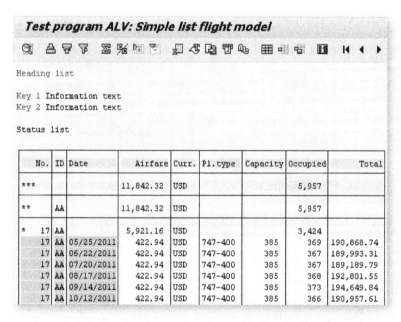

Figure 1.3: ALV list using function module

1.2.2   ALV grid display function modules

A step forward in graphical appearance is evident with the RE-USE_ALV_GRID_DISPLAY function module (Figure 1.4). Pre-programmed buttons made the use of the REUSE_ALV_GRID_* function modules very attractive despite their status of not being released for customer use.

Airline	No.	Flight Date	Airfare	Curr.	Plane Type	Capacity	Occupied	Total	Capacity	Occupied	Capacity	Occupied
AA	17	05/25/2011	422.94	USD	747-400	385	369	190,868.74	31	31	21	19
AA	17	06/22/2011	422.94	USD	747-400	385	367	189,993.31	31	30	21	20
AA	17	07/20/2011	422.94	USD	747-400	385	367	189,189.79	31	28	21	21
AA	17	08/17/2011	422.94	USD	747-400	385	368	192,801.55	31	30	21	21
AA	17	09/14/2011	422.94	USD	747-400	385	373	194,649.84	31	31	21	21
AA	17	10/12/2011	422.94	USD	747-400	385	366	190,957.61	31	30	21	21

Figure 1.4: ALV grid using function module

1.3 Object-oriented techniques

1.3.1 ALV control framework

The application of object-oriented concepts resulted in the ALV control framework, also called grid control (Figure 1.5). The ALV control framework was similar enough to function-module ALVs that it served as a good introduction to object-oriented programming. Developers used classes and methods instead of function modules and gained knowledge of syntax and navigation that they could apply later to non-ALV development efforts.

SAP

Airline	No.	Flight Date	Airfare	Curr.	Plane Type	Capacity	Occupied	Total	Capacity	Occupied	Capacity	Occupied
AA	17	05/25/2011	422.94	USD	747-400	385	369	190,868.74	31	31	21	19
AA	17	06/22/2011	422.94	USD	747-400	385	367	189,993.31	31	30	21	20
AA	17	07/20/2011	422.94	USD	747-400	385	367	189,189.79	31	28	21	21
AA	17	08/17/2011	422.94	USD	747-400	385	368	192,801.55	31	30	21	21
AA	17	09/14/2011	422.94	USD	747-400	385	373	194,649.84	31	31	21	21
AA	17	10/12/2011	422.94	USD	747-400	385	366	190,957.61	31	30	21	21

Figure 1.5: Output using ALV control framework

1.3.2 ALV object model

SAP has provided a more mature object-oriented ALV technique based on SALV classes called ALV object model, also described as an "ALV wrapper" (Figure 1.6).

ALV Object Model

Agency No.	Travel agency name	Currency	Airline	Flight No.	Flight Date	Book. no.	Amount	Currency	Airline	Amount	Currency
102	Hot Socks Travel	AUD	AZ	789	02/01/2012	9659	1,469.88	AUD	Alitalia	1,957.00	EUR
102	Hot Socks Travel	AUD	AZ	789	02/01/2012	9699	696.26	AUD	Alitalia	927.00	EUR
102	Hot Socks Travel	AUD	AZ	789	02/01/2012	9729	696.26	AUD	Alitalia	927.00	EUR
102	Hot Socks Travel	AUD	AZ	789	02/01/2012	9751	750.41	AUD	Alitalia	999.10	EUR
107	Ben McCloskey Ltd.	GBP	AZ	789	02/01/2012	9653	1,277.92	GBP	Alitalia	2,060.00	EUR
107	Ben McCloskey Ltd.	GBP	AZ	789	02/01/2012	9757	575.06	GBP	Alitalia	927.00	EUR
109	Kangeroos	GBP	AZ	789	02/01/2012	9656	1,214.02	GBP	Alitalia	1,957.00	EUR
109	Kangeroos	GBP	AZ	789	02/01/2012	9684	638.96	GBP	Alitalia	1,030.00	EUR
112	Super Agency	GBP	AZ	789	02/01/2012	9702	607.01	GBP	Alitalia	978.50	EUR
123	Aussie Travel	GBP	AZ	789	02/01/2012	9760	638.96	GBP	Alitalia	1,030.00	EUR
295	The Ultimate Answer	GBP	AZ	789	02/01/2012	9671	638.96	GBP	Alitalia	1,030.00	EUR

Figure 1.6: Output using ALV object model

1.3.3   ALV with integrated data access

SAP S/4HANA has its own ALV functionality for customers wishing to use it (Figure 1.7). It is called ALV with integrated data access (IDA), and it permits you to provide the familiar ALV interface to users when displaying in-memory data.

IDA ALV Sample: Simplest Example - show data with one line of code

ID	No.	Flight Date	Airfare	Cu	Pl.type	Capac	Occupi	Total	Capac	Occupi	Capac	Occupi
AA	17	05/25/2011	422.94	USD	747-400	385	369	190,868.74	31	31	21	19
AA	17	06/22/2011	422.94	USD	747-400	385	367	189,993.31	31	30	21	20
AA	17	07/20/2011	422.94	USD	747-400	385	367	189,189.79	31	28	21	21
AA	17	08/17/2011	422.94	USD	747-400	385	368	192,801.55	31	30	21	21
AA	17	09/14/2011	422.94	USD	747-400	385	373	194,649.84	31	31	21	21
AA	17	10/12/2011	422.94	USD	747-400	385	366	190,957.61	31	30	21	21

Figure 1.7: Output using ALV with integrated data access (IDA)

1.4   Web Dynpro

SAP List Viewer for Web Dynpro is available for ABAP and Java platforms.

1.5 Summary

Business users have gained more flexibility when displaying and extracting data. Developers have gained more powerful, re-usable tools that continue to evolve.

Be aware that the two ALV function module techniques described in Chapter 1.2 are not released by SAP for customer use. The ALV grid display function module examples are included in this book to help you make the connection between a technique you may already know and the objects-based technology you may be learning. These examples may also help you modify a legacy ALV program that uses one of the function module techniques when a re-write isn't possible.

The SAP Community Network forums contain many questions across all the ALV techniques. The responses are sometimes accurate for the ALV technique the poster is using, but sometimes they are not. Because of similarities in the ALV techniques, however, a wrong answer can sometimes be helpful—if you know how to "transpose" it to your technique. (For instance, an incorrect response of COLWIDTH-OPTIMIZE might lead you to CWIDTH_OPT in your ALV layout structure.)

Key points:

▶ New tools and techniques for SAP report development have been introduced over time.

▶ Older techniques often continue to function (to reduce the impact upon existing programs) and are still appropriate for some situations. This concept is called *backwards compatibility*.

▶ For new SAP List Viewer programs, avoid using the unsupported, "not released" function module techniques. Instead, use ABAP objects techniques such as ALV control framework.

For more information about these techniques, including how to find SAP-provided sample programs, refer to the Appendix.

2 Writing an ALV program using function modules

In this chapter, you'll learn how to write a report using an ALV function module technique, specifically, the REUSE_ALV_GRID_DISPLAY function module. For the training scenario, you'll retrieve data from the SAP Flight Application tables in order to evaluate the amount of income that various travel agencies have generated booking airline flights. The retrieved data will include two currency amounts and three currency keys.

2.1 Create the ABAP program

A preview of the ALV output from this initial program is shown in Figure 2.1.

ALV Function Module (Start)

Agency...	Travel agency name	Curr...	ID	No.	Flight Date	Booking	Amount (for.currency)	Curr.	Airline	Amount (loc.currncy)	Curr.
123	Aussie Travel	GBP	AA	17	05/25/2011	113	243.09	GBP	American Airlines	359.50	USD
123	Aussie Travel	GBP	AA	17	05/25/2011	230	285.98	GBP	American Airlines	422.94	USD
123	Aussie Travel	GBP	AA	17	05/25/2011	265	271.68	GBP	American Airlines	401.79	USD
123	Aussie Travel	GBP	AA	17	05/25/2011	270	271.68	GBP	American Airlines	401.79	USD
123	Aussie Travel	GBP	AA	17	05/25/2011	279	285.98	GBP	American Airlines	422.94	USD
123	Aussie Travel	GBP	AA	17	05/25/2011	394	285.98	GBP	American Airlines	422.94	USD

Figure 2.1: Preview (function module – FM)

Using transaction code se38 (or se80, if you prefer), type a name for the new program, then click on the CREATE button. (I have used the name ZKK_ALV_FM for this initial program.) Complete the TYPE and STATUS fields (Figure 2.2), then click on the SAVE button. When prompted for the Package, click on the LOCAL OBJECT button. This fills the Package field with $TMP and positions your cursor in the new program.

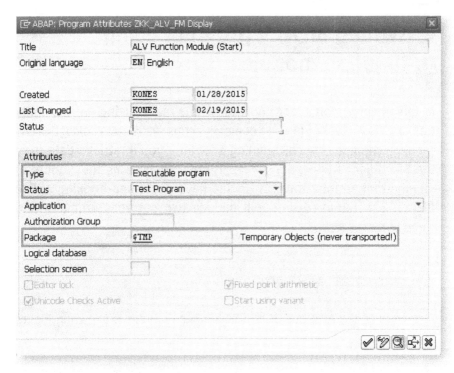

Figure 2.2: Program attributes (FM)

2.2 Data declarations

As shown in Figure 2.3, begin the data declarations section of the program by listing the database tables used in the SELECT-OPTIONS statement: SBOOK and STRAVELAG (Figure 2.4). This will prevent a syntax error.

A local *TYPE* called LTY_OUTPUT lists the fields to be displayed in this ALV. A single-line structure and matching internal tables (GS_OUTPUT and GT_OUTPUT) are declared next, based on the local TYPE LTY_OUTPUT.

```
REPORT zkk_alv_fm NO STANDARD PAGE HEADING.

TABLES: sbook,                              "bookings
        stravelag.                          "travel agencies

TYPES: BEGIN OF lty_output,
         agencynum TYPE stravelag-agencynum, "agency number
         name      TYPE stravelag-name,      "agency name
         currency  TYPE stravelag-currency,  "agency currency
         carrid    TYPE sbook-carrid,        "booked carrier
         connid    TYPE sbook-connid,        "booked connection
         fldate    TYPE sbook-fldate,        "booked date
         bookid    TYPE sbook-bookid,        "booking ID
         forcuram  TYPE sbook-forcuram,      "price in foreign currency
         forcurkey TYPE sbook-forcurkey,     "foreign currency key
         carrname  TYPE scarr-carrname,      "carrier name
         loccuram  TYPE sbook-loccuram,      "price in airline curr
         loccurkey TYPE sbook-loccurkey,     "local currency of airline
       END OF lty_output.

DATA: gs_output    TYPE lty_output,          "local structure (line)
      gt_output    TYPE STANDARD TABLE OF lty_output,
      gt_fieldcat  TYPE slis_t_fieldcat_alv.

DATA: gv_lines TYPE i.
```

Figure 2.3: Data declarations (FM)

Local TYPE vs. data dictionary structure

 Instead of defining your output structure as a local TYPE in your program, you can define it as a structure in the data dictionary. The technique you use may depend upon your employer's or client's standards and practices, the number of changes you expect to make over time to the output structure, and the ease of making those changes.

Currency keys

 Some types of data require a "partner" field for clarity—for instance, currency amounts require currency keys, count and weight amounts require units of measure, and texts that can be stored in multiple languages require language keys. To facilitate troubleshooting and flexibility, we will provide all of the applicable currency keys in the ALV interface. In Chapter 6.1, you will see how you can hide fields on initial display of the ALV.

Referring again to Figure 2.3, you'll see a global table called GT_FIELDCAT. The *field catalog table* is used to pass information (such as output length or data type) about the fields included in the output structure.

Field catalog table (SLIS_T_FIELDCAT_ALV)

 The field catalog table contains information about each of the fields (or columns) in the ALV output. If your structure is not already defined in the data dictionary, you will need to populate this information into the field catalog table yourself. You will see later in this chapter, though, that you can refer to metadata in the data dictionary when populating your field catalog table.

The final data item declared in this simple program is a global variable GV_LINES that will be used to verify that records were found for display using the ALV interface.

2.3   Select-Options

After the data declarations, type three SELECT-OPTIONS as shown in Figure 2.4. Save, check, and activate your program.

```
SELECT-OPTIONS: s_agnum FOR stravelag-agencynum DEFAULT '123',
                s_carid FOR sbook-carrid,
                s_fldat FOR sbook-fldate.
```

Figure 2.4: Selection-options declaration (FM)

Change the SELECT-OPTIONS labels that will be displayed to the user from question marks to the texts stored in the data dictionary by using the menu path GOTO • TEXT ELEMENTS • SELECTION TEXTS. Check the checkboxes (Figure 2.5). Activate the selection texts, then go back to your program source code.

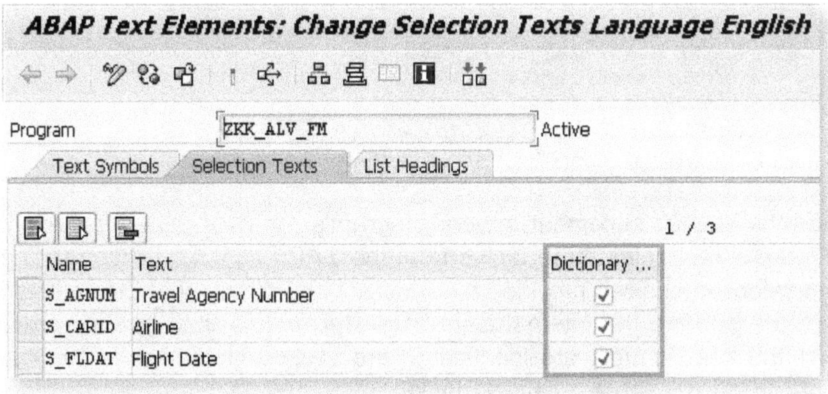

Figure 2.5: Copying selection texts from the data dictionary (FM)

The selection screen should look like Figure 2.6 when done.

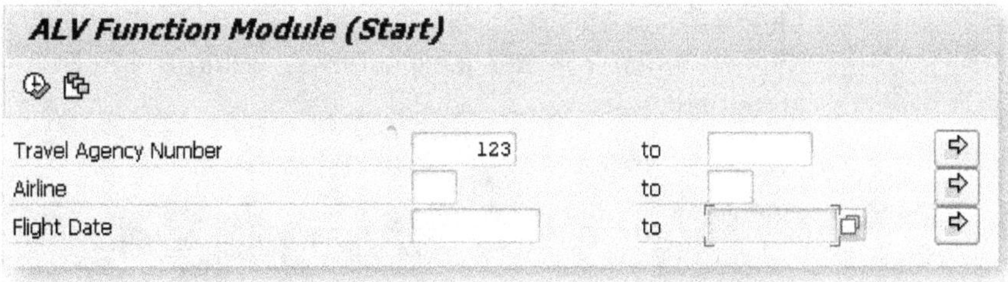

Figure 2.6: Selection screen (FM)

2.4   Selection of data for ALV output

We will type placeholders for the INITIALIZATION and the AT SELECTION-SCREEN events, but will leave them empty for this initial program (Figure 2.7).

```
INITIALIZATION.

AT SELECTION-SCREEN.

START-OF-SELECTION.                      "retrieve data

  SELECT stravelag~agencynum stravelag~name stravelag~currency
         sbook~carrid sbook~connid sbook~fldate sbook~bookid
         sbook~forcuram sbook~forcurkey
         scarr~carrname
         sbook~loccuram sbook~loccurkey
    FROM stravelag join sbook
                   on stravelag~agencynum = sbook~agencynum
                join scarr
                   on sbook~carrid         = scarr~carrid
    INTO TABLE gt_output
         WHERE stravelag~agencynum IN s_agnum
         AND sbook~carrid          IN s_carid
         AND sbook~fldate          IN s_fldat.
```

Figure 2.7: Retrieval of data for ALV output (FM)

Add the SELECT statement to your program's START-OF-SELECTION event (Figure 2.7). It joins three tables from the SAP Flight Application (using the selection choices provided by the user) and directs that the selected data be put into the internal table GT_OUTPUT. Note that the field order and the field formats are identical in the SELECT statement and in the local TYPE LTY_OUTPUT defined earlier.

Tilde for joins

The symbol between the table names and field names in Figure 2.7 is a tilde ~. Use the tilde instead of the usual hyphen when you are joining tables within a SELECT statement.

Optimization of SELECT statements

Optimizing a SELECT statement can make a tremendous improvement in your program's performance. Utilize SAP tools such as *runtime analysis* (transaction codes sat or se30) and *performance trace* (transaction code st05) to make improvements.

End the START-OF-SELECTION section by adding the lines of code shown in Figure 2.8. If data was retrieved, you will sort the table using the fields of the internal table that make each row unique. (Advanced sorting is covered in Chapter 5.) If no data was retrieved, the program is ended here with a message to the user.

```
DESCRIBE TABLE gt_output LINES gv_lines.
IF gv_lines NE 0.                          "data was retrieved
   SORT gt_output BY agencynum
                     carrid
                     connid
                     fldate
                     bookid.
ELSE.
   MESSAGE ID '00' TYPE 'I' NUMBER 001 WITH 'No data retrieved'.
   RETURN.
ENDIF.

END-OF-SELECTION.
```

Figure 2.8: Verify that data was retrieved (FM)

2.5   Main logic section

I'll use *subroutines* in this program to break the logic into smaller parts for demonstration purposes, both for simplicity and because many of the programs that you support use this older syntax.

(If your employer's or client's standards for new and/or modified programs require the use of *methods* syntax, adjust the examples accordingly.)

```
************** Start of main program logic *****************************

   PERFORM zf_build_fieldcatalog USING gt_fieldcat[].

   PERFORM zf_display_alv.

************** End of main program logic *****************************
```

Figure 2.9: Two subroutines (FM)

In the first subroutine in Figure 2.9, you will populate the field catalog table with information about the fields to be displayed. You may recall that this is necessary because the internal table uses a local TYPE instead of a structure defined in the data dictionary. The global table GT_FIELDCAT is passed to the subroutine ZF_BUILD_FIELDCATALOG, and it is returned to the main program with content.

With no field catalog information, the ALV will display the data records with blank column headings and with none of the data dictionary features that provide context for developers and users alike: check tables (F4 dropdowns), field help (F1), and forward navigation within the data dictionary.

Use of data dictionary structure for ALV

 If the internal table of data that you will be displaying corresponds to a table or structure defined in the data dictionary, you can build your field catalog by calling function module REUSE_ALV_FIELDCATALOG_MERGE at the start of the ZF_BUILD_FIELDCATALOG subroutine, then update only those retrieved field attributes that require a change. If none of your fields require a change (no pre-summing, no hiding of fields, no hotspots, etc.), you can omit the building of the field catalog entirely and pass the structure name to the REUSE_ALV_GRID_DISPLAY function module in the I_STRUCTURE_NAME parameter.

In the second subroutine, you will call the REUSE_ALV_GRID_DISPLAY function module.

2.6   Building the field catalog table

Within this subroutine (Figure 2.10), first define a local structure called LS_FIELDCAT. LS_FIELDCAT is based on structure SLIS_FIELDCAT_ALV.

Table 2.1 shows how the naming convention frequently uses a "t" to differentiate tables from their underlying structures.

Type-pool SLIS		
Structure	slis_fieldcat_alv	ls_fieldcat (local)
Table	slis_t_fieldcat_alv	lt_fieldcat (local) gt_fieldcat[] (global)

Table 2.1: Naming convention (FM)

```
FORM zf_build_fieldcatalog USING lt_fieldcat TYPE slis_t_fieldcat_alv.

  DATA: ls_fieldcat TYPE slis_fieldcat_alv.      "single row

  CLEAR ls_fieldcat.
  ls_fieldcat-fieldname     = 'AGENCYNUM'.
  ls_fieldcat-ref_fieldname = 'AGENCYNUM'.       "data dict info
  ls_fieldcat-ref_tabname   = 'STRAVELAG'.
  APPEND ls_fieldcat TO lt_fieldcat.

  CLEAR ls_fieldcat.
  ls_fieldcat-fieldname     = 'NAME'.
  ls_fieldcat-ref_fieldname = 'NAME'.
  ls_fieldcat-ref_tabname   = 'STRAVELAG'.
  APPEND ls_fieldcat TO lt_fieldcat.

  CLEAR ls_fieldcat.
  ls_fieldcat-fieldname     = 'CURRENCY'.
  ls_fieldcat-ref_fieldname = 'CURRENCY'.
  ls_fieldcat-ref_tabname   = 'STRAVELAG'.
  APPEND ls_fieldcat TO lt_fieldcat.
```

Figure 2.10: Building the field catalog, part 1 (FM)

For each of the fields in the output table GT_OUTPUT, complete the following steps:

1. Clear LS_FIELDCAT.

2. Fill FIELDNAME with the LTY_OUTPUT fieldname.

3. Fill REF_FIELDNAME with the fieldname from our original data source. (Note: you can omit REF_FIELDNAME if the FIELDNAME from the internal table matches the name of the field from the REF_TABNAME table, as it does in the program.)

4. Fill REF_TABNAME with the table name of our original data source.

5. Append LS_FIELDCAT to the table LT_FIELDCAT.

In this program, the fieldnames from the local type LTY_OUTPUT match the fieldnames of the database data, but that is not a requirement. Under some circumstances, you may decide to use names that are different. You may also decide to create your own name for fields with a custom function (for example, a counter or traffic light field).

Continue through the fields of local TYPE LTY_OUTPUT, as shown in Figure 2.11.

The SELECT statement to fill the internal table GT_OUTPUT retrieved two amount fields and three currency keys.

```
CLEAR ls_fieldcat.
ls_fieldcat-fieldname     = 'CARRID'.
ls_fieldcat-ref_fieldname = 'CARRID'.
ls_fieldcat-ref_tabname   = 'SBOOK'.
APPEND ls_fieldcat TO lt_fieldcat.

CLEAR ls_fieldcat.
ls_fieldcat-fieldname     = 'CONNID'.
ls_fieldcat-ref_fieldname = 'CONNID'.
ls_fieldcat-ref_tabname   = 'SBOOK'.
APPEND ls_fieldcat TO lt_fieldcat.

CLEAR ls_fieldcat.
ls_fieldcat-fieldname     = 'FLDATE'.
ls_fieldcat-ref_fieldname = 'FLDATE'.
ls_fieldcat-ref_tabname   = 'SBOOK'.
APPEND ls_fieldcat TO lt_fieldcat.

CLEAR ls_fieldcat.
ls_fieldcat-fieldname     = 'BOOKID'.
ls_fieldcat-ref_fieldname = 'BOOKID'.
ls_fieldcat-ref_tabname   = 'SBOOK'.
APPEND ls_fieldcat TO lt_fieldcat.
```

Figure 2.11: Building the field catalog, part 2 (FM)

The two amount fields (FORCURAM, LOCCURAM) need a pair of additional fields populated into the field catalog: CFIELDNAME and CTABNAME as shown in Figure 2.12 and Figure 2.13.

```
CLEAR ls_fieldcat.
ls_fieldcat-fieldname     = 'FORCURAM'.    "amount field !
ls_fieldcat-cfieldname    = 'FORCURKEY'.   "associated currency key
ls_fieldcat-ctabname      = 'SBOOK'.
ls_fieldcat-ref_fieldname = 'FORCURAM'.
ls_fieldcat-ref_tabname   = 'SBOOK'.
APPEND ls_fieldcat TO lt_fieldcat.

CLEAR ls_fieldcat.
ls_fieldcat-fieldname     = 'FORCURKEY'.
ls_fieldcat-ref_fieldname = 'FORCURKEY'.
ls_fieldcat-ref_tabname   = 'SBOOK'.
APPEND ls_fieldcat TO lt_fieldcat.

CLEAR ls_fieldcat.
ls_fieldcat-fieldname     = 'CARRNAME'.
ls_fieldcat-ref_fieldname = 'CARRNAME'.
ls_fieldcat-ref_tabname   = 'SCARR'.
APPEND ls_fieldcat TO lt_fieldcat.
```

Figure 2.12: Building the field catalog, part 3 (FM)

The three fields containing currency keys (CURRENCY, FORCURKEY, and LOCCURKEY) do **not** need any additional attributes populated. (Chapter 5.1 contains more information about the three currency key fields.)

```
CLEAR ls_fieldcat.
ls_fieldcat-fieldname     = 'LOCCURAM'.    "amount field !
ls_fieldcat-cfieldname    = 'LOCCURKEY'.   "currency key here
ls_fieldcat-ctabname      = 'SBOOK'.
ls_fieldcat-ref_fieldname = 'LOCCURAM'.
ls_fieldcat-ref_tabname   = 'SBOOK'.
APPEND ls_fieldcat TO lt_fieldcat.

CLEAR ls_fieldcat.
ls_fieldcat-fieldname     = 'LOCCURKEY'.
ls_fieldcat-ref_fieldname = 'LOCCURKEY'.
ls_fieldcat-ref_tabname   = 'SBOOK'.
APPEND ls_fieldcat TO lt_fieldcat.

ENDFORM.
```

Figure 2.13: Building the field catalog, final (FM)

2.7 Calling the ALV function module

The REUSE_ALV_GRID_DISPLAY function module can accept many import parameters. As shown in Figure 2.14, you can generate a simple ALV display by passing only three items: the report name (SY-REPID), the field catalog table just populated (GT_FIELDCATALOG[]), and the internal table of data that was selected from three joined database tables (GT_OUTPUT).

```
*------------------------------------------------------------
FORM zf_display_alv.

  CALL FUNCTION 'REUSE_ALV_GRID_DISPLAY'
    EXPORTING
      i_callback_program = sy-repid
      it_fieldcat        = gt_fieldcat[]
    TABLES
      t_outtab           = gt_output
    EXCEPTIONS
      program_error      = 1
      OTHERS             = 2.

  IF sy-subrc <> 0.
    MESSAGE ID '00' TYPE 'I' NUMBER 001
      WITH 'REUSE_ALV_GRID_DISPLAY call error: ' sy-subrc.
    RETURN.
  ENDIF.

ENDFORM.
```

Figure 2.14: Calling the ALV function module (FM)

Finally, include error-handling to send the user a pop-up message if the function module call fails with a return code (SY-SUBRC) other than 0.

Run the program to display the data (Figure 2.1).

2.8 Summary

In this chapter, an SAP List Viewer (ALV) report was generated by calling function module REUSE_ALV_GRID_DISPLAY. With very little coding, data was presented with an ALV application toolbar that lets the user reorganize the report (sort, filter, change column order, sum, etc.), print it, or download it to another application.

Key points:

- ▶ Data declaration, selection-screen definition, retrieval of data, creation of field catalog, and ALV call
- ▶ Local type instead of data dictionary structure
- ▶ SELECT statement with multiple joins
- ▶ For new SAP List Viewer programs, use an ABAP objects technique (Chapter 3)

In Chapter 3, you'll create a report similar to this chapter's report, but instead of using the unsupported function module technique shown in this chapter, you'll use the ALV control framework, an ABAP objects technique.

3 Writing an ALV program using the ALV control framework

In this chapter, you'll learn to write a report using the ALV control framework. As in Chapter 2, this program retrieves data from the SAP Flight Application tables in order to evaluate the amount of income that various travel agencies have generated booking airline flights. The retrieved data will include two currency amounts and three currency keys.

3.1 Create the ABAP program

Much of the program code written in Chapter 2 can be re-used for this chapter's exercise, and vice versa. A simple way to copy your program is to use the COPY button from the initial screen of the ABAP editor, transaction code se38.

To create a new program, use transaction code se38 (or se80, if you prefer) to type a name for the program, then click on the CREATE button. (I have named this program ZKK_ALV_CTRLFW.) Complete the TYPE and STATUS fields (Figure 3.1), then click on the SAVE button. When prompted for the Package, click on the LOCAL OBJECT button. This fills the Package field with $TMP and positions your cursor in the new program.

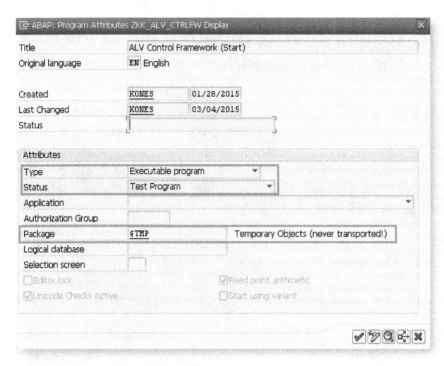

Figure 3.1: Program attributes (CF)

Figure 3.2 is a preview of the ALV output from this first example program using the ALV control framework.

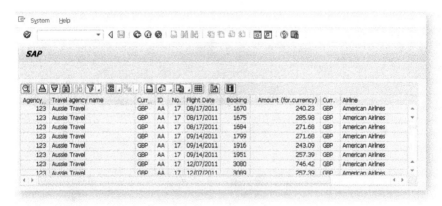

Figure 3.2: Preview (ALV control framework)

3.2   Data declarations

As shown in Figure 3.3, begin the data declarations section of the program by listing the database tables used in the SELECT-OPTIONS statement: SBOOK and STRAVELAG (Figure 3.4). This will prevent a syntax error.

```
REPORT zkk_alv_ctrlfw.

TABLES: sbook,                            "bookings
        stravelag.                        "travel agencies

TYPES: BEGIN OF lty_output,
        agencynum TYPE stravelag-agencynum, "agency number
        name      TYPE stravelag-name,      "agency name
        currency  TYPE stravelag-currency,  "agency currency
        carrid    TYPE sbook-carrid,        "booked carrier
        connid    TYPE sbook-connid,        "booked connection
        fldate    TYPE sbook-fldate,        "booked date
        bookid    TYPE sbook-bookid,        "booking ID
        forcuram  TYPE sbook-forcuram,      "price in foreign currency
        forcurkey TYPE sbook-forcurkey,     "foreign currency key
        carrname  TYPE scarr-carrname,      "carrier name
        loccuram  TYPE sbook-loccuram,      "price in airline curr
        loccurkey TYPE sbook-loccurkey,     "local currency of airline
      END OF lty_output.

DATA: gs_output   TYPE lty_output,          "local structure (line)
      gt_output   TYPE STANDARD TABLE OF lty_output,
      gt_fieldcat TYPE lvc_t_fcat.          "table

DATA: gv_lines            TYPE i,
      ok_code             LIKE sy-ucomm,
      g_container         TYPE scrfname VALUE 'ZKK_ALV_CTRLFW_9100_CONT1',
      grid1               TYPE REF TO cl_gui_alv_grid,
      g_custom_container  TYPE REF TO cl_gui_custom_container.
```

Figure 3.3: Data declarations (CF)

A local *TYPE* called LTY_OUTPUT lists the fields to be displayed in this ALV. A structure and matching internal table (GS_OUTPUT and GT_OUTPUT) are declared next, based on the local TYPE LTY_OUTPUT.

Local TYPE vs. data dictionary structure

 Instead of defining your output structure as a local TYPE in your program, you can define it as a structure in the data dictionary. The technique you use may depend upon your employer's or client's standards and practices, the number of changes you expect to make over time to the output structure, and the ease of making those changes.

Currency keys

 Some types of data require a "partner" field for clarity—for instance, currency amounts require currency keys, count and weight amounts require units of measure, and texts that can be stored in multiple languages require language keys. To facilitate troubleshooting and flexibility, we will provide all of the applicable currency keys in the ALV interface. In Chapter 6.1, you will see how you can hide fields on initial display of the ALV.

Referring again to Figure 3.3, you'll see a field catalog table GT_FIELDCAT to pass information (such as output length or data type) about the fields of the output structure. This time the table is based on the ALV control framework format LVC_T_FCAT.

Field catalog table (LVC_T_FCAT)

 The field catalog table contains information about each of the fields (or columns) in the ALV output. If your structure is not already defined in the data dictionary, you will need to populate this information into the field catalog table yourself. You will see later in this chapter, though, that you can refer to metadata in the data dictionary when populating your field catalog table.

You'll use variable GV_LINES to verify that records were retrieved for display.

The final four variables declared in Figure 3.3 are part of the ALV control framework. You will use OK_CODE and G_CONTAINER to set up the output screen. The screen setup is one of the biggest differences between this technique and the function module technique. The text value for G_CONTAINER is a concatenation of the program name, the screen number, and CONT1 for "container 1". The text value aligned with G_CONTAINER is not as important as making sure that you match the value exactly in the ELEMENT LIST tab of the screen that you'll build later. (Even when you expect to only use one container, it is good practice to include a number.)

GRID1 and G_CUSTOM_CONTAINER are declared with *TYPE REF TO* classes that are part of the ALV control framework. You'll add the logic for the custom container in Chapter 3.8.

3.3 Select-Options

After the data declarations, type three *SELECT-OPTIONS* as shown in Figure 3.4. Save, check, and activate your program.

```
SELECT-OPTIONS: s_agnum FOR stravelag-agencynum DEFAULT '123',
                s_carid FOR sbook-carrid,
                s_fldat FOR sbook-fldate.
```

Figure 3.4: SELECT-OPTIONS declaration (CF)

Change the SELECT-OPTIONS labels that will be displayed to the user from question marks to the texts stored in the data dictionary by using the menu path GOTO • TEXT ELEMENTS • SELECTION TEXTS. Check the checkboxes as shown in Figure 3.5. Activate the selection texts then go back to your program source code.

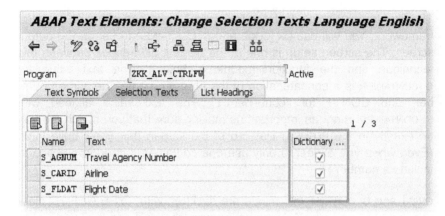

Figure 3.5: Copying selection texts from the data dictionary (CF)

The selection screen should look like Figure 3.6 when done.

Figure 3.6: Selection screen (CF)

3.4 Selection of data for ALV output

We will type placeholders for the INITIALIZATION and the AT SELECTION-SCREEN events, but will leave them empty for this initial program.

Add the SELECT statement to your program's START-OF-SELECTION event (Figure 3.7). It joins three tables from the SAP Flight Application (using the selection choices provided by the user) and directs that the selected data be put into the internal table GT_OUTPUT. Note that the field order and the field formats are identical in the SELECT statement and in the local TYPE LTY_OUTPUT defined earlier.

```
INITIALIZATION.

AT SELECTION-SCREEN.

START-OF-SELECTION.                    "retrieve data

   SELECT stravelag~agencynum stravelag~name stravelag~currency
          sbook~carrid sbook~connid sbook~fldate sbook~bookid
          sbook~forcuram sbook~forcurkey
          scarr~carrname
          sbook~loccuram sbook~loccurkey
     FROM stravelag JOIN sbook
                        ON stravelag~agencynum = sbook~agencynum
                   JOIN scarr
                        ON sbook~carrid        = scarr~carrid
     INTO TABLE gt_output
       WHERE stravelag~agencynum IN s_agnum
         AND sbook~carrid        IN s_carid
         AND sbook~fldate        IN s_fldat.

END-OF-SELECTION.
```

Figure 3.7: Retrieval of data for ALV output (CF)

Tilde for joins

The symbol between the table names and field names in Figure 3.7 is a tilde ~. Use the tilde instead of the usual hyphen when you are joining tables within a SELECT statement.

Optimization of SELECT statements

Optimizing a SELECT statement can make a tremendous improvement in your program's performance. Utilize SAP tools such as *runtime analysis* (transaction codes sat or se30) and *performance trace* (transaction code st05) to make improvements.

3.5 Main logic section

Add the lines of code shown in Figure 3.8. If data was retrieved, sort the table using the fields of the internal table that make each row unique.

(Advanced sorting is covered in Chapter 5.) Build the field catalog and then call the screen. Much of the ALV control framework logic is aligned with the screen, as you will see.

(If your employer's or client's standards for new and/or modified programs require the use of *methods* syntax instead of *subroutines*, adjust the examples accordingly.)

```
DESCRIBE TABLE gt_output LINES gv_lines.
IF gv_lines NE 0.                         "data was retrieved
   SORT gt_output BY agencynum
                      carrid
                      connid
                      fldate
                      bookid.

   PERFORM zf_build_fieldcatalog USING gt_fieldcat[].

   CALL SCREEN 9100.
ELSE.
   MESSAGE ID '00' TYPE 'I' NUMBER 001 WITH 'No data retrieved'.
   RETURN.
ENDIF.
```

Figure 3.8: Verify that data was retrieved and perform main program logic (CF)

If no data was retrieved, the program is ended here with a message to the user.

3.6   Building the field catalog table

Within this subroutine (Figure 3.9), first define a local structure called LS_FIELDCAT. We are only interacting with single lines of the field catalog table while inside this subroutine so that is why we have declared the structure locally. LS_FIELDCAT is based on the ALV control framework structure LVC_S_FCAT.

Use of data dictionary structure for ALV

 If the internal table of data that you will be displaying corresponds to a table or structure defined in the data dictionary, you can build your field catalog by calling function module LVC_FIELDCATALOG_MERGE at the start of the ZF_BUILD_FIELDCATALOG subroutine, then update only those retrieved field attributes that require a change. If none of your fields require a change (no pre-summing, no hiding of fields, no hotspots, etc.), you can omit the building of the field catalog entirely and pass the structure name to the SET_TABLE_FOR_FIRST_DISPLAY method in the I_STRUCTURE_NAME parameter.

```
FORM zf_build_fieldcatalog USING lt_fieldcat TYPE lvc_t_fcat.

  DATA: ls_fieldcat TYPE lvc_s_fcat.     "single row

  CLEAR ls_fieldcat.
  ls_fieldcat-fieldname = 'AGENCYNUM'.
  ls_fieldcat-ref_table = 'STRAVELAG'.
  APPEND ls_fieldcat TO lt_fieldcat.

  CLEAR ls_fieldcat.
  ls_fieldcat-fieldname = 'NAME'.
  ls_fieldcat-ref_table = 'STRAVELAG'.
  APPEND ls_fieldcat TO lt_fieldcat.

  CLEAR ls_fieldcat.
  ls_fieldcat-fieldname = 'CURRENCY'.
  ls_fieldcat-ref_table = 'STRAVELAG'.
  APPEND ls_fieldcat TO lt_fieldcat.
```

Figure 3.9: Building the field catalog, part 1 (CF)

Table 3.1 shows how the naming convention frequently uses a "t" to differentiate tables from their underlying structures.

ALV control framework		
Structure	lvc_s_fieldcat	ls_fieldcat (local)
Table	lvc_t_fieldcat	lt_fieldcat (local) gt_fieldcat[] (global)

Table 3.1: Naming convention (CF)

For each of the fields in the output table GT_OUTPUT, complete the following steps:

1. Clear LS_FIELDCAT.

2. Fill FIELDNAME with the LTY_OUTPUT fieldname.

3. Fill REF_TABLE with the table name of the original data source.

4. Append LS_FIELDCAT to the table LT_FIELDCAT.

In this program, the fieldnames from the local type LTY_OUTPUT match the fieldnames of the database data, but that is not a requirement. Under some circumstances, you may decide to use names that are different. You may also decide to create your own name for fields with a custom function (for example, a counter or traffic light field).

Continue through the fields of local TYPE LTY_OUTPUT, as shown in Figure 3.10.

```
CLEAR ls_fieldcat.
ls_fieldcat-fieldname = 'CARRID'.
ls_fieldcat-ref_table = 'SBOOK'.
APPEND ls_fieldcat TO lt_fieldcat.

CLEAR ls_fieldcat.
ls_fieldcat-fieldname = 'CONNID'.
ls_fieldcat-ref_table = 'SBOOK'.
APPEND ls_fieldcat TO lt_fieldcat.

CLEAR ls_fieldcat.
ls_fieldcat-fieldname = 'FLDATE'.
ls_fieldcat-ref_table = 'SBOOK'.
APPEND ls_fieldcat TO lt_fieldcat.

CLEAR ls_fieldcat.
ls_fieldcat-fieldname = 'BOOKID'.
ls_fieldcat-ref_table = 'SBOOK'.
APPEND ls_fieldcat TO lt_fieldcat.
```

Figure 3.10: Building the field catalog, part 2 (CF)

The SELECT statement to fill the internal table GT_OUTPUT retrieved two amount fields and three currency keys.

The two amount fields (FORCURAM, LOCCURAM) need one additional field populated into the field catalog: CFIELDNAME as shown in Figure 3.11 and Figure 3.12.

```
CLEAR ls_fieldcat.
ls_fieldcat-fieldname  = 'FORCURAM'.      "amount field !
ls_fieldcat-cfieldname = 'FORCURKEY'.     "associated currency key
ls_fieldcat-ref_table  = 'SBOOK'.
APPEND ls_fieldcat TO lt_fieldcat.

CLEAR ls_fieldcat.
ls_fieldcat-fieldname  = 'FORCURKEY'.
ls_fieldcat-ref_table  = 'SBOOK'.
APPEND ls_fieldcat TO lt_fieldcat.

CLEAR ls_fieldcat.
ls_fieldcat-fieldname  = 'CARRNAME'.
ls_fieldcat-ref_table  = 'SCARR'.
APPEND ls_fieldcat TO lt_fieldcat.
```

Figure 3.11: Building the field catalog, part 3 (CF)

The three fields containing currency keys (CURRENCY, FORCURKEY, and LOCCURKEY) do **not** need any additional attributes populated. (Chapter 5.1 contains more information about the three currency key fields.)

```
CLEAR ls_fieldcat.
ls_fieldcat-fieldname  = 'LOCCURAM'.      "amount field !
ls_fieldcat-cfieldname = 'LOCCURKEY'.     "currency key here
ls_fieldcat-ref_table  = 'SBOOK'.
APPEND ls_fieldcat TO lt_fieldcat.

CLEAR ls_fieldcat.
ls_fieldcat-fieldname  = 'LOCCURKEY'.
ls_fieldcat-ref_table  = 'SBOOK'.
APPEND ls_fieldcat TO lt_fieldcat.

ENDFORM.
```

Figure 3.12: Building the field catalog, final (CF)

Order of remaining tasks

 A number of tasks need to be done in order to use the ALV control framework. It may seem a bit confusing the first time, but the tasks should be easier with the instructions in this chapter. The order in which you perform many of these tasks is not rigid, though some tasks have a natural order. For instance, you need to create the ALV display screen before you can add the custom control or the PF-status to that screen. If your ALV doesn't display when you finish the exercise (Figure 3.27), use transaction code se80 to check the components of your program against Figure 3.32, looking for any omissions—there is no need to delete and start over.

3.7 Screen call

The last statement executed in the main program logic is the CALL SCREEN command (Figure 3.8). To avoid conflicts with SAP-provided screens, it is standard practice for developers to number their screens between 9000 and 9999. (I have used 9100 for this program.)

Double-click on the number 9100 in the CALL SCREEN 9100 statement, then click YES when asked if you want to create the object (Figure 3.13).

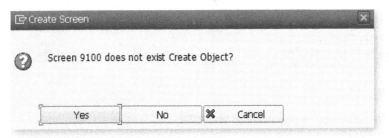

Figure 3.13: Create the display screen (CF)

Forward navigation brings you into the SAP Screen Painter. On the AT-TRIBUTES tab, provide a short description such as "ALV Initial Screen" (Figure 3.14).

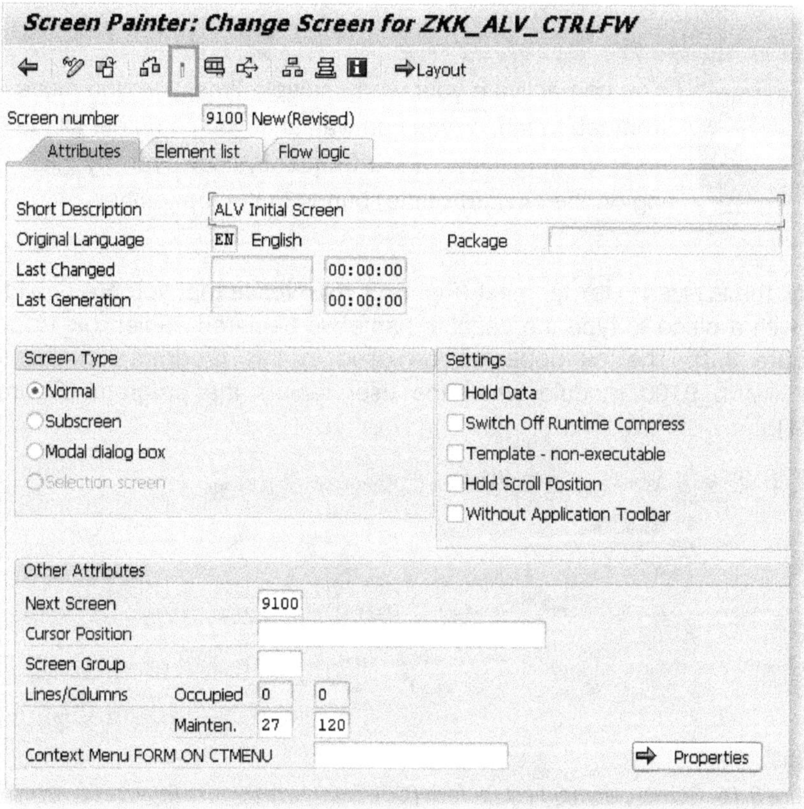

Figure 3.14: Screen attributes (CF)

Click the ACTIVATE button in the toolbar. Highlight the object DYNP (dynpro) in the list (Figure 3.15), then click the green checkmark.

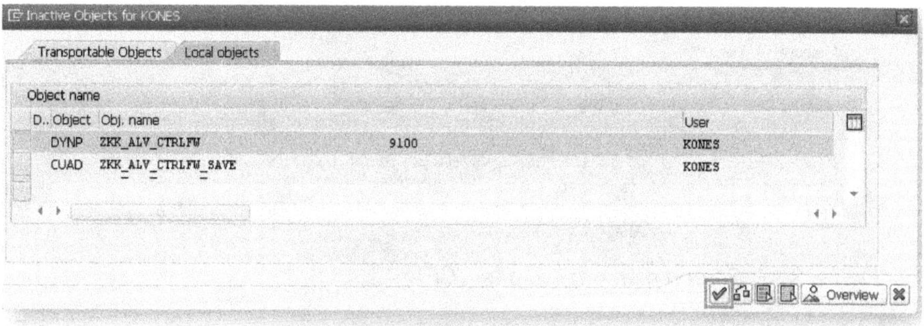

Figure 3.15: Activate objects (CF)

Screen activation

You can activate your work multiple times, as you move from tab to tab, or you can wait until you complete all the work, then activate. Save frequently, however, by clicking on the SAVE (diskette) button in the top toolbar.

Click the ELEMENT LIST tab next (Figure 3.16). Notice that you are provided with a place to type the variable name we declared earlier: OK_CODE (Figure 3.3). The OK_CODE will be used in this program's ZM_USER _COMMAND_9100 module when the user leaves the program (Figure 3.21).

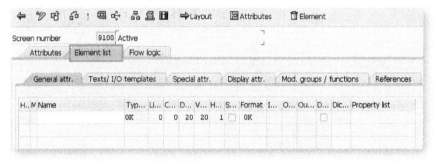

Figure 3.16: Screen element list, before (CF)

After adding your variable, the ELEMENT LIST will appear as it does in Figure 3.17. You'll return to this screen to add one more element later.

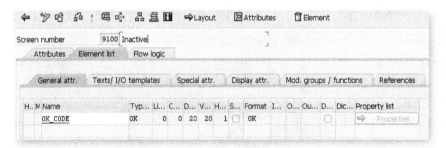

Figure 3.17: Screen element list, after (CF)

3.8 Process before output (PBO) and process after input (PAI) module logic

Click the FLOW LOGIC tab next. By default, SAP will propose names for a *process before output* (PBO) module and a *process after input* (PAI) module as shown in Figure 3.18.

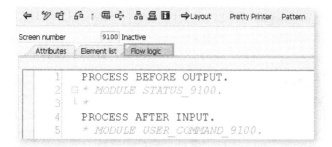

Figure 3.18: Proposed module names (CF)

Code will be added to the ABAP

 With the exception of the two module names on the FLOW LOGIC tab (Figure 3.19), your code will reside in the main logic of your ABAP. There is no need to create *includes* for these simple exercises.

Remove the asterisks to uncomment these proposed module names, then type ZM_ in front of each as shown in Figure 3.19. This naming convention (Z for custom, M for module) helps them stand out from SAP-provided modules in the debugger.

Screen Painter: Change Screen for ZKK_ALV_CTRLFW

```
Screen number        9100 Active
    Attributes    Element list    Flow logic

    1      PROCESS BEFORE OUTPUT.
    2         MODULE zm_status_9100.
    3
    4      PROCESS AFTER INPUT.
    5         MODULE zm_user_command_9100.
```

Figure 3.19: Modified module names (CF)

SE80 object navigator

 The *object navigator* (transaction code se80) is an alternative to forward navigation for accessing the various components of your program. Click on the REPOSITORY BROWSER bar near the top of transaction se80's left-hand navigation panel, then choose PROGRAM from the first dropdown. Type your program name in the next box down and press ⌈Enter⌋. The components of your program will display (Figure 3.32).

Double-click on ZM_STATUS_9100. Forward navigation will place you back into your program source code. Type the content shown in Figure 3.20, then save. (You can use the PATTERN button in the editor to insert text, if you wish.) PBO modules such as ZM_STATUS_9100 run before the first ALV screen display and before each subsequent re-display.

```
*-----------------------------------------------------------------
MODULE zm_status_9100 OUTPUT.

  SET PF-STATUS 'MAIN9100'.
  IF g_custom_container IS INITIAL.
    CREATE OBJECT g_custom_container
      EXPORTING
        container_name = g_container.
    CREATE OBJECT grid1
      EXPORTING
        i_parent = g_custom_container.

    CALL METHOD grid1->set_table_for_first_display
      EXPORTING
        i_structure_name = 'LTY_OUTPUT'
      CHANGING
        it_fieldcatalog  = gt_fieldcat
        it_outtab        = gt_output.
  ENDIF.

ENDMODULE.
```

Figure 3.20: Process before output (PBO) logic (CF)

The last items that we included in our data declarations (Figure 3.3) are used in the PBO module: G_CUSTOM_CONTAINER, G_CONTAINER, and GRID1. The *CALL METHOD* serves the same purpose as the function module call in the Chapter 2 program (Figure 2.14). The SET_TABLE _FOR_FIRST_DISPLAY method will be using your local type definition, the field catalog table you populated, and the data you retrieved for output.

Running RS_ABAP_SOURCE_SCAN to find text strings

 To find additional code examples within your SAP environment, run program RS_ABAP_SOURCE_SCAN. Use transaction code se38 or sa38 to display the selection screen for this program, provide a text string such as SET_TABLE_FOR_FIRST_DISPLAY, restrict the search further if you wish, then run the program by clicking on the clock button (F8 key). You can click on any of the returned items to view the program code.

You'll create the *PF-status* for the 9100 screen in a later step. For now, return to the FLOW LOGIC screen (Figure 3.19) to create your PAI module. There are several ways to get there, depending upon your preference and how you reached your current location in the program.

- ▶ Green BACK arrow
- ▶ Or double-click on 9100 in the CALL 9100 statement in the main logic section, then click the FLOW LOGIC tab
- ▶ Or use the object navigator transaction code se80

Once there, double-click on ZM_USER_COMMAND_9100. This takes you back into your program source code. Type the content shown in Figure 3.21, then save.

The PAI module reacts to user input. You will provide an exit from the ALV screen when the user clicks the BACK, EXIT, or CANCEL buttons. You will configure these buttons later in the PF-STATUS called MAIN9100 (Figure 3.26).

```
MODULE zm_user_command_9100 INPUT.

  CALL METHOD cl_gui_cfw=>dispatch.

  CASE ok_code.
    WHEN 'BACK'
      OR 'EXIT'
      OR 'CANC'.

      PERFORM zf_exit_program.
    WHEN OTHERS.
*       do nothing
  ENDCASE.

  CLEAR ok_code.

ENDMODULE.
```

Figure 3.21: Process after input (PAI) logic (CF)

While you are still in the ZM_USER_COMMAND_9100 PAI module, double-click on the subroutine name ZF_EXIT_PROGRAM. Type the content shown in Figure 3.22 into your source code.

```
FORM zf_exit_program.

  LEAVE PROGRAM.

ENDFORM.
```

Figure 3.22: Exit subroutine (CF)

Save, then click the ACTIVATE button in the toolbar. Select all objects in the pop-up window that are associated with this program, then click the green checkmark.

Only two tasks remain: creating the PF-STATUS and putting the custom control on the screen.

3.9   PF-status for screen

Return again to the PBO module ZM_STATUS_9100 (Figure 3.20). Double-click on MAIN9100, then click YES when asked if you want to create this GUI status object (Figure 3.23).

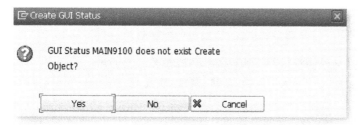

Figure 3.23: Create PF-status (CF)

Type a description into the short text field on the attributes screen (Figure 3.24), then click on the green checkmark. (Keep the default status type NORMAL SCREEN.)

Create Status		
Program	ZKK_ALV_CTRLFW	
Status	MAIN9100	

Status Attributes

Short Text	Main Status

Status type
- ◉ Normal Screen
- ○ Dialog Box
- ○ Context Menu

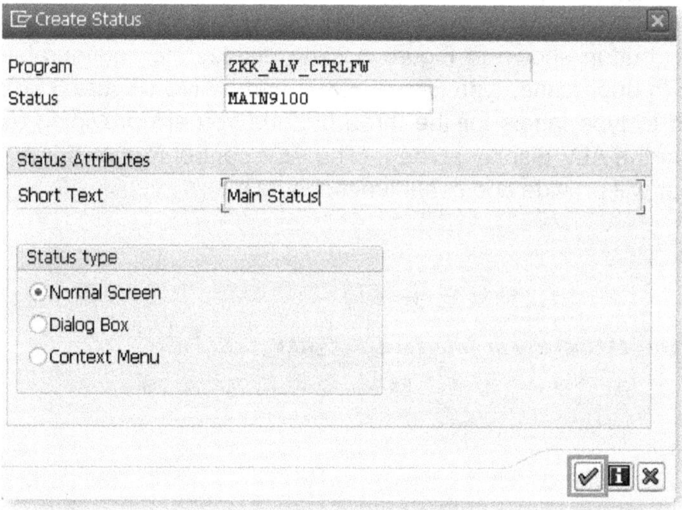

Figure 3.24: PF-status attributes (CF)

Remember the three OK_CODE values that you included in the PAI module ZM_USER_INPUT_9100 (Figure 3.21)? You'll now align those values with three toolbar buttons in the FUNCTION KEYS section of the PF-status.

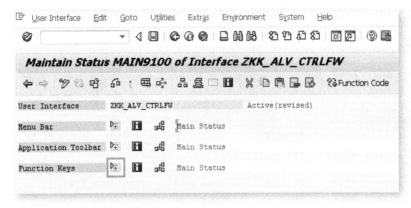

Figure 3.25: Function keys dropdown (CF)

Click the OPEN button shown in Figure 3.25 to display the configurable function keys. In uppercase, type BACK, EXIT, and CANC (Figure 3.26). You only need to type labels for the three buttons you are providing as exit points from the ALV display screen. (The ALV control framework application toolbar will provide additional functionality.)

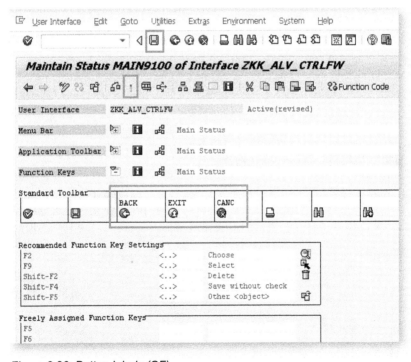

Figure 3.26: Button labels (CF)

Save by clicking the SAVE (diskette) button at the top, then activate.

Status labels must match PAI module OK_CODE values

Be sure to match the values exactly in both places (Figure 3.26 and Figure 3.21), including the case (uppercase, lowercase, or mixed case). Since our response to the user action is the same (LEAVE PROGRAM) regardless of which button is clicked, we can repeat an identical label (for instance, EXIT) for all three buttons and include only one OK_CODE value (EXIT) in the PAI module's CASE statement. As long as we are consistent in both places, it will work as intended.

3.10 Custom control on screen

If you were to run your program now, without completing this final part, a blank screen would display (Figure 3.27) instead of data records.

Figure 3.27: Missing custom control = no ALV data display (CF)

To finish the program, go to screen 9100 again, either by using the object navigator (transaction code se80) or by double-clicking on the number 9100 in your source code statement CALL SCREEN 9100. Click the LAYOUT icon (Figure 3.28) in the toolbar to launch the graphical portion of the SAP Screen Painter.

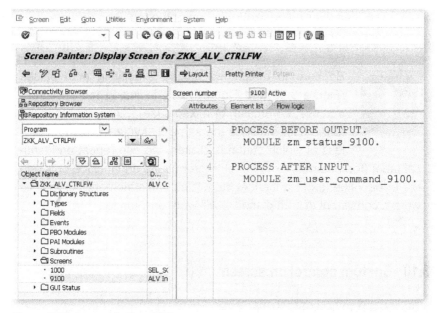

Figure 3.28: Layout button (CF)

You are now in the graphical portion of the SAP Screen Painter (Figure 3.29). Find the CUSTOM CONTROL button on the left side of the screen. It is near the bottom of the column of buttons and has a small C in the corner.

You will use this button to draw a large box on the canvas to indicate the space available for your ALV data output (Figure 3.30).

1. Click once on the CUSTOM CONTROL button.

2. Position the mouse cursor in the upper left corner of the blank canvas. The cursor changes to a new shape: a small rectangle with an upside-down L.

3. Hold the left mouse button down while dragging the mouse cursor to the lower right corner of the canvas.

4. Release the mouse button. If your screen does not look like Figure 3.30, delete the image with the SCISSORS button and try again.

In the NAME field above the canvas, type the value you aligned with G_CONTAINER at the start of program (Figure 3.3). In the example program, it is called ZKK_ALV_CTRLFW_9100_CONT1.

Figure 3.29: Custom control button (CF)

Figure 3.30: Custom control on the layout canvas (CF)

Save and activate. Use the green BACK arrow to return to the ELEMENT
LIST tab (Figure 3.31). Notice that the custom control name you provided
on the layout canvas screen has been added to the list that previously
showed only OK_CODE (Figure 3.17).

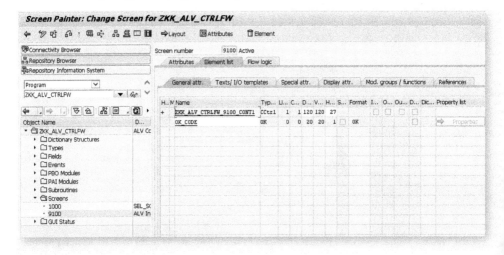

Figure 3.31: Element list, final (CF)

To verify that you have all the components, use the object navigator (transaction code se80) to compare your program to the list in Figure 3.32.

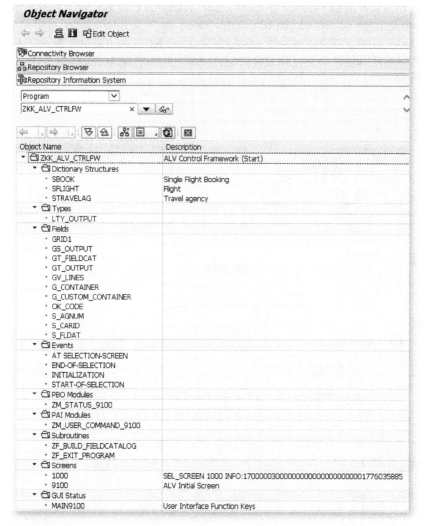

Figure 3.32: All components in object navigator (CF)

You are now ready to run the program and display the data (Figure 3.2).

3.11 Enabling background execution

The ALV control framework can be run in the background with the addition of a few lines of code (Figure 3.33). With this change, your ALV program can be scheduled to run immediately, or at a future time, with the report output sent to the SAP print spool. (The function module version of the ALV program does not require this special coding in order to work in background or batch mode.)

```
*-------------------------------------------------------------------
MODULE zm_status_9100 OUTPUT.
  DATA: g_dock_container TYPE REF TO cl_gui_docking_container.

  SET PF-STATUS 'MAIN9100'.
  IF g_custom_container IS INITIAL.

    IF cl_gui_alv_grid=>offline( ) IS INITIAL.      "online/foreground
      CREATE OBJECT g_custom_container
        EXPORTING
          container_name = g_container.
      CREATE OBJECT grid1
        EXPORTING
          i_parent = g_custom_container.
    ELSE.                                            "background
      CREATE OBJECT grid1
        EXPORTING i_parent = g_dock_container.
    ENDIF.

    CALL METHOD grid1->set_table_for_first_display
      EXPORTING
        i_structure_name = 'LTY_OUTPUT'
      CHANGING
        it_fieldcatalog  = gt_fieldcat
        it_outtab        = gt_output.
  ENDIF.
ENDMODULE.
```

Figure 3.33: Enabling the program for background execution (CF)

G_DOCK_CONTAINER should be defined in the main data area of the program, but it is shown in the ZM_STATUS_9100 module for convenience. Figures in the remainder of the book will omit the docking container logic, but feel free to add it to your program and retain it as you add new features.

Anticipating background execution in advance of need

Some developers add these background execution lines of code proactively even if there is no immediate requirement, avoiding program changes later.

Without the additional code, an attempted background program run will be cancelled (Figure 3.34).

Job log overview for job: ZKK_ALV_CTRLFW_LAYOUT_SORT_MOR / 22201200

Date	Time	Message text
06/22/2015	22:20:12	Job started
06/22/2015	22:20:12	Step 001 started (program ZKK_ALV_CTRLFW_LAYOUT_SORT_MOR, variant DREAM TRAVEL
06/22/2015	22:20:12	Control Framework: Fatal error - GUI cannot be reached
06/22/2015	22:20:13	Internal session terminated with a runtime error RAISE_EXCEPTION (see ST22)
06/22/2015	22:20:13	Job cancelled

Figure 3.34: Background job log with error message (CF)

3.12 Summary

In this chapter, you generated an SAP List Viewer report using the ALV control framework. With very little coding on your part (and a few additional screen setup steps), you presented the data and an ALV application toolbar that lets the user reorganize the report (sort, filter, change column order, sum, etc.), print it, and download it to another application.

Key points:

▶ Data declaration, selection-screen definition, retrieval of data, creation of a field catalog, and ALV call

▶ Additional components: screen call, custom control, PBO and PAI modules, and PF-status

▶ Local type instead of data dictionary structure

▶ SELECT statement with multiple joins

▶ Background execution

In Chapter 4, you'll explore ways to make the output more meaningful on initial display, reducing the amount of reformatting the user must do. You'll also see how to meet other requirements that may be presented.

4 Adding layout features to an ALV program

The SAP List Viewer has great flexibility and can be configured in ways that meet current needs and anticipate future needs. This chapter shows a few ways to tailor the initial display using features provided at the layout level. Example code will be shown for each of the two ALV types covered in this book.

4.1 Training scenario

You may recall that the user of this report is retrieving data from the SAP Flight Application tables in order to evaluate the amount of income that various travel agencies have generated booking airline flights.

For the remaining examples, we will imagine that the owner of several travel agencies in the United Kingdom has acquired an additional agency in Australia. The owner wishes to evaluate the bookings made by all of her agencies (Figure 4.1) and has requested a monthly data extract.

AGENCYNUM	NAME	COUNTRY	CURRENCY
102	Hot Socks Travel	AU	AUD
107	Ben McCloskey Ltd.	GB	GBP
109	Kangeroos	GB	GBP
112	Super Agency	GB	GBP
123	Aussie Travel	GB	GBP
295	The Ultimate Answer	GB	GBP

Figure 4.1: Travel agencies

Selection screen variant

For convenience, you can add these travel agency numbers (102, 107, 109, 112, 123, and 295) to your selection screen (Figure 2.6 or Figure 3.6), then save it as a selection screen variant using the SAVE (diskette) button.

As you work through the sections of this chapter, you can incorporate the new features into the program you've already begun or into a copy of that program. Save and activate as you go. (My example programs are called ZKK_ALV_FM_LAYOUT and ZKK_ALV_CTRLFW_LAYOUT.)

Extracting to Microsoft Excel and to local file formats

 Depending upon your SAP environment and upon which techniques you are using to generate the SAP List Viewer, the ALV features seen on screen may or may not be available after extract to Microsoft Excel (or to one of the *local file* formats). As a developer, it is a good practice to check the behavior of your program and communicate to the appropriate stakeholder early in order to manage expectations about data extract behavior.

4.2 Layout features

Layout features are those that affect the overall appearance or behavior of the ALV display.

Layout features vs. layout variants

 The layout features described in this chapter are coded into the ALV program by the developer, based on specifications provided when the program was created. *Layout variants*, on the other hand, are configured and saved by the user or developer *after* the display of an ALV report.

In order to enable layout features within the two types of programs we've covered (function module and ALV control framework), you first perform three tasks.

▶ Declare an additional data structure

▶ Create a subroutine to populate the structure

▶ Pass the structure to the function module or ALV control framework method

4.2.1 Function module

For programs using the function module technique described in Chapter 2, first add a layout data structure based on the type SLIS_LAYOUT_ALV (Figure 4.2).

```
DATA: gs_output   TYPE lty_output,          "local structure (line)
      gt_output   TYPE STANDARD TABLE OF lty_output,
      gt_fieldcat TYPE slis_t_fieldcat_alv,
      gs_layout   TYPE slis_layout_alv.
```

Figure 4.2: Define the layout structure (FM)

View all the available layout features

Take a moment to double-click SLIS_LAYOUT_ALV. Forward navigation will take you to the definition where you can see all the options available to you as layout features. Return by clicking once on the green BACK arrow.

Second, add a PERFORM statement (Figure 4.3). In subroutine ZF_BUILD_LAYOUT, you will code the features to be enabled. For now, double-click on ZF_BUILD_LAYOUT to add the FORM and ENDFORM statements of the subroutine to this program (Figure 4.9).

```
************** Start of main program logic **************

  PERFORM zf_build_layout USING gs_layout.

  PERFORM zf_build_fieldcatalog USING gt_fieldcat[].

  PERFORM zf_display_alv.

************** End of main program logic **************
```

Figure 4.3: Populate the layout structure (FM)

Finally, include the layout structure GS_LAYOUT in the function module call (Figure 4.4).

```
/--------------------------------------------------------------
FORM zf_display_alv.

  CALL FUNCTION 'REUSE_ALV_GRID_DISPLAY'
    EXPORTING
      i_callback_program = sy-repid
      is_layout          = gs_layout
      it_fieldcat        = gt_fieldcat[]
    TABLES
      t_outtab           = gt_output
    EXCEPTIONS
      program_error      = 1
      OTHERS             = 2.

  IF sy-subrc <> 0.
    MESSAGE ID '00' TYPE 'I' NUMBER 001
      WITH 'REUSE_ALV_GRID_DISPLAY call error: ' sy-subrc.
    RETURN.
  ENDIF.

ENDFORM.
```

Figure 4.4: Pass the layout structure (FM)

Now that these elements have been added to your program, you can begin adding individual layout features. For programs that call the RE-USE_ALV_GRID_DISPLAY function module, follow the "Function Module" examples in each sub-section. The relevant figure captions are denoted (FM).

4.2.2 ALV control framework

For programs using the ALV control framework technique (Chapter 3), first add a layout data structure based on the type LVC_S_LAYO (Figure 4.5).

```
DATA: gs_layout   TYPE lvc_s_layo,              "layout params
      gs_output   TYPE lty_output,              "local structure (line)
      gt_output   TYPE STANDARD TABLE OF lty_output,
      gt_fieldcat TYPE lvc_t_fcat.              "table
```

Figure 4.5: Define the layout structure (CF)

View all the available layout features

Take a moment to double-click LVC_S_LAYO. Forward navigation will take you to the definition where you can see all the options available to you as layout features. Return by clicking once on the green BACK arrow.

Second, add a PERFORM statement (Figure 4.6). In subroutine ZF_BUILD _LAYOUT, you will code the features to be enabled. For now, double-click on ZF_BUILD_LAYOUT to add the FORM and ENDFORM statements of the subroutine to this program (Figure 4.11).

```
DESCRIBE TABLE gt_output LINES gv_lines.
IF gv_lines NE 0.                          "data was retrieved
   SORT gt_output BY agencynum
                    carrid
                    connid
                    fldate
                    bookid.

   PERFORM zf_build_layout        USING gs_layout.

   PERFORM zf_build_fieldcatalog USING gt_fieldcat[].

   CALL SCREEN 9100.
ELSE.
   MESSAGE ID '00' TYPE 'I' NUMBER 001 WITH 'No data retrieved'.
   RETURN.
ENDIF.
```

Figure 4.6: Populate the layout structure (CF)

Finally, include the layout structure GS_LAYOUT in the method call in the ZM_STATUS_9100 module (Figure 4.7).

```
*-----------------------------------------------------------------
MODULE zm_status_9100 OUTPUT.

  SET PF-STATUS 'MAIN9100'.
  IF g_custom_container IS INITIAL.
    CREATE OBJECT g_custom_container
      EXPORTING
        container_name = g_container.
    CREATE OBJECT grid1
      EXPORTING
        i_parent = g_custom_container.

    CALL METHOD grid1->set_table_for_first_display
      EXPORTING
        i_structure_name = 'LTY_OUTPUT'
        is_layout        = gs_layout
      CHANGING
        it_fieldcatalog  = gt_fieldcat
        it_outtab        = gt_output.
  ENDIF.

ENDMODULE.
```

Figure 4.7: Pass the layout structure (CF)

Now that these elements have been added to your program, you can begin adding individual layout features. Follow the "ALV control framework" examples in each sub-section. The relevant figure captions are denoted (CF).

4.3   Alternating shaded and non-shaded lines

The alternating shaded and non-shaded lines of Figure 4.8 and Figure 4.10 are also known as *zebra stripe*. When turned on, the even rows are shaded slightly darker than the odd rows, making it easier for readers to visually follow a line of data from left to right.

4.3.1   Function module

To turn on the alternate row shading, fill the ZEBRA field of the layout structure with X as shown in Figure 4.9.

ALV Function Module (Layout Changes)

Agency	Travel agency name	Curr.	ID	No.	Flight Date	Booking	Amount (for.currency)	Curr.	Airline
102	Hot Socks Travel	AUD	AA	17	05/25/2011	12	657.88	AUD	American Airlines
102	Hot Socks Travel	AUD	AA	17	05/25/2011	52	1,038.77	AUD	American Airlines
102	Hot Socks Travel	AUD	AA	17	05/25/2011	82	328.94	AUD	American Airlines
102	Hot Socks Travel	AUD	AA	17	05/25/2011	104	311.63	AUD	American Airlines
102	Hot Socks Travel	AUD	AA	17	05/25/2011	240	346.26	AUD	American Airlines

Figure 4.8: Example of alternating shading (FM)

```
*------------------------------------------------------
FORM zf_build_layout USING ls_layout TYPE slis_layout_alv.

* shade every other line of the display table for readability
  ls_layout-zebra = 'X'.

ENDFORM.
```

Figure 4.9: Enable the zebra feature (FM)

4.3.2   ALV control framework

To turn on the alternate row shading, fill the ZEBRA field of the layout structure with X as shown in Figure 4.11.

SAP

Agency	Travel agency name	Curr.	ID	No.	Flight Date	Booking	Amount (for.currency)	Curr.	Airline
102	Hot Socks Travel	AUD	AA	17	05/25/2011	12	657.88	AUD	American Airlines
102	Hot Socks Travel	AUD	AA	17	05/25/2011	52	1,038.77	AUD	American Airlines
102	Hot Socks Travel	AUD	AA	17	05/25/2011	82	328.94	AUD	American Airlines
102	Hot Socks Travel	AUD	AA	17	05/25/2011	104	311.63	AUD	American Airlines
102	Hot Socks Travel	AUD	AA	17	05/25/2011	240	346.26	AUD	American Airlines

Figure 4.10: Example of alternating shading (CF)

```
*------------------------------------------------------
FORM zf_build_layout USING ls_layout TYPE lvc_s_layo.

  ls_layout-zebra = 'X'.

ENDFORM.
```

Figure 4.11: Enable the zebra feature (CF)

4.4   Optimizing column widths

By default, ALV columns are displayed at their full width, regardless of whether any of the retrieved data requires a column that wide. Look again at Figure 4.8 or Figure 4.10 to see displays with default column widths. When column optimization is turned on, the columns will be displayed only as wide as necessary for the set of data chosen for display (Figure 4.12 and Figure 4.14). This reduces left-right scrolling by the online user.

Impact of optimized columns on heading texts

When you enable column width optimization, your column heading text may be reduced to a shorter text from the data dictionary, as shown in Figure 4.12 and Figure 4.14. In these examples, we now have two fields called "Amount" on the screen. A mouse hover over the column heading allows the user to see the longer text, but other options for you to consider would be passing an explicit column heading or explicit column width for those fields in the field catalog table.

4.4.1   Function module

To optimize the column widths of the ALV display, fill the COLWIDTH _OPTIMIZE field of the layout structure with X as shown in Figure 4.13.

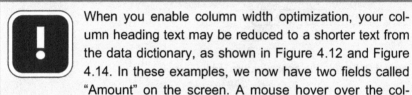

Figure 4.12: Example of optimized column widths (FM)

```
FORM zf_build_layout USING ls_layout TYPE slis_layout_alv.

* shade every other line of the display table for readability
  ls_layout-zebra              = 'X'.
* optimize column-widths to save space on-screen
  ls_layout-colwidth_optimize = 'X'.

ENDFORM.
```

Figure 4.13: Enable column optimization feature (FM)

4.4.2   ALV control framework

To optimize the column widths of the ALV display, fill the CWIDTH_OPT field of the layout structure with X as shown in Figure 4.15.

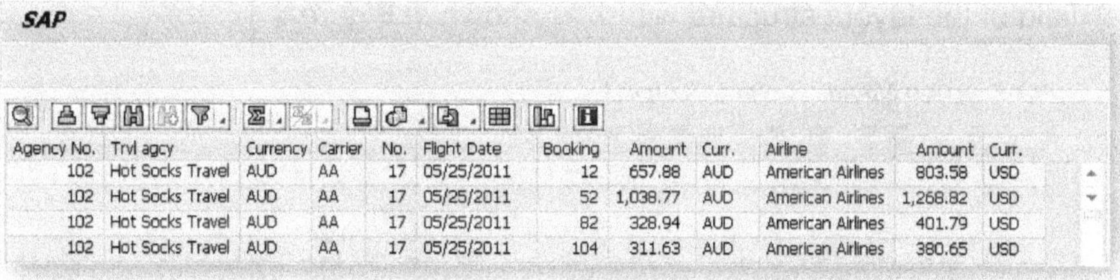

Figure 4.14: Example of optimized column widths (CF)

```
FORM zf_build_layout USING ls_layout TYPE lvc_s_layo.

  ls_layout-zebra       = 'X'.

  ls_layout-cwidth_opt = 'X'.

ENDFORM.
```

Figure 4.15: Enable column optimization feature (CF)

4.5   Displaying totals at the top

By default, ALV data is displayed at a detail (item) level with no totals. Without additional coding, the user wishing to see totals can highlight a summable column such as "Amount (for currency)" and click on the TOTAL button. One or more lines of totals are appended to the bottom of the data display. To see the totals, the user must scroll to the bottom of the data display.

For greater convenience for the user, you can add a layout feature that will show totals at the top of the data display instead.

Other settings used to configure subtotals are specified in the sort table and will be described in Chapter 5.

Take a moment to notice in Figure 4.16 and Figure 4.18 how SAP provides separate totals for each of the currency keys associated with the column we've summed: one total for bookings stored in Australian dollars (AUD), another total for bookings stored in British pounds (GBP).

4.5.1 Function module

To move totals to the top of the ALV display, fill the TOTALS_BEFORE_ITEMS field of the layout structure with X as shown in Figure 4.17.

ALV Function Module (Layout Changes)

Agency No.	Trvl agcy	Currency	Carrier	No.	Flight Date	Booking	Σ Amount	Curr.	Airline	Amount	Curr.
							▪ 1,028,...	AUD			
							4,364,1...	GBP			
102	Hot Socks Travel	AUD	AA	17	05/25/2011	12	657.88	AUD	American Airlines	803.58	USD
102	Hot Socks Travel	AUD	AA	17	05/25/2011	52	1,038.77	AUD	American Airlines	1,268.82	USD
102	Hot Socks Travel	AUD	AA	17	05/25/2011	82	328.94	AUD	American Airlines	401.79	USD
102	Hot Socks Travel	AUD	AA	17	05/25/2011	104	311.63	AUD	American Airlines	380.65	USD

Figure 4.16: Example of totals on top (FM)

```
FORM zf_build_layout USING ls_layout TYPE slis_layout_alv.

  ls_layout-zebra                 = 'X'.
  ls_layout-colwidth_optimize     = 'X'.

  ls_layout-totals_before_items = 'X'.

ENDFORM.
```

Figure 4.17: Enable totals on top feature (FM)

4.5.2 ALV control framework

To move totals to the top of the ALV display, fill the TOTALS_BEF field of the layout structure with X as shown in Figure 4.19.

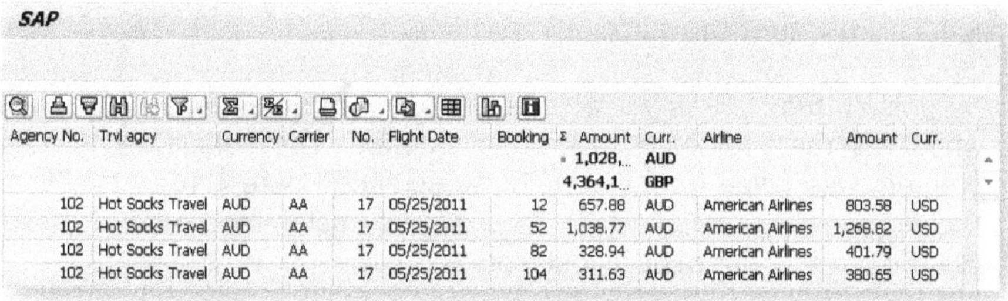

SAP

Agency No.	Trvl agcy	Currency	Carrier	No.	Flight Date	Booking	Σ Amount	Curr.	Airline	Amount	Curr.
							• 1,028,..	AUD			
							4,364,1..	GBP			
102	Hot Socks Travel	AUD	AA	17	05/25/2011	12	657.88	AUD	American Airlines	803.58	USD
102	Hot Socks Travel	AUD	AA	17	05/25/2011	52	1,038.77	AUD	American Airlines	1,268.82	USD
102	Hot Socks Travel	AUD	AA	17	05/25/2011	82	328.94	AUD	American Airlines	401.79	USD
102	Hot Socks Travel	AUD	AA	17	05/25/2011	104	311.63	AUD	American Airlines	380.65	USD

Figure 4.18: Example of totals on top (CF)

```
*---------------------------------------------------------------
FORM zf_build_layout USING ls_layout TYPE lvc_s_layo.

  ls_layout-zebra         = 'X'.
  ls_layout-cwidth_opt = 'X'.

  ls_layout-totals_bef = 'X'.

ENDFORM.
```

Figure 4.19: Enable totals on top feature (CF)

4.6 Displaying a title at the top

You can control the 70-character title displayed at the top of your ALV screen using a layout feature (Figure 4.20 and Figure 4.25). You can provide information there that will be meaningful to the business user (and at the same time helpful to developers and testers). For instance, the title can be used to differentiate periodic runs (like quarterly) from ad hoc runs or can be used to denote the SAP system used (SY-SYSID).

For the training scenario, we'll imagine that the owner of multiple travel agencies wants to see the data two different ways: with and without her recent Australian acquisition, Hot Socks Travel. We can manage this several ways, but let's also imagine that the person running these reports is using selection screen variants (SY-SLSET) and has been using a naming convention suffix of _Z to denote the previous version of the selection screen variant.

4.6.1 Function module

By default, the system value SY-TITLE appears at the top of the screen when you run your function module program. The default title for the program was taken from the attributes screen (Figure 4.16): ALV Function Module (Layout Changes). To provide a custom and more dynamic title (Figure 4.20), use the layout feature called WINDOW_TITLEBAR.

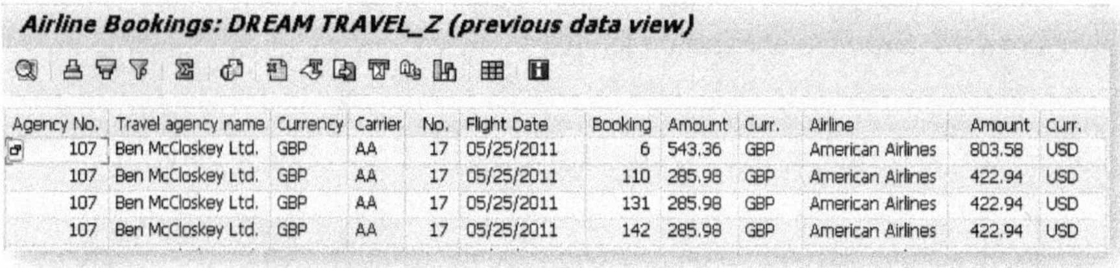

| Airline Bookings: DREAM TRAVEL_Z (previous data view) |

Agency No.	Travel agency name	Currency	Carrier	No.	Flight Date	Booking	Amount	Curr.	Airline	Amount	Curr.
107	Ben McCloskey Ltd.	GBP	AA	17	05/25/2011	6	543.36	GBP	American Airlines	803.58	USD
107	Ben McCloskey Ltd.	GBP	AA	17	05/25/2011	110	285.98	GBP	American Airlines	422.94	USD
107	Ben McCloskey Ltd.	GBP	AA	17	05/25/2011	131	285.98	GBP	American Airlines	422.94	USD
107	Ben McCloskey Ltd.	GBP	AA	17	05/25/2011	142	285.98	GBP	American Airlines	422.94	USD

Figure 4.20: Example of custom title (FM)

Add a variable to your program to contain the custom text (Figure 4.21).

```
DATA: gv_lines    TYPE i,
      gv_title    TYPE syst-title.
```

Figure 4.21: Variable for new custom title (FM)

Create a new subroutine ZF_START to contain the logic for this one-time population of the title variable (Figure 4.22).

```
START-OF-SELECTION.

  PERFORM zf_start.
```

Figure 4.22: New subroutine for one-time population (FM)

Fill the variable with the desired text. In the example in Figure 4.23, the title begins with static text (Airline Bookings:) followed by the variant name. If the variant name contains the _Z naming convention described in the training exercise, more static text (previous data view) is appended to signify that the older variant content was used to select the data. (This example shows that titles can be built during program execution; it is not a recommendation of this particular naming convention.)

```
*------------------------------------------------------------
FORM zf_start.

* populate screen title using selection variant name
  CONCATENATE 'Airline Bookings:'(001)
              syst-slset                    "variant name
  INTO gv_title SEPARATED BY space.
  IF syst-slset CS '_Z'.
    CONCATENATE gv_title
              '(previous data view)'(002)
    INTO gv_title SEPARATED BY space.
  ENDIF.

ENDFORM.
```

Figure 4.23: Fill the variable for the title (FM)

Text symbols

As a best practice to support language flexibility, store static texts on the *text symbols* tab of the program's Text Elements area. You can use forward navigation for this by double-clicking on the text, then clicking the SAVE and ACTIVATE buttons. This technique will add the number of the text symbol to your source code as shown in Figure 4.23, in this example (001) and (002).

To display the custom title on the ALV screen, fill the WINDOW_TITLEBAR field of the layout structure with the variable as shown in Figure 4.24.

```
*------------------------------------------------------------
FORM zf_build_layout USING ls_layout TYPE slis_layout_alv.

  ls_layout-zebra               = 'X'.
  ls_layout-colwidth_optimize   = 'X'.
  ls_layout-totals_before_items = 'X'.

  ls_layout-window_titlebar     = gv_title.

ENDFORM.
```

Figure 4.24: Fill the variable for the title (FM)

4.6.2 ALV control framework

By default, there is no title above the column headings when you run the ALV control framework program (Figure 4.18). To provide a custom title as shown in Figure 4.25, use the layout feature called GRID_TITLE.

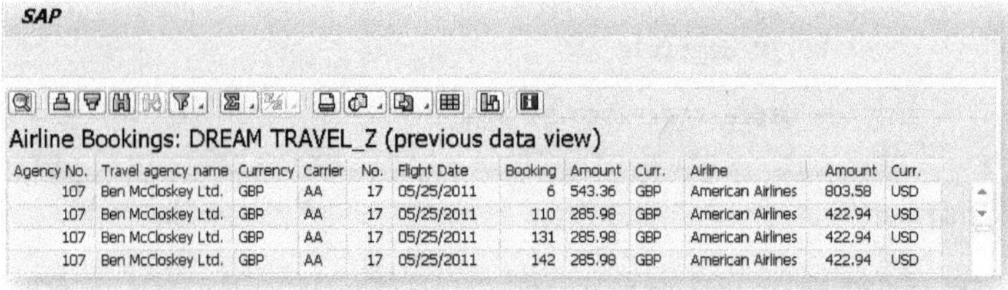

Figure 4.25: Example of custom title (CF)

Add a variable to your program to contain the custom text (Figure 4.26).

```
DATA: gv_lines            TYPE i,
      gv_title            TYPE syst-title,
      ok_code             LIKE sy-ucomm,
      g_container         TYPE scrfname VALUE 'ZKK_ALV_CTRLFW_9100_CONT1',
      grid1               TYPE REF TO cl_gui_alv_grid,
      g_custom_container  TYPE REF TO cl_gui_custom_container.
```

Figure 4.26: Variable for new custom title (CF)

Create a new subroutine ZF_START to contain the logic for this one-time population of the title variable (Figure 4.27).

```
START-OF-SELECTION.

    PERFORM zf_start.
```

Figure 4.27: New subroutine for one-time population (CF)

Fill the variable with the desired text. In the example in Figure 4.28, the title begins with static text (Airline Bookings:) followed by the variant name. If the variant name contains the _Z naming convention described in the training exercise, more static text (previous data view) is appended to signify that the older variant content was used to select the data. (This example shows that titles can be built during program execution; it is not a recommendation of this particular naming convention.)

```
*------------------------------------------------------
FORM zf_start.

* populate screen title using selection variant name
  CONCATENATE 'Airline Bookings:' (001)
                syst-slset                    "variant name
  INTO gv_title SEPARATED BY space.
  IF syst-slset CS '_Z'.
    CONCATENATE gv_title
                '(previous data view)' (002)
    INTO gv_title SEPARATED BY space.
  ENDIF.

ENDFORM.
```

Figure 4.28: Fill the variable for the title (CF)

Text symbols

 As a best practice to support language flexibility, store static texts on the *text symbols* tab of the program's text elements area. You can use forward navigation for this by double-clicking on the text, then clicking the SAVE and ACTIVATE buttons. This technique will add the number of the text symbol to your source code as shown in Figure 4.28, in this example (001) and (002).

To display the custom title on the ALV screen, fill the GRID_TITLE field of the layout structure with the variable as shown in Figure 4.29.

```
*------------------------------------------------------
FORM zf_build_layout USING ls_layout TYPE lvc_s_layo.

  ls_layout-zebra       = 'X'.
  ls_layout-cwidth_opt  = 'X'.
  ls_layout-totals_bef  = 'X'.

  ls_layout-grid_title  = gv_title.

ENDFORM.
```

Figure 4.29: Enable custom title (CF)

4.7 Previewing layout features

You can preview some layout features prior to coding them by executing any ALV program, then clicking on the CHANGE LAYOUT button shown in Figure 4.30 and Figure 4.31. This is handy for demonstrating the behavior to those writing the program specification and can help you identify the structure component you need to populate to enable one of these features by default.

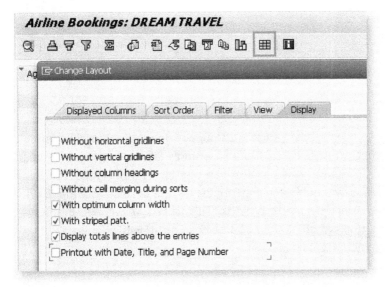

Figure 4.30: Layout features in change layout (FM)

One additional feature is available to the user in the ALV control framework (Figure 4.31): WITH SMALL HEADING.

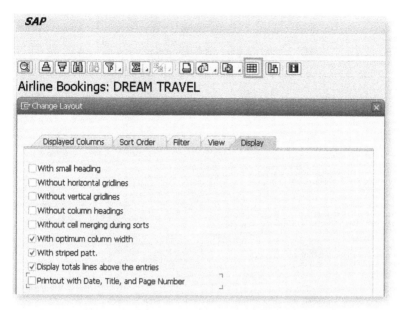

Figure 4.31: Layout features in change layout (CF)

4.8 Summary

In this chapter, you saw how layout features affect the overall appearance and behavior of the ALV display. You added several lines of code to both types of SAP List Viewer programs covered in this book, then you populated the appropriate predefined structure field to enable several layout features.

Even though the syntax varies by SAP List Viewer type, the coding is very similar.

Key points:

► Shading alternate rows
► Optimizing column widths
► Putting totals at the top of the report
► Adding a title
► Previewing layout features

5 Adding sort features to an ALV program

Just as you can enable various layout features prior to displaying the SAP List Viewer output to the user, you can enable sort features that influence the initial display. Grouping and subtotaling are also controlled by the settings passed in the sort table.

5.1 Training scenario

We'll continue working with the travel agency scenario described in Chapter 4.1.

Copy your in-progress program before continuing

In order to better compare the default sort behavior of your earlier program to the sort-related code you'll be adding in this chapter, consider copying your earlier program now (with all its components such as saved variants). Save and activate changes as you go. If you need to recreate the selection screen variant, refer to the tip in Chapter 4.1. (I called my program copies ZKK_ALV_FM_LAYOUT_SORT and ZKK_ALV_CTRLFW_LAYOUT_SORT.)

Your program's internal table of selected data includes three currency keys (CURRENCY, FORCURKEY, and LOCCURKEY). The first of these is the currency key associated with each travel agency. There is a one-to-one relationship between the travel agency and the value in the CURRENCY field. It was selected from the table of travel agency information (STRAVELAG) and is considered *master data*. A travel agency's currency key rarely changes, but it sometimes does. An example of this would be a country switching to or from the Euro.

To simplify the definition of groups for subtotals, you will move the travel agency CURRENCY field from the initial display of the transactional report, but will retain it in the ALV. To hide the CURRENCY field, add the NO_OUT setting to the field catalog table (Chapter 6.1).

The FORCURKEY and the LOCCURKEY currency keys, on the other hand, are *transactional data*. Because you aligned these two currency keys with the appropriate amount field (FORCURAM, LOCCURAM) using the CFIELDNAME setting in the field catalog (Chapter 2.6 and Chapter 3.6), totals and subtotals will be automatically grouped by currency key.

5.2   Sort features

Sort features affect the order of the records displayed, how the records are grouped, and how subtotals are shown.

- ▶ Record order is controlled by the sort table.
- ▶ Column order is controlled by the field catalog table.

Use of the sort table is optional. If you don't pass grouping instructions using the sort table, the program will display only grand totals when the user highlights an amount column and clicks the TOTAL button. To provide additional insights to the user in the training scenario, you will pass a sort table that contains groups for subtotals.

Display totals on initial display

See Chapter 6.2 to see how to display totals on initial display (without user action) using the DO_SUM feature in the field catalog.

Do not pass 'X' as the value for GROUP in sort table

Valid GROUP values include UL (underline) and * (page feed with underline), interchangeable for many programs. Avoid passing an invalid value such as 'X' in the GROUP field of the sort table.

Pass explicit sort direction values in sort table

Sort direction is an optional field in the sort table. For ease of support and assurance of consistent behavior over time, do include the appropriate UP or DOWN parameter for sorted fields in the sort table.

As with the layout features, there are three elements to set up in your program in order to use the sort features:

▶ Declare an additional table

▶ Create a subroutine to populate the table

▶ Pass the table to the function module or ALV control framework method

5.2.1 Function module

For programs using the function module technique described in Chapter 2, first add a sort table based on the type SLIS_T_SORTINFO_ALV (Figure 5.1).

```
DATA: gs_output   TYPE lty_output,          "local structure (line)
      gt_output   TYPE STANDARD TABLE OF lty_output,
      gt_sort     TYPE slis_t_sortinfo_alv,
      gt_fieldcat TYPE slis_t_fieldcat_alv,
      gs_layout   TYPE slis_layout_alv.
```

Figure 5.1: Define the sort table (FM)

View all the available sort table features

Take a moment to double-click SLIS_T_SORTINFO_ALV. Forward navigation will take you to the definition where you can see all the options available to you as sort features. Return by clicking once on the green BACK arrow.

Second, add a PERFORM statement (Figure 5.2). In subroutine ZF_BUILD _SORT_TABLE, you will code the features to be enabled. For now, double-click on ZF_BUILD_SORT_TABLE to add the form and endform statements of the subroutine to this program (Figure 5.9).

```
************* Start of main program logic *************

  PERFORM zf_build_layout USING gs_layout.

  PERFORM zf_build_fieldcatalog USING gt_fieldcat[].

  PERFORM zf_build_sort_table USING gt_sort[].

  PERFORM zf_display_alv.

************* End of main program logic *************
```

Figure 5.2: Populate the sort table (FM)

Finally, include the sort table GT_SORT in the function module call (Figure 5.3).

```
*----------------------------------------------------------------
FORM zf_display_alv.

  CALL FUNCTION 'REUSE_ALV_GRID_DISPLAY'
    EXPORTING
      i_callback_program = sy-repid
      is_layout          = gs_layout
      it_fieldcat        = gt_fieldcat[]
      it_sort            = gt_sort[]
    TABLES
      t_outtab           = gt_output
    EXCEPTIONS
      program_error      = 1
      OTHERS             = 2.

  IF sy-subrc <> 0.
    MESSAGE ID '00' TYPE 'I' NUMBER 001
      WITH 'REUSE_ALV_GRID_DISPLAY call error: ' sy-subrc.
    RETURN.
  ENDIF.

ENDFORM.
```

Figure 5.3: Pass the sort table (FM)

Now that these elements have been added to your program, you can begin adding individual sort features. For programs that call the REUSE _ALV_GRID_DISPLAY function module, follow the "Function Module" examples in each sub-section. The relevant figure captions are denoted (FM).

5.2.2 ALV control framework

For programs using the ALV control framework described in Chapter 3, first add a sort table structure based on the type LVC_T_SORT (Figure 5.4).

```
DATA: gs_layout   TYPE lvc_s_layo,           "layout params
      gs_output   TYPE lty_output,           "local structure (line)
      gt_output   TYPE STANDARD TABLE OF lty_output,
      gt_sort     TYPE lvc_t_sort,
      gt_fieldcat TYPE lvc_t_fcat.           "table
```

Figure 5.4: Define the sort table (CF)

View all the available sort features

Take a moment to double-click LVC_T_SORT. Forward navigation will take you to the definition where you can see all the options available to you as sort features. Return by clicking once on the green BACK arrow.

Second, add a PERFORM statement (Figure 5.5). In subroutine ZF_BUILD_SORT, you will code the features to be enabled. For now, double-click on ZF_BUILD_SORT to add the FORM and ENDFORM statements of the subroutine to this program (Figure 5.12).

```
DESCRIBE TABLE gt_output LINES gv_lines.
IF gv_lines NE 0.                          "data was retrieved
   SORT gt_output BY agencynum
                     carrid
                     connid
                     fldate
                     bookid.
   PERFORM zf_build_layout       USING gs_layout.
   PERFORM zf_build_fieldcatalog USING gt_fieldcat[].

   PERFORM zf_build_sort         USING gt_sort[].

   CALL SCREEN 9100.
ELSE.
   MESSAGE ID '00' TYPE 'I' NUMBER 001 WITH 'No data retrieved'.
   RETURN.
ENDIF.
```

Figure 5.5: Populate the sort table (CF)

Finally, include the sort table GT_SORT in the method call in the ZM_STATUS_9100 module (Figure 5.6).

```
*----------------------------------------------------------
MODULE zm_status_9100 OUTPUT.

  SET PF-STATUS 'MAIN9100'.
  IF g_custom_container IS INITIAL.
    CREATE OBJECT g_custom_container
      EXPORTING
        container_name = g_container.
    CREATE OBJECT grid1
      EXPORTING
        i_parent = g_custom_container.

    CALL METHOD grid1->set_table_for_first_display
      EXPORTING
        i_structure_name = 'LTY_OUTPUT'
        is_layout        = gs_layout
      CHANGING
        it_fieldcatalog  = gt_fieldcat
        it_sort          = gt_sort
        it_outtab        = gt_output.
  ENDIF.

ENDMODULE.
```

Figure 5.6: Pass the sort table (CF)

Now that these elements have been added to your program, you can begin adding the individual sort features. Follow the "ALV control framework" examples in each sub-section for an ALV control framework program. The relevant figure captions are denoted (CF).

5.3   Configuring a sort group

For the first sort example, you'll group the agency number (AGENCYNUM) and agency name (NAME) together, sorting by agency number.

5.3.1   Function module

With the sort table values passed in Figure 5.9, the data in the cells of this two-column group will merge as shown in Figure 5.7 instead of re-peating on every line as they did in Figure 4.12. All fields of the group must be specified in the sort table for the cell merge to act on all the columns of the group you have defined.

Airline Bookings: DREAM TRAVEL

Agency No.	Trvl agcy	Carrier	No.	Flight Date	Booking	Amount	Curr.	Airline	Amount	Curr.
102	Hot Socks Travel	AA	17	05/25/2011	12	657.88	AUD	American Airlines	803.58	USD
		AA	17	05/25/2011	52	1,038.77	AUD	American Airlines	1,268.82	USD
		AA	17	05/25/2011	82	328.94	AUD	American Airlines	401.79	USD
		AA	17	05/25/2011	104	311.63	AUD	American Airlines	380.65	USD
		AA	17	05/25/2011	240	346.26	AUD	American Airlines	422.94	USD

Figure 5.7: Group defined in sort table, before user action (FM)

When the user selects the first amount column and clicks the TOTAL button, subtotals and totals are displayed (Figure 5.8).

Airline Bookings: DREAM TRAVEL

Agency No.	Trvl agcy	Carrier	No.	Flight Date	Booking Σ	Amount	Curr.	Airline	Amount	Curr.
						1,028,775.04	AUD			
						4,364,153.15	GBP			
102	Hot Socks Tr...					1,028,775.04	AUD			
107	Ben McCloske...					856,941.48	GBP			
109	Kangeroos					981,205.58	GBP			
112	Super Agency					848,529.40	GBP			
123	Aussie Travel					836,886.68	GBP			
295	The Ultimate...					840,590.01	GBP			

Figure 5.8: Group defined in sort table, after user action (FM)

For both fields in Figure 5.9, provide:

- ▶ SPOS: sort position, can be incremented rather than static (for instance, LV_SPOS = LV_SPOS + 1)
- ▶ FIELDNAME: from the internal table

TABNAME: the internal table name For field(s) to be sorted, provide:

- ▶ UP or DOWN: ascending or descending sort direction

Because there is a one-to-one relationship between the agency number and the agency name, we will only sort by AGENCYNUM.

```
FORM zf_build_sort_table USING lt_sort TYPE slis_t_sortinfo_alv.

  DATA: ls_sort TYPE slis_sortinfo_alv.        "single row

  CLEAR lt_sort.

  CLEAR ls_sort.
  ls_sort-spos      = '1'.
  ls_sort-fieldname = 'AGENCYNUM'.
  ls_sort-tabname   = 'GT_OUTPUT'.
  ls_sort-up        = 'X'.
  APPEND ls_sort TO lt_sort.

  CLEAR ls_sort.
  ls_sort-spos      = '2'.
  ls_sort-fieldname = 'NAME'.
  ls_sort-tabname   = 'GT_OUTPUT'.
  ls_sort-group     = 'UL'.        "end of agencynum/name group
  ls_sort-subtot    = 'X'.         "sub-total amounts at this group
  ls_sort-expa      = 'X'.         "expandable to detail
  APPEND ls_sort TO lt_sort.

ENDFORM.
```

Figure 5.9: Define group for subtotals (FM)

For the final field of the group (also known as the control break), provide:

▶ GROUP: either UL (underline) or * (page feed)

▶ SUBTOT: level at which the subtotal will be provided

▶ EXPA: expandable, groups are closed when totaled (Figure 5.8) then can be expanded individually to view detail records

5.3.2   ALV control framework

With the sort table values passed in Figure 5.12, the data in the cells of this two-column group will merge as shown in Figure 5.10 instead of repeating on every line as they did in Figure 4.14. All fields of the group must be specified in the sort table for the cell merge to act on all the columns of the group.

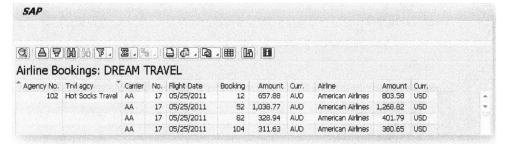

Figure 5.10: Group defined in sort table, before user action (CF)

When the user selects the first amount column and clicks the TOTAL button, subtotals and totals are displayed (Figure 5.11).

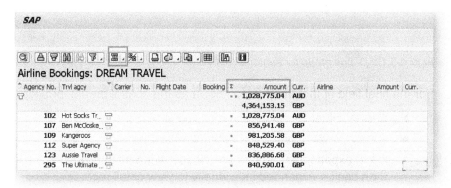

Figure 5.11: Group defined in sort table, after user action (CF)

For both fields in Figure 5.12, provide:

▶ SPOS: sort position, can be incremented rather than static (for instance, LV_SPOS = LV_SPOS + 1)

FIELDNAME: from the internal table For field(s) to be sorted, provide:

▶ UP or DOWN: ascending or descending sort direction

Because there is a one-to-one relationship between the agency number and the agency name, we will only sort by AGENCYNUM.

```
FORM zf_build_sort USING lt_sort TYPE lvc_t_sort.

  DATA: ls_sort TYPE lvc_s_sort.      "single row

  CLEAR lt_sort.

  CLEAR ls_sort.
  ls_sort-spos       = '1'.
  ls_sort-fieldname = 'AGENCYNUM'.
  ls_sort-up         = 'X'.
  APPEND ls_sort TO lt_sort.

  CLEAR ls_sort.
  ls_sort-spos       = '2'.
  ls_sort-fieldname = 'NAME'.
  ls_sort-group      = 'UL'.       "end of agencynum/name group
  ls_sort-subtot     = 'X'.       "sub-total amounts at this group
  ls_sort-expa       = 'X'.       "expandable to detail
  APPEND ls_sort TO lt_sort.

ENDFORM.
```

Figure 5.12: Define group for subtotals (CF)

For the final field of the group (also known as the control break), provide:

► GROUP: either UL (underline) or * (page feed)

► SUBTOT: level at which the subtotal will be provided

► EXPA: expandable, groups are closed when totaled (Figure 5.11) then can be expanded individually to view detail records

5.4   Changing the sort field in a sort group

Suppose you need to display the table in a different order, sorted by agency name instead of agency number. Without changing the sort order or the field order in the internal table, change the output using the ALV sort table.

5.4.1   Function module

With the sort table values passed in Figure 5.15, the data in the cells of this two-column group will merge as shown in Figure 5.13 instead of repeating on every line as they did in Figure 4.12. All fields of the group must be specified in the sort table for the cell merge to act on all the columns of the group.

Airline Bookings: DREAM TRAVEL

Agency No.	Trvl agcy	Carrier	No.	Flight Date	Booking	Amount	Curr.	Airline	Amount	Curr.
123	Aussie Travel	AA	17	05/25/2011	113	243.09	GBP	American Airlines	359.50	USD
		AA	17	05/25/2011	230	285.98	GBP	American Airlines	422.94	USD
		AA	17	05/25/2011	265	271.68	GBP	American Airlines	401.79	USD
		AA	17	05/25/2011	270	271.68	GBP	American Airlines	401.79	USD

Figure 5.13: Group defined in sort table, before user action (FM)

When the user selects the first amount column and clicks the TOTAL button, subtotals and totals are displayed (Figure 5.14).

Airline Bookings: DREAM TRAVEL

Agency No.	Trvl agcy	Carrier	No.	Flight Date	Booking Σ	Amount	Curr.	Airline	Amount	Curr.
						1,028,775.04	AUD			
						4,364,153.15	GBP			
123	Aussie Trav...					836,886.68	GBP			
107	Ben McClos...					856,941.48	GBP			
102	Hot Socks ...					1,028,775.04	AUD			
109	Kangeroos					981,205.58	GBP			
112	Super Age...					848,529.40	GBP			
295	The Ultima...					840,590.01	GBP			

Figure 5.14: Group defined in sort table, after user action (FM)

For both fields in Figure 5.15, provide:

▶ SPOS: sort position, can be incremented rather than static (for instance, LV_SPOS = LV_SPOS + 1)

▶ FIELDNAME: from the internal table

TABNAME: the internal table name For field(s) to be sorted, provide:

▶ UP or DOWN: ascending or descending sort direction

Because there is a one-to-one relationship between the agency name and the agency number, we will only sort by NAME.

```
*------------------------------------------------------------------
FORM zf_build_sort_table USING lt_sort TYPE slis_t_sortinfo_alv.

  DATA: ls_sort TYPE slis_sortinfo_alv.        "single row

  CLEAR lt_sort.

  CLEAR ls_sort.
  ls_sort-spos      = '1'.
  ls_sort-fieldname = 'NAME'.
  ls_sort-tabname   = 'GT_OUTPUT'.
  ls_sort-UP        = 'X'.
  APPEND ls_sort TO lt_sort.

  CLEAR ls_sort.
  ls_sort-spos      = '2'.
  ls_sort-fieldname = 'AGENCYNUM'.
  ls_sort-tabname   = 'GT_OUTPUT'.
  ls_sort-GROUP     = 'UL'.         "end of agencynum/name group
  ls_sort-subtot    = 'X'.          "sub-total amounts at this group
  ls_sort-expa      = 'X'.          "expandable to detail
  APPEND ls_sort TO lt_sort.

ENDFORM.
```

Figure 5.15: Define group for subtotals (FM)

For the final field of the group (also known as the control break), provide:

▶ GROUP: either UL (underline) or * (page feed with underline)

▶ SUBTOT: X. level at which the subtotal will be provided

▶ EXPA: expandable, groups are collapsed when totaled (Figure 5.14) then can be expanded individually to view detail records

5.4.2 ALV control framework

With the sort table values passed in Figure 5.18, the data in the cells of this two-column group will merge as shown in Figure 5.16 instead of repeating on every line as they did in Figure 4.14. All fields of the group must be specified in the sort table for the cell merge to act on all the columns of the group.

Agency No.	Trvl agcy	Carrier	No.	Flight Date	Booking	Amount	Curr.	Airline	Amount	Curr.
123	Aussie Travel	AA	17	05/25/2011	113	243.09	GBP	American Airlines	359.50	USD
		AA	17	05/25/2011	230	285.98	GBP	American Airlines	422.94	USD
		AA	17	05/25/2011	265	271.68	GBP	American Airlines	401.79	USD
		AA	17	05/25/2011	270	271.68	GBP	American Airlines	401.79	USD

Figure 5.16: Group defined in sort table, before user action (CF)

When the user selects the first amount column and clicks the TOTAL button, subtotals and totals are displayed (Figure 5.17).

Agency No.	Trvl agcy	Carrier	No.	Flight Date	Booking	Σ	Amount	Curr.	Airline	Amount	Curr.
						■ ■	1,028,775.04	AUD			
							4,364,153.15	GBP			
123	Aussie Trav...					■	836,886.68	GBP			
107	Ben McClos...					■	856,941.48	GBP			
102	Hot Socks...					■	1,028,775.04	AUD			
109	Kangeroos					■	981,205.58	GBP			
112	Super Age...					■	848,529.40	GBP			
295	The Ultima...					■	840,590.01	GBP			

Figure 5.17: Group defined in sort table, after user action (CF)

For both fields in Figure 5.18, provide:

▶ SPOS: sort position, can be incremented rather than static (for instance, lv_spos = lv_spos + 1)

FIELDNAME: from the internal table For field(s) to be sorted, provide:

▶ UP or DOWN: ascending or descending sort direction

Because there is a one-to-one relationship between the agency name and the agency number, we will only sort by NAME.

89

```
*--------------------------------------------------------------------*
FORM zf_build_sort USING lt_sort TYPE lvc_t_sort.

  DATA: ls_sort TYPE lvc_s_sort.        "single row

  CLEAR lt_sort.

  CLEAR ls_sort.
  ls_sort-spos      = '1'.
  ls_sort-fieldname = 'NAME'.
  ls_sort-up        = 'X'.
  APPEND ls_sort TO lt_sort.

  CLEAR ls_sort.
  ls_sort-spos      = '2'.
  ls_sort-fieldname = 'AGENCYNUM'.
  ls_sort-group     = 'UL'.      "end of agencynum/name group
  ls_sort-subtot    = 'X'.       "sub-total amounts at this group
  ls_sort-expa      = 'X'.       "expandable to detail
  APPEND ls_sort TO lt_sort.

ENDFORM.
```

Figure 5.18: Define group for subtotals (CF)

For the final field of the group (also known as the control break), provide:

▶ GROUP: either UL (underline) or * (page feed with underline)

▶ SUBTOT: X, level at which the subtotal will be provided

▶ EXPA: expandable, groups are collapsed when totaled (Figure 5.17) then can be expanded individually to view detail records

5.5 Changing column order to reflect sort order

Generally, it is a best practice to display data with the sorted columns ordered from left to right. In Chapter 5.4, you changed the program to output the ALV records in ascending order by agency name instead of by agency number. To visually reinforce this sort order for the user, you will now change the field catalog so that NAME is output to the left of AGENCYNUM.

5.5.1 Function module

The original sort and column order is shown in Figure 5.8. The revised output, reflecting the new agency name sort order, is shown in Figure 5.19.

Airline Bookings: DREAM TRAVEL

Travel agency name ▲▼		Agency No.	Carrier	No.	Flight Date	Booking	Amount	Curr.	Airline	Amount	Curr.
▽							▪▪ 1,028,775.04	AUD			
							4,364,153.15	GBP			
Aussie Travel	🖵	123					▪ 836,886.68	GBP			
Ben McCloskey Ltd.	🖵	107					▪ 856,941.48	GBP			
Hot Socks Travel	🖵	102					▪ 1,028,775.04	AUD			
Kangeroos	🖵	109					▪ 981,205.58	GBP			
Super Agency	🖵	112					▪ 848,529.40	GBP			
The Ultimate Answer	🖵	295					▪ 840,590.01	GBP			

Figure 5.19: Sorted column moved to the left (FM)

Since the field catalog controls column order, the change is made there. Simply change the order of the two fields (Figure 5.20).

```
FORM zf_build_fieldcatalog USING lt_fieldcat TYPE slis_t_fieldcat_alv.

  DATA: ls_fieldcat TYPE slis_fieldcat_alv.    "single row

  CLEAR ls_fieldcat.
  ls_fieldcat-fieldname     = 'NAME'.
  ls_fieldcat-ref_fieldname = 'NAME'.
  ls_fieldcat-ref_tabname   = 'STRAVELAG'.
  APPEND ls_fieldcat TO lt_fieldcat.

  CLEAR ls_fieldcat.
  ls_fieldcat-fieldname     = 'AGENCYNUM'.
  ls_fieldcat-ref_fieldname = 'AGENCYNUM'.
  ls_fieldcat-ref_tabname   = 'STRAVELAG'.     "data dict info
  APPEND ls_fieldcat TO lt_fieldcat.

  CLEAR ls_fieldcat.
  ls_fieldcat-fieldname     = 'CURRENCY'.
  ls_fieldcat-ref_fieldname = 'CURRENCY'.
  ls_fieldcat-ref_tabname   = 'STRAVELAG'.
  ls_fieldcat-no_out        = 'X'.             "hide field
  APPEND ls_fieldcat TO lt_fieldcat.
```

Figure 5.20: Changing the order of the columns (FM)

Changing column order using COL_POS

 You can also change column order by populating an explicit number in the COL_POS field for each record included in your field catalog.

If you have not yet hidden the travel agency CURRENCY field, consider doing so now with the NO_OUT setting (Figure 5.20).

5.5.2 ALV control framework

The original sort and column order is shown in Figure 5.11. The revised output, reflecting the new agency name sort order, is shown in Figure 5.21.

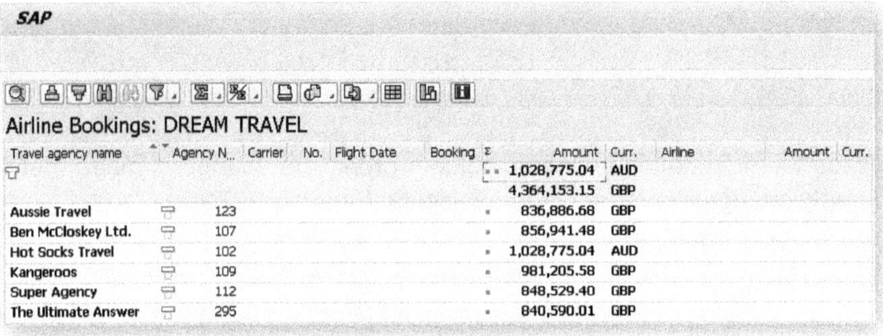

Figure 5.21: Sorted column moved to the left (CF)

Since the field catalog controls column order, the change is made there. Simply change the order of the two fields (Figure 5.22).

```
FORM zf_build_fieldcatalog USING lt_fieldcat TYPE lvc_t_fcat.

  DATA: ls_fieldcat TYPE lvc_s_fcat.      "single row

  CLEAR ls_fieldcat.
  ls_fieldcat-fieldname = 'NAME'.
  ls_fieldcat-ref_table = 'STRAVELAG'.
  APPEND ls_fieldcat TO lt_fieldcat.

  CLEAR ls_fieldcat.
  ls_fieldcat-fieldname = 'AGENCYNUM'.
  ls_fieldcat-ref_table = 'STRAVELAG'.
  APPEND ls_fieldcat TO lt_fieldcat.

  CLEAR ls_fieldcat.
  ls_fieldcat-fieldname = 'CURRENCY'.
  ls_fieldcat-ref_table = 'STRAVELAG'.
  ls_fieldcat-no_out    = 'X'.            "hide field
  APPEND ls_fieldcat TO lt_fieldcat.
```

Figure 5.22: Changing the order of the columns (CF)

Changing column order using COL_POS

You can also change column order by populating an explicit number in the COL_POS field for each record included in your field catalog.

If you have not yet hidden the travel agency CURRENCY field, consider doing so now with the NO_OUT setting (Figure 5.22).

5.6   Configuring a two-level sort

Sometimes a single-level subtotal is adequate, but often data can be grouped multiple ways and the ability to view subtotals across multiple levels is desirable.

The training scenario ALV program currently provides a subtotal by travel agency and currency-specific totals for all the agencies specified in the selection screen (Figure 5.19 and Figure 5.21). You'll now add a subtotal within each agency to show the amount of income by airline.

5.6.1   Function module

The field that provides the desired subtotal by airline is the third column of your output table: CARRID (labeled ID in Figure 5.23). Comparing the single-level sort of Figure 5.13 to the two-level sort of Figure 5.23, you'll notice that the third column is now displayed with cell merge.

Airline Bookings: DREAM TRAVEL

Trvl agcy	Agency No.	ID	No.	Flight Date	Booking	Amount	Curr.	Airline	Amount	Curr.
Aussie Travel	123	AA	17	05/25/2011	113	243.09	GBP	American Airlines	359.50	USD
			17	05/25/2011	230	285.98	GBP	American Airlines	422.94	USD
			17	05/25/2011	265	271.68	GBP	American Airlines	401.79	USD
			17	05/25/2011	270	271.68	GBP	American Airlines	401.79	USD

Figure 5.23: Second sort group defined, before user action (FM)

With the two-level sort, the user will see airline subtotals within each travel agency when selecting an amount column and clicking on the TO-TAL button (Figure 5.24).

Airline Bookings: DREAM TRAVEL

Trvl agcy	Agency No.	ID	No.	Flight Date	Booking	Σ	Amount	Curr.	Airline	Amount	Curr.
						▪▪	1,028,775.04	AUD			
							4,364,153.15	GBP			
Aussie Tra...	123	AA				▪	36,368.59	GBP			
		AZ				▪	143,794.85	GBP			
		DL				▪	57,342.94	GBP			
		JL				▪	99,522.00	GBP			
		LH				▪	109,707.54	GBP			
		QF				▪	64,387.22	GBP			
		SQ				▪	159,901.80	GBP			
		UA				▪	165,861.74	GBP			
Ben McClo...	107	AA				▪	37,297.99	GBP			
		AZ				▪	151,795.04	GBP			

Figure 5.24: Second sort group defined, after user action (FM)

To add an additional group for subtotals (Figure 5.25), add the field(s) that comprise the next group and provide:

▶ SPOS: sort position, can be incremented rather than static (for instance, lv_spos = lv_spos + 1)

▶ FIELDNAME: from the internal table

TABNAME: the internal table name For field(s) to be sorted, provide:

UP or DOWN: ascending or descending sort direction For the final field of each group, provide:

▶ GROUP: either UL (underline) or * (page feed with underline)

For the final field of the final group, provide:

▶ SUBTOT: X, level at which the subtotal will be provided

▶ EXPA: expandable, groups are collapsed when totaled (Figure 5.24) then can be expanded individually to view detail records

```
*
FORM zf_build_sort_table USING lt_sort TYPE slis_t_sortinfo_alv.

  DATA: ls_sort TYPE slis_sortinfo_alv.
  CLEAR lt_sort.

  CLEAR ls_sort.
  ls_sort-spos      = '1'.
  ls_sort-fieldname = 'NAME'.
  ls_sort-tabname   = 'GT_OUTPUT'.
  ls_sort-up        = 'X'.            "explicit sort
  APPEND ls_sort TO lt_sort.

  CLEAR ls_sort.
  ls_sort-spos      = '2'.
  ls_sort-fieldname = 'AGENCYNUM'.
  ls_sort-tabname   = 'GT_OUTPUT'.
  ls_sort-group     = 'UL'.          "end of name/agencynum group
  APPEND ls_sort TO lt_sort.

  CLEAR ls_sort.
  ls_sort-spos      = '3'.
  ls_sort-fieldname = 'CARRID'.
  ls_sort-tabname   = 'GT_OUTPUT'.
  ls_sort-up        = 'X'.            "explicit sort
  ls_sort-group     = 'UL'.          "end of carrid group
  ls_sort-subtot    = 'X'.            "sub-total amounts at this group
  ls_sort-expa      = 'X'.            "initially closed, expandable
  APPEND ls_sort TO lt_sort.

ENDFORM.
```

Figure 5.25: Defining a second group for subtotals (FM)

Because AGENCYNUM is no longer part of the **last** group defined, the SUB-TOT and EXPA settings move from AGENCYNUM to CARRID (Figure 5.25). AGENCYNUM is still the last field of a group so it retains its GROUP setting for inclusion in the NAME/AGENCYNUM group subtotal.

5.6.2   ALV control framework

The field that provides the desired subtotal by airline is the third column of your output table: CARRID (labeled ID in Figure 5.26). Comparing the single-level sort of Figure 5.16 to the two-level sort of Figure 5.26, you'll notice that the third column is now displayed with cell merge.

SAP

Airline Bookings: DREAM TRAVEL

Trvl agcy	Agency No.	ID	No.	Flight Date	Booking	Amount	Curr.	Airline	Amount	Curr.
Aussie Travel	123	AA	17	05/25/2011	113	243.09	GBP	American Airlines	359.50	USD
			17	05/25/2011	230	285.98	GBP	American Airlines	422.94	USD
			17	05/25/2011	265	271.68	GBP	American Airlines	401.79	USD
			17	05/25/2011	270	271.68	GBP	American Airlines	401.79	USD

Figure 5.26: Second sort group defined, before user action (CF)

With the two-level sort, the user will see airline subtotals within each travel agency when selecting an amount column and clicking on the TO-TAL button (Figure 5.27).

SAP

Airline Bookings: DREAM TRAVEL

Trvl agcy	Agency No.	ID	No.	Flight Date	Booking	Σ Amount	Curr.	Airline	Amount	Curr.
▽						1,028,775.04	AUD			
						4,364,153.15	GBP			
Aussie Tra...	123	AA ▽				36,368.59	GBP			
		AZ ▽				143,794.85	GBP			
		DL ▽				57,342.94	GBP			
		JL ▽				99,522.00	GBP			
		LH ▽				109,707.54	GBP			
		QF ▽				64,387.22	GBP			
		SQ ▽				159,901.80	GBP			
		UA ▽				165,861.74	GBP			
Ben McClo...	107	AA ▽				37,297.99	GBP			
		AZ ▽				151,795.04	GBP			

Figure 5.27: Second sort group defined, after user action (CF)

To add an additional group for subtotals (Figure 5.28), add the field(s) that comprise the next group and provide:

- ▶ SPOS: sort position, can be incremented rather than static (for instance, lv_spos = lv_spos + 1)

FIELDNAME: from the internal table For field(s) to be sorted, provide:

UP or DOWN: ascending or descending sort direction For the final field of each group, provide:

- ▶ GROUP: either UL (underline) or * (page feed with underline)

For the final field of the final group, provide:

▶ SUBTOT: X, level at which the subtotal will be provided

▶ EXPA: expandable, groups are collapsed when totaled (Figure 5.27) then can be expanded individually to view detail records

```
FORM zf_build_sort USING lt_sort TYPE lvc_t_sort.

  DATA: ls_sort TYPE lvc_s_sort.
  CLEAR lt_sort.

  CLEAR ls_sort.
  ls_sort-spos      = '1'.
  ls_sort-fieldname = 'NAME'.
  ls_sort-up        = 'X'.          "explicit sort
  APPEND ls_sort TO lt_sort.

  CLEAR ls_sort.
  ls_sort-spos      = '2'.
  ls_sort-fieldname = 'AGENCYNUM'.
  ls_sort-group     = 'UL'.         "end of name/agencynum
  APPEND ls_sort TO lt_sort.

  CLEAR ls_sort.
  ls_sort-spos      = '3'.
  ls_sort-fieldname = 'CARRID'.
  ls_sort-up        = 'X'.          "explicit sort
  ls_sort-group     = 'UL'.         "end of carrid group
  ls_sort-subtot    = 'X'.          "sub-total amounts at this group
  ls_sort-expa      = 'X'.          "initially closed, expandable
  APPEND ls_sort TO lt_sort.
ENDFORM.
```

Figure 5.28: Defining a second group for subtotals (CF)

Because AGENCYNUM is no longer part of the **last** group defined, the SUB-TOT and EXPA settings move from AGENCYNUM to CARRID (Figure 5.28). AGENCYNUM is still the last field of a group so it retains its GROUP setting for inclusion in the NAME/AGENCYNUM group subtotal.

5.7   Populating the sort table from the selection screen

If desired, you can populate the sort table based on a user preference from the selection screen. For this exercise, you'll provide the user with a choice of two subtotal groups coded earlier:

▶ By agency name

▶ By airline carrier within agency

Reorder columns to support subtotals options

If you provide a subtotal option that would be better supported visually by a different column order, be sure to add an IF statement to the field catalog to provide the alternative column order. In this section, both of the subtotal options begin with an agency name sort. The agency name is the leftmost column of the display so the column order in the field catalog works for both options. If we were to include a subtotal option of "by airline carrier, then by agency name", we would sort first by CARRID when building the sort table and would list CARRID as the first field in the field catalog as described in Chapter 5.5.

5.7.1 Function module

The selection screen will provide the user with a choice between subtotals by agency or by airline within each agency (Figure 5.29).

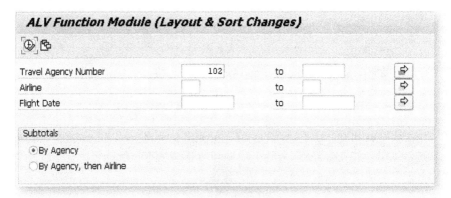

Figure 5.29: Subtotal options for user selection (FM)

Add the code shown in Figure 5.30 to create the radio buttons on the selection screen.

```
SELECT-OPTIONS: s_agnum FOR stravelag-agencynum DEFAULT '123',
                s_carid FOR sbook-carrid,
                s_fldat FOR sbook-fldate.
SELECTION-SCREEN: SKIP.
SELECTION-SCREEN: BEGIN OF BLOCK b1 WITH FRAME TITLE text-003.
SELECTION-SCREEN: BEGIN OF LINE.      "Agency
  PARAMETERS:      rb_1 RADIOBUTTON GROUP rad1 DEFAULT 'X'.
  SELECTION-SCREEN COMMENT 5(25) TEXT-004 FOR FIELD rb_1.
SELECTION-SCREEN: END OF LINE.

SELECTION-SCREEN: BEGIN OF LINE.      "Agency, Airline
  PARAMETERS:      rb_2 RADIOBUTTON GROUP rad1.
  SELECTION-SCREEN COMMENT 5(25) TEXT-005 FOR FIELD rb_2.
SELECTION-SCREEN: END OF LINE.
SELECTION-SCREEN: END OF BLOCK b1.
```

Figure 5.30: Radio buttons for subtotal options (FM)

Provide new labels on the selection screen by double-clicking on each TEXT-nnn in Figure 5.30 to navigate to the TEXT SYMBOLS tab (Figure 5.31). Type the text, save, and activate. Use the green BACK arrow to return to your source code.

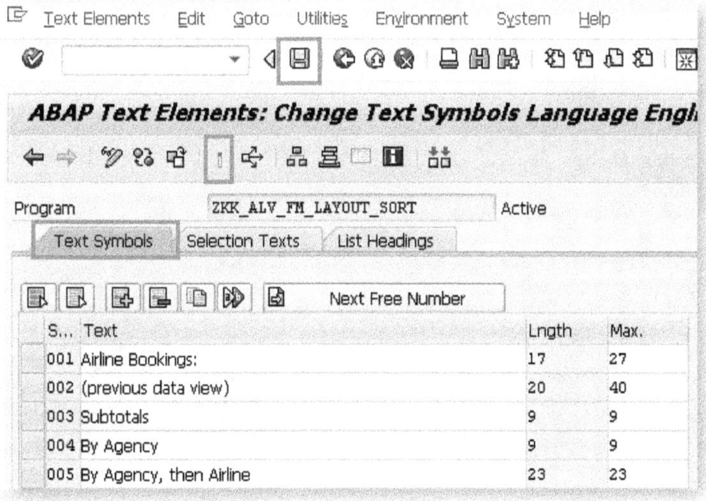

Figure 5.31: Radio button text symbols (FM)

Add an IF statement to the ZF_BUILD_SORT_TABLE logic based on radio button 1 having been chosen. The code for this choice (Figure 5.32) matches the single-level sort previously coded (Figure 5.15).

```
*-----------------------------------------------------------------*
FORM zf_build_sort_table USING lt_sort TYPE slis_t_sortinfo_alv.

  DATA: ls_sort TYPE slis_sortinfo_alv.
  CLEAR lt_sort.

  IF rb_1 = 'X'.                      "by agency
    CLEAR ls_sort.
    ls_sort-spos        = '1'.
    ls_sort-fieldname   = 'NAME'.
    ls_sort-tabname     = 'GT_OUTPUT'.
    ls_sort-up          = 'X'.        "explicit sort
    APPEND ls_sort TO lt_sort.

    CLEAR ls_sort.
    ls_sort-spos        = '2'.
    ls_sort-fieldname   = 'AGENCYNUM'.
    ls_sort-tabname     = 'GT_OUTPUT'.
    ls_sort-group       = 'UL'.       "end of name/agencynum group
    ls_sort-subtot      = 'X'.        "sub-total amounts at this group
    ls_sort-expa        = 'X'.        "initially closed, expandable
    APPEND ls_sort TO lt_sort.
```

Figure 5.32: Logic for first subtotal option (FM)

For the ELSE portion of the ZF_BUILD_SORT_TABLE logic based on radio button 2 having been chosen, add the code shown in Figure 5.33. This code matches the two-level sort previously coded (Figure 5.25).

```
  ELSE.                              "by agency, airline
    CLEAR ls_sort.
    ls_sort-spos        = '1'.
    ls_sort-fieldname   = 'NAME'.
    ls_sort-tabname     = 'GT_OUTPUT'.
    ls_sort-UP          = 'X'.        "explicit sort
    APPEND ls_sort TO lt_sort.

    CLEAR ls_sort.
    ls_sort-spos        = '2'.
    ls_sort-fieldname   = 'AGENCYNUM'.
    ls_sort-tabname     = 'GT_OUTPUT'.
    ls_sort-GROUP       = 'UL'.       "end of name/agencynum group
    APPEND ls_sort TO lt_sort.

    CLEAR ls_sort.
    ls_sort-spos        = '3'.
    ls_sort-fieldname   = 'CARRID'.
    ls_sort-tabname     = 'GT_OUTPUT'.
    ls_sort-up          = 'X'.        "explicit sort
    ls_sort-group       = 'UL'.       "end of carrid group
    ls_sort-subtot      = 'X'.        "sub-total amounts at this group
    ls_sort-expa        = 'X'.        "initially closed, expandable
    APPEND ls_sort TO lt_sort.
  ENDIF.
ENDFORM.
```

Figure 5.33: Logic for second subtotal option (FM)

Execute the program with each of the radio button choices to see the difference. If you have not yet added the DO_SUM setting to an amount field in the field catalog (Chapter 6.2), you will need to highlight an amount column in the ALV display and click on the TOTAL button to view the subtotal.

The displays with subtotals should match Figure 5.19 and Figure 5.24, respectively.

5.7.2 ALV control framework

The selection screen will provide the user with a choice between subtotals by agency or by airline within each agency (Figure 5.34).

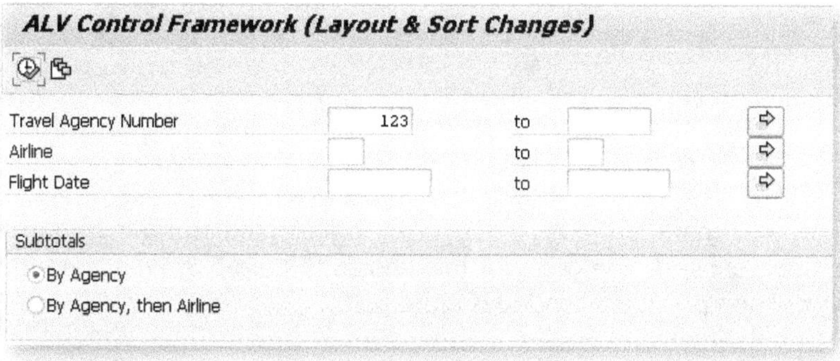

Figure 5.34: Subtotal options for user selection (CF)

Add the code shown in Figure 5.35 to create the radio buttons on the selection screen.

```
SELECT-OPTIONS: s_agnum FOR stravelag-agencynum DEFAULT '123',
                s_carid FOR sbook-carrid,
                s_fldat FOR sbook-fldate.
SELECTION-SCREEN: SKIP.
SELECTION-SCREEN: BEGIN OF BLOCK b1 WITH FRAME TITLE TEXT-003.
  SELECTION-SCREEN: BEGIN OF LINE.      "Agency
    PARAMETERS:     rb_1 RADIOBUTTON GROUP rad1 DEFAULT 'X'.
    SELECTION-SCREEN COMMENT 5(25) TEXT-004 FOR FIELD rb_1.
  SELECTION-SCREEN: END OF LINE.

  SELECTION-SCREEN: BEGIN OF LINE.      "Agency, Airline
    PARAMETERS:     rb_2 RADIOBUTTON GROUP rad1.
    SELECTION-SCREEN COMMENT 5(25) TEXT-005 FOR FIELD rb_2.
  SELECTION-SCREEN: END OF LINE.
SELECTION-SCREEN: END OF BLOCK b1.
```

Figure 5.35: Radio buttons for subtotal options (CF)

Provide new labels on the selection screen by double-clicking on each TEXT-nnn in Figure 5.35 to navigate to the TEXT SYMBOLS tab (Figure 5.36). Type the text, save, and activate. Use the green BACK arrow to return to your source code.

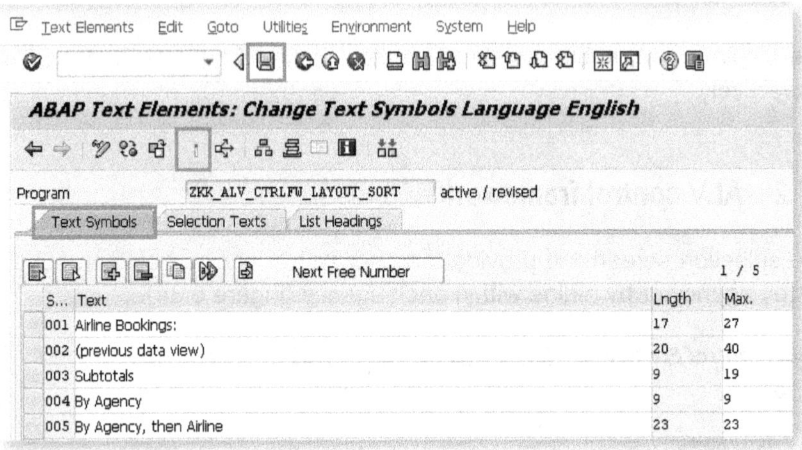

Figure 5.36: Radio button text symbols (CF)

Add an IF statement to the ZF_BUILD_SORT logic based on radio button 1 having been chosen. The code for this choice (Figure 5.37) matches the single-level sort previously coded (Figure 5.18).

```
*-----------------------------------------------------------------*
FORM zf_build_sort USING lt_sort TYPE lvc_t_sort.

  DATA: ls_sort TYPE lvc_s_sort.
  CLEAR lt_sort.

  IF rb_1 = 'X'.                      "by agency
    CLEAR ls_sort.
    ls_sort-spos       = '1'.
    ls_sort-fieldname = 'NAME'.
    ls_sort-UP        = 'X'.          "explicit sort
    APPEND ls_sort TO lt_sort.

    CLEAR ls_sort.
    ls_sort-spos       = '2'.
    ls_sort-fieldname = 'AGENCYNUM'.
    ls_sort-GROUP      = 'UL'.         "end of name/agencynum group
    ls_sort-subtot    = 'X'.          "sub-total amounts at this group
    ls_sort-expa       = 'X'.          "initially closed, expandable
    APPEND ls_sort TO lt_sort.
```

Figure 5.37: Logic for first subtotal option (CF)

For the ELSE portion of the ZF_BUILD_SORT logic based on radio button 2 having been chosen, add the code shown in Figure 5.38. This code matches the two-level sort previously coded (Figure 5.28).

```
ELSE.                                    "by agency, airline
  CLEAR ls_sort.
  ls_sort-spos        = '1'.
  ls_sort-fieldname = 'NAME'.
  ls_sort-up          = 'X'.             "explicit sort
  APPEND ls_sort TO lt_sort.

  CLEAR ls_sort.
  ls_sort-spos        = '2'.
  ls_sort-fieldname = 'AGENCYNUM'.
  ls_sort-group       = 'UL'.            "end of name/agencynum group
  APPEND ls_sort TO lt_sort.

  CLEAR ls_sort.
  ls_sort-spos        = '3'.
  ls_sort-fieldname = 'CARRID'.
  ls_sort-up          = 'X'.             "explicit sort
  ls_sort-group       = 'UL'.            "end of carrid group
  ls_sort-subtot      = 'X'.             "sub-total amounts at this group
  ls_sort-expa        = 'X'.             "initially closed, expandable
  APPEND ls_sort TO lt_sort.
ENDIF.

ENDFORM.
```

Figure 5.38: Logic for second subtotal option (CF)

Execute the program with each of the radio button choices to see the difference. If you have not yet added the DO_SUM setting to an amount field in the field catalog (Chapter 6.2), you will need to highlight an amount column in the ALV display and click on the TOTAL button to view the subtotal.

The displays with subtotals should match Figure 5.21 and Figure 5.27, respectively.

5.8   Summary

In this chapter, you learned how to use the ALV sort table to control sorting, grouping, and subtotal behavior. You added three foundational lines of code to both types of SAP List Viewer programs covered in this book, then populated the sort table to meet various requirements.

Key points:

- ▶ Record order is controlled by the sort table
- ▶ Column order is controlled by the field catalog table
- ▶ More than one GROUP can be defined in the sort table
- ▶ Valid values for GROUP are UL and * (not X)
- ▶ EXPA displays subtotals with the detail lines hidden yet allows the user to expand those lines to see the detail
- ▶ The field catalog setting NO_OUT can be used to hide nonessential fields and provide a simpler group for subtotal display
- ▶ The field catalog setting DO_SUM can be used to provide subtotals on initial display

Best practices:

- ▶ Populate the GROUP setting on the "rightmost" field of each grouping of related fields.
- ▶ Populate SUBTOT and EXPA settings only on the final group.
- ▶ Identify the currency key field for each currency amount using CFIELDNAME when populating the field catalog table.
- ▶ Identify the unit of measure field for each quantity in using QFIELDNAME when populating the field catalog table.

6 Adding more features to an ALV program

In this chapter, you'll add even more features to the two types of ALV programs. Some features activate additional functionality. Other features configure the initial display of data so the user can gain insight with less manual effort.

As before, you may wish to make a copy of your in-progress program and variants now, then add the features described in this chapter to the new copy. This will allow you to compare previous behavior to new behavior. Activate and save as you go. (I called my program copies ZKK_ALV_FM_LAYOUT_SORT_MORE and ZKK_ALV_CTRLFW_LAYOUT _SORT_MOR.)

6.1   Passing hidden columns of data

Some fields that are included in ALV output can be useful for trouble-shooting, for special analysis, or for future use, but are not needed by most users. For the training scenario, the master data currency key associated with each travel agency (CURRENCY) can be hidden from the initial display of data. The currency keys associated with the two transactional booking amounts (FORCURKEY and LOCCURKEY) are essential for understanding and summing those amounts so they must be retained.

Users of the ALV data can reveal hidden columns by using the CHANGE LAYOUT button to change the displayed columns (Figure 6.1).

Figure 6.1: Users can re-display hidden fields

6.1.1 Function module

Comparing Figure 6.2 to Figure 4.20, you'll see that the currency column that had appeared between the travel agency name and the carrier code is no longer present.

Airline Bookings: DREAM TRAVEL

Agency No.	Trvl agcy	Carrier	No.	Flight Date	Booking	Amount	Curr.	Airline	Amount	Curr.
102	Hot Socks Travel	AA	17	05/25/2011	12	657.88	AUD	American Airlines	803.58	USD
		AA	17	05/25/2011	52	1,038.77	AUD	American Airlines	1,268.82	USD
		AA	17	05/25/2011	82	328.94	AUD	American Airlines	401.79	USD
		AA	17	05/25/2011	104	311.63	AUD	American Airlines	380.65	USD

Figure 6.2: Example of field hidden on initial display (FM)

To hide a field, fill the NO_OUT field of the field catalog with X as shown in Figure 6.3.

```
CLEAR ls_fieldcat.
ls_fieldcat-fieldname     = 'CURRENCY'.
ls_fieldcat-ref_fieldname = 'CURRENCY'.
ls_fieldcat-ref_tabname   = 'STRAVELAG'.
ls_fieldcat-no_out        = 'X'.            "hide field
APPEND ls_fieldcat TO lt_fieldcat.
```

Figure 6.3: Value to set for hidden field (FM)

6.1.2 ALV control framework

Comparing Figure 6.4 to Figure 4.25, you'll see that the currency column that had appeared between the travel agency name and the carrier code is no longer present.

SAP

Airline Bookings: DREAM TRAVEL

Agency No.	Trvl agcy	Carrier	No.	Flight Date	Booking	Amount	Curr.	Airline	Amount	Curr.
102	Hot Socks Travel	AA	17	05/25/2011	12	657.88	AUD	American Airlines	803.58	USD
102	Hot Socks Travel	AA	17	05/25/2011	52	1,038.77	AUD	American Airlines	1,268.82	USD
102	Hot Socks Travel	AA	17	05/25/2011	82	328.94	AUD	American Airlines	401.79	USD
102	Hot Socks Travel	AA	17	05/25/2011	104	311.63	AUD	American Airlines	380.65	USD

Figure 6.4: Example of field hidden on initial display (CF)

To hide a field, fill the NO_OUT field of the field catalog with X as shown in Figure 6.5.

```
CLEAR ls_fieldcat.
ls_fieldcat-fieldname = 'CURRENCY'.
ls_fieldcat-ref_table = 'STRAVELAG'.
ls_fieldcat-no_out    = 'X'.            "hide field
APPEND ls_fieldcat TO lt_fieldcat.
```

Figure 6.5: Value to set for hidden field (CF)

6.2 Displaying totals and subtotals immediately

In Chapter 5, we first displayed the ALV data grouped, but unsummed (Figure 5.7 and Figure 5.10). User action was necessary to display totals—an amount column had to be selected and the TOTAL button had to be clicked in order to view the subtotals (Figure 5.8 and Figure 5.11).

For the training scenario, the owner of the Dream Travel group of agencies prefers to see the data already summed by "Amount in foreign currency" (FORCURAM), the amount that corresponds to each travel agency's working currency. You can provide this automatic summing by enabling a setting in the field catalog: DO_SUM.

"Not enabling" is different than disabling

 The DO_SUM setting in the field catalog provides a default behavior without disabling the ability of the user to over-ride it after display. This is generally desirable, supporting both standardization and flexibility. For some reports, however, it may be necessary to prevent some user actions. "Not enabling" a feature (by omitting it from the field catalog or by passing a blank value) may not be sufficient. In those situations, the developer should look for an SAP-provided setting in the structure that will truly disable the feature. NO_SUM is an example of a field catalog setting that prevents the user from using the TOTAL button on a specified amount column (Figure 6.6).

Airline Bookings: DREAM TRAVEL

Travel agency name	Agency No.	ID	No.	Date	Booking	Amount	Curr.	Airline	Amount	Curr.
Aussie Travel	123	A	17	05/...	113	243.09	GBP	Ame...	359.50	USD
		A	17	05/...	230	285.98	GBP	Ame...	422.94	USD
		A	17	05/...	265	271.68	GBP	Ame...	401.79	USD
		A	17	05/...	270	271.68	GBP	Ame...	401.79	USD
		A	17	05/	279	285.98	GBP	Ame	422.94	USD

☑ Desired operation cannot be performed for column 'Amount (loc.currncy)'

Figure 6.6: Use of no_sum to prevent manual summing (FM)

6.2.1 Function module

Your program provides a selection screen option (Figure 5.29.) for displaying subtotals "By Agency" or "By Agency, then Airline". The desired result for the "By Agency" option is shown in Figure 6.7.

Airline Bookings: DREAM TRAVEL

Travel agency name	Agency No.	ID No.	Date	Booking	Σ	Amount	Curr.	Airline	Amount	Curr.
					▪▪	1,028,775.04	AUD			
						4,364,153.15	GBP			
Aussie Travel		123			▪	836,886.68	GBP			
Ben McCloskey Ltd.		107			▪	856,941.48	GBP			
Hot Socks Travel		102			▪	1,028,775.04	AUD			
Kangeroos		109			▪	981,205.58	GBP			
Super Agency		112			▪	848,529.40	GBP			
The Ultimate Answer		295			▪	840,590.01	GBP			

Figure 6.7: Automating the display of totals, one level (FM)

The desired result for the "By Agency, then Airline" option is shown in Figure 6.8.

Airline Bookings: DREAM TRAVEL

Travel agency name	Agency No.	ID	No.	Date	Booking	Σ	Amount	Curr.	Airline	Amount	Curr.
						▪▪	1,028,775.04	AUD			
							4,364,153.15	GBP			
Aussie Travel		123	AA			▪	36,368.59	GBP			
			AZ			▪	143,794.85	GBP			
			DL			▪	57,342.94	GBP			
			JL			▪	99,522.00	GBP			
			LH			▪	109,707.54	GBP			
			QF			▪	64,387.22	GBP			
			SQ			▪	159,901.80	GBP			
			UA			▪	165,861.74	GBP			
Ben McCloskey Ltd.		107	AA			▪	37,297.99	GBP			
			AZ			▪	151,795.04	GBP			

Figure 6.8: Automating the display of totals, two levels (FM)

The initial display of subtotals for both of these groupings (previously coded into the sort table based upon the user choice) was accomplished by adding the DO_SUM setting for this amount field (FORCURAM) in the field catalog (Figure 6.9).

```
CLEAR ls_fieldcat.
ls_fieldcat-fieldname      = 'FORCURAM'.    "amount field !
ls_fieldcat-cfieldname     = 'FORCURKEY'.   "associated currency key
ls_fieldcat-ctabname       = 'SBOOK'.
ls_fieldcat-ref_fieldname  = 'FORCURAM'.
ls_fieldcat-ref_tabname    = 'SBOOK'.
ls_fieldcat-do_sum         = 'X'.           "display summed
APPEND ls_fieldcat TO lt_fieldcat.
```

Figure 6.9: Value to set for automatic summing of an amount field (FM)

Know your data and the user needs

 Take care not to overdo the use of DO_SUM. Identify the subtotals that will provide value and meet user requirements. In Figure 6.10, both the foreign currency (associated with the travel agency) and the local currency (associated with the airline) have been totaled, providing a confusing display.

In Chapter 5.7, you learned how to obtain user preferences from the selection screen and use IF statements to manage which settings were passed to the ALV function module. To avoid the confusion of two summed amounts (Figure 6.10), you can provide the user with the option of displaying amounts in foreign currency, local currency, or a single "report currency" of their choice. Based on the user choice, you can add IF statements in the field catalog subroutine to set DO_SUM for the chosen amount field, and hide the unneeded amount field and its associated currency key (Chapter 7.3).

Airline Bookings: DREAM TRAVEL

Travel agency name	Agency No.	Carrier	No.	Date	Booking	Σ	Amount	Curr.	Airline	Σ	Amount	Curr.
						▪▪	1,028,775.04	AUD		▪▪	501,583.25	AUD
							4,364,153.15	GBP			2,599,334.96	EUR
											109,448,450	JPY
											2,589,878.89	SGD
											2,369,495.63	USD
Aussie Travel	123	AA				▪	36,368.59	GBP		▪	53,785.39	USD
		AZ				▪	143,794.85	GBP		▪	231,796.85	EUR
		DL				▪	57,342.94	GBP		▪	84,804.23	USD
		JL				▪	99,522.00	GBP		▪	17,740,622	JPY
		LH				▪	109,707.54	GBP		▪	176,847.48	EUR
		QF				▪	64,387.22	GBP		▪	77,957.15	AUD
		SQ				▪	159,901.80	GBP		▪	426,541.53	SGD
		UA				▪	165,861.74	GBP		▪	245,291.96	USD
Ben McCloskey Ltd.	107	AA				▪	37,297.99	GBP		▪	55,159.89	USD
		AZ				▪	151,795.04	GBP		▪	244,693.09	EUR

Figure 6.10: Example of excessive subtotals (FM)

6.2.2 ALV control framework

Your program provides a selection screen option (Figure 5.34) for displaying subtotals "By Agency" or "By Agency, then Airline". The desired result for the "By Agency" option is shown in Figure 6.11.

SAP

Airline Bookings: DREAM TRAVEL

Travel agency name	Agency No.	ID No.	Date	Booking	Σ	Amount	Curr.	Airline	Amount	Curr.
					▪▪	1,028,775.04	AUD			
						4,364,153.15	GBP			
Aussie Travel		123			▪	836,886.68	GBP			
Ben McCloskey Ltd.		107			▪	856,941.48	GBP			
Hot Socks Travel		102			▪	1,028,775.04	AUD			
Kangeroos		109			▪	981,205.58	GBP			
Super Agency		112			▪	848,529.40	GBP			
The Ultimate Answer		295			▪	840,590.01	GBP			

Figure 6.11: Automating the display of totals, one level (CF)

The desired result for the "By Agency, then Airline" option is shown in Figure 6.12.

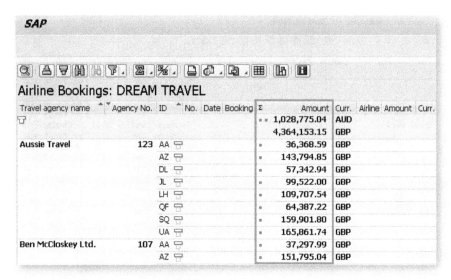

Figure 6.12: Automating the display of totals, two levels (CF)

The initial display of subtotals for both of these groupings (previously coded into the sort table based upon the user choice) was accomplished by adding the DO_SUM setting for this amount field (FORCURAM) in the field catalog (Figure 6.13).

```
CLEAR ls_fieldcat.
ls_fieldcat-fieldname  = 'FORCURAM'.      "amount field !
ls_fieldcat-cfieldname = 'FORCURKEY'.     "associated currency key
ls_fieldcat-ref_table  = 'SBOOK'.
ls_fieldcat-do_sum     = 'X'.             "display summed
APPEND ls_fieldcat TO lt_fieldcat.
```

Figure 6.13: Value to set for automatic summing of an amount field (CF)

Know your data and the user needs

Take care not to overdo the use of DO_SUM. Identify the subtotals that will provide value and meet user requirements. In Figure 6.14, both the foreign currency (associated with the travel agency) and the local currency (associated with the airline) have been totaled, providing a confusing display.

In Chapter 5.7, you learned how to obtain user preferences from the selection screen and use IF statements to manage which settings were passed to the ALV engine. To avoid the confusion of two summed amounts (Figure 6.14), you can provide the user with the option of displaying amounts in foreign currency, local currency, or a single "report currency" of their choice. Based on the user choice, you can add IF statements in the field catalog subroutine to set DO_SUM for the chosen amount field and hide the unneeded amount field and its associated currency key (Chapter 7.3).

Airline Bookings: DREAM TRAVEL

Travel agency name	Agency No.	ID	No.	Date	Booking Σ	Amount	Curr.	Airline Σ	Amount	Curr.
						1,028,775.04	AUD		501,583.25	AUD
						4,364,153.15	GBP		2,599,334.96	EUR
									109,448,450	JPY
									2,589,878.89	SGD
									2,369,495.63	USD
Aussie Travel	123	AA				36,368.59	GBP		53,785.39	USD
		AZ				143,794.85	GBP		231,796.85	EUR
		DL				57,342.94	GBP		84,804.23	USD
		JL				99,522.00	GBP		17,740,622	JPY
		LH				109,707.54	GBP		176,847.48	EUR
		QF				64,387.22	GBP		77,957.15	AUD
		SQ				159,901.80	GBP		426,541.53	SGD
		UA				165,861.74	GBP		245,291.96	USD
Ben McCloskey Ltd.	107	AA				37,297.99	GBP		55,159.89	USD
		AZ				151,795.04	GBP		244,693.09	EUR

Figure 6.14: Example of excessive subtotals (CF)

6.3 Adding record counts

Using two different techniques, record counts can be added to an ALV. Both techniques update the totals if the user applies a filter to the displayed data.

1. Layout structure technique (the COUNT option will be enabled in a menu or toolbar button dropdown list, Figure 6.15 and Figure 6.27)

   ▶ Pros: Users expose the record counts to view only if needed, no coding to populate the count field (remains initial), no disabled options on the dropdown list

   ▶ Cons: Column heading is always "Count." regardless of name you provide, requires user action to expose it to view, count field is not populated for users who export the data to spreadsheets

2. Field catalog technique (explicit count field on each record, Figure 6.23 and Figure 6.34)

   ▶ Pros: User action is not necessary to expose the record counts to view, the count field for every record is populated with '1' which may be preferred by users who export the data to spreadsheets, column heading other than "Count." can be defined

   ▶ Cons: Requires coding to populate the count field for every record, the COUNT option on the dropdown list remains disabled

The technique you use may depend upon a business requirement or user preference so both will be described here.

6.3.1 Function module

By default, the count functionality is disabled in the menu at the top of the ALV screen (Figure 6.15). Select EDIT • CALCULATE to see this.

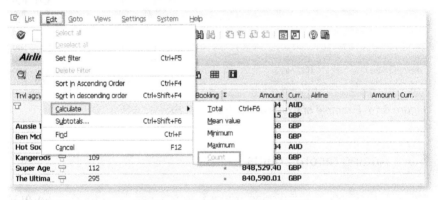

Figure 6.15: Count menu option is disabled by default (FM)

For the layout structure count technique, you make two changes:

1. Add a new integer field at the end of the internal table structure

2. Specify the new field as a "count" field in the layout structure

After those two code changes, the EDIT • CALCULATE • COUNT menu option is no longer disabled and record counts can be displayed by the user (Figure 6.16).

Airline Bookings: DREAM TRAVEL

Travel agency name		Agency No.	ID	No.	Date	Booking	Σ	Amount	Curr.	Airline	Amount	Curr.	Σ	Count.
								1,028,775.04	AUD					10,262
								4,364,153.15	GBP					
Aussie Travel		123						836,886.68	GBP					1,662
Ben McCloskey Ltd.		107						856,941.48	GBP					1,662
Hot Socks Travel		102						1,028,775.04	AUD					1,665
Kangeroos		109						981,205.58	GBP					1,949
Super Agency		112						848,529.40	GBP					1,661
The Ultimate Answer		295						840,590.01	GBP					1,663

Figure 6.16: Record counts displayed by user (FM)

When you add the new integer field to the internal table structure type, place it at the end of the structure (Figure 6.17). By doing so, you can continue to use the SELECT statement coded earlier. Even though you will not be populating this integer field, it must be present with this technique to avoid a runtime error (short dump). In the example, it is called "count", but other names are acceptable.

```
TYPES: BEGIN OF lty_output,
        agencynum TYPE stravelag-agencynum,  "agency number
        name      TYPE stravelag-name,       "agency name
        currency  TYPE stravelag-currency,   "agency currency
        carrid    TYPE sbook-carrid,         "booked carrier
        connid    TYPE sbook-connid,         "booked connection
        fldate    TYPE sbook-fldate,         "booked date
        bookid    TYPE sbook-bookid,         "booking ID
        forcuram  TYPE sbook-forcuram,       "price in foreign currency
        forcurkey TYPE sbook-forcurkey,      "foreign currency key
        carrname  TYPE scarr-carrname,       "carrier name
        loccuram  TYPE sbook-loccuram,       "price in airline curr
        loccurkey TYPE sbook-loccurkey,      "local currency of airline
        count     TYPE i,           "empty field for rec count, required
      END OF lty_output.
```

Figure 6.17: Count field added to internal table structure (FM)

Next, pass the name of this new field in COUNTFNAME of the layout structure (Figure 6.18). The text you pass in single quotes:

▶ Does not have to be "Count", but must match the name of the field you added to the internal table structure

▶ Is not case sensitive

▶ Is not used for the column label (COUNT. will be displayed as the column label regardless of the name you provide)

```
*------------------------------------------------------------
FORM zf_build_layout USING ls_layout TYPE slis_layout_alv.

  ls_layout-zebra                   = 'X'.
  ls_layout-colwidth_optimize       = 'X'.
  ls_layout-totals_before_items     = 'X'.
  ls_layout-window_titlebar         = gv_title.
* internal table placeholder field for menu-driven Counts
  ls_layout-countfname              = 'Count'.

ENDFORM.
```

Figure 6.18: Specify the field to be used for menu-driven record counts (FM)

Instead of using the menu path, the user can click on the CHANGE LAYOUT button (Figure 6.19) to display this new count subtotal which is hidden on initial display.

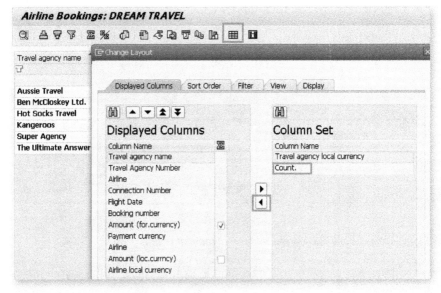

Figure 6.19: Count field is also available in change layout (FM)

If the user of the report applies filtering criteria after displaying the data, the count column will reflect the number of records matching the filter (Figure 6.20).

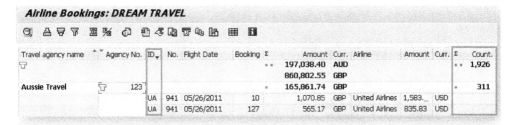

Figure 6.20: Record counts after user filter action, detail (FM)

For the field catalog count technique, you make three changes:

1. Add a new integer field at the end of the internal table structure (Figure 6.17)

2. Add the field to the field catalog

3. Populate the count field on each record in the internal table with '1'

If you have already added the COUNTFNAME line of code to the layout while coding the first technique (Figure 6.18), comment it or delete it now. You don't need two columns of record counts.

Add the new count field to the field catalog (Figure 6.21). Because this field was not selected from an existing database table, you can't reference an existing table and field from the data dictionary. Supply short, medium, and long texts to avoid displaying a blank column heading. Pass 'I' (integer) in the internal data type structure component INTTYP. Add the familiar DO_SUM line so that the record counts display immediately at the group levels predefined in the sort table.

```
FORM zf_build_fieldcatalog USING lt_fieldcat TYPE slis_t_fieldcat_alv.

  DATA: ls_fieldcat TYPE slis_fieldcat_alv.
  CLEAR lt_fieldcat.

  CLEAR ls_fieldcat.
  ls_fieldcat-fieldname     = 'NAME'.
  ls_fieldcat-ref_fieldname = 'NAME'.
  ls_fieldcat-ref_tabname   = 'STRAVELAG'.
  APPEND ls_fieldcat TO lt_fieldcat.

** adding the counter field at the end of the fieldcatalog

  CLEAR ls_fieldcat.
  ls_fieldcat-fieldname     = 'COUNT'.    "matches internal table
  ls_fieldcat-seltext_l     = 'RecCount'.        "up to 40 chars
  ls_fieldcat-seltext_m     = 'RecCount'.        "up to 20 chars
  ls_fieldcat-seltext_s     = 'RecCount'.        "up to 10 chars
  ls_fieldcat-inttype       = 'I'.
  ls_fieldcat-do_sum        = 'X'.
  APPEND ls_fieldcat TO lt_fieldcat.
ENDFORM.
```

Figure 6.21: Adding a record count to the field catalog (FM)

```
  DESCRIBE TABLE gt_output LINES gv_lines.
  IF gv_lines NE 0.                        "data was retrieved

    CLEAR gs_output.
    gs_output-count = 1.

    MODIFY gt_output FROM gs_output
      TRANSPORTING count WHERE NOT agencynum IS INITIAL.

    SORT gt_output BY agencynum
                      carrid
                      connid
                      fldate
                      bookid.
  ELSE.
    MESSAGE ID '00' TYPE 'I' NUMBER 001 WITH 'No data retrieved'.
    EXIT.
  ENDIF.

END-OF-SELECTION.
```

Figure 6.22: Populating the count field in the internal table (FM)

Unlike the first technique, this technique requires that you populate the COUNT field with '1' for record. You can do that, without looping through the internal table, by using a MODIFY/TRANSPORTING command (Figure

118

6.22). The GS_OUTPUT structure is based on local type LTY_OUTPUT (Figure 2.3), but was not referenced until now.

The report with record count totals provided using the second technique appears in Figure 6.23.

Airline Bookings: DREAM TRAVEL

Travel agency name	Agency No.	ID No.	Date	Booking	Σ	Amount	Curr.	Airline	Amount	Curr.	Σ RecCount
						1,028,775.04	AUD				10,262
						4,364,153.15	GBP				
Aussie Travel	123					836,886.68	GBP				1,662
Ben McCloskey Ltd.	107					856,941.48	GBP				1,662
Hot Socks Travel	102					1,028,775.04	AUD				1,665
Kangeroos	109					981,205.58	GBP				1,949
Super Agency	112					848,529.40	GBP				1,661
The Ultimate Answer	295					840,590.01	GBP				1,663

Figure 6.23: Record counts display immediately (FM)

When the detail records are exposed, you can see the '1' that you populated for each table row (Figure 6.24). Compare this to the detail records in Figure 6.20.

Airline Bookings: DREAM TRAVEL

Travel agency name	Agency No.	ID No.	Date	Booking	Σ	Amount	Curr.	Airline	Amount	Curr.	Σ RecCount
						1,028,775.04	AUD				10,26...
						4,364,153.15	GBP				
Aussie Travel	123					836,886.68	GBP				1,662
Ben McCloskey Ltd.	107					856,941.48	GBP				1,662
		A	17	05/...	6	543.36	GBP	Ame...	803.58	USD	1
		A	17	05/...	110	285.98	GBP	Ame...	422.94	USD	1

Figure 6.24: Detail records show count of 1 (FM)

The COUNT option on the EDIT • CALCULATE menu is grey again. The CHANGE LAYOUT pop-up reflects the label you provided and shows it in the list of displayed and summed columns (Figure 6.25).

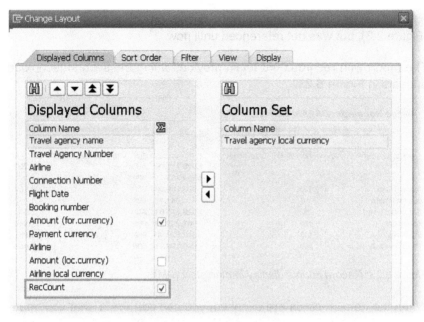

Figure 6.25: Record count is visible in change layout (FM)

6.3.2 ALV control framework

By default, there is no count functionality in the dropdown list next to the TOTAL button (Figure 6.26).

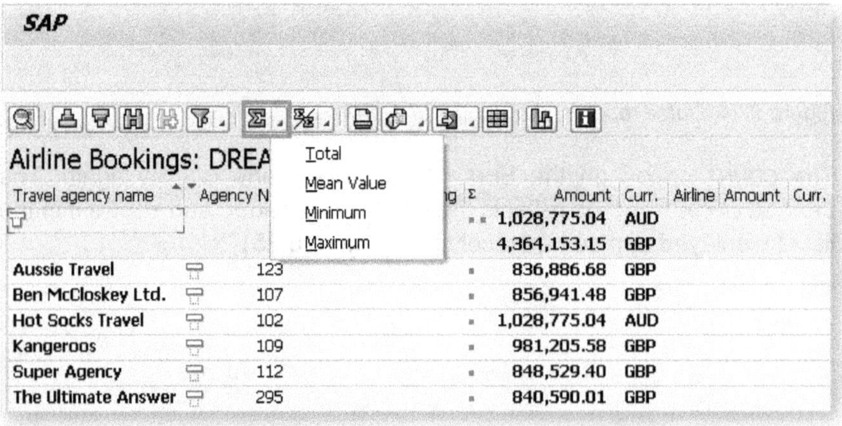

Figure 6.26: Count menu option is absent (CF)

For the layout structure count technique, you make two changes:

1. Add a new integer field at the end of the internal table structure

2. Specify the new field as a count field in the layout structure

After those two code changes, COUNT appears on the dropdown list next to the TOTAL button and record counts can be displayed by the user (Figure 6.27).

Airline Bookings: DREA	Total									
Travel agency name	Agency N	Mean Value	king ∑	Amount	Curr.	Airline	Amount	Curr.	∑	Count.
		Minimum		1,028,775.04	AUD					10,262
		Maximum		4,364,153.15	GBP					
Aussie Travel	1	Count		836,886.68	GBP					1,662
Ben McCloskey Ltd.	107			856,941.48	GBP					1,662
Hot Socks Travel	102			1,028,775.04	AUD					1,665
Kangeroos	109			981,205.58	GBP					1,949
Super Agency	112			848,529.40	GBP					1,661
The Ultimate Answer	295			840,590.01	GBP					1,663

Figure 6.27: Record counts displayed by user (CF)

When you add the new integer field to the internal table structure type, place it at the end of the structure (Figure 6.28). By doing so, you can continue to use the efficient SELECT statement coded earlier. In the example, it is called "count", but other names are acceptable.

```
TYPES: BEGIN OF lty_output,
          agencynum TYPE stravelag-agencynum,  "agency number
          name      TYPE stravelag-name,       "agency name
          currency  TYPE stravelag-currency,   "agency currency
          carrid    TYPE sbook-carrid,         "booked carrier
          connid    TYPE sbook-connid,         "booked connection
          fldate    TYPE sbook-fldate,         "booked date
          bookid    TYPE sbook-bookid,         "booking ID
          forcuram  TYPE sbook-forcuram,       "price in foreign currency
          forcurkey TYPE sbook-forcurkey,      "foreign currency key
          carrname  TYPE scarr-carrname,       "carrier name
          loccuram  TYPE sbook-loccuram,       "price in airline curr
          loccurkey TYPE sbook-loccurkey,      "local currency of airline
          count     TYPE i,                    "for record count
        END OF lty_output.
```

Figure 6.28: Count field added to internal table structure (CF)

Next, pass the name of this new field in COUNTFNAME of the layout structure (Figure 6.29). The text you pass in single quotes:

- ▶ Does not have to be "Count", but must match the name of the field you added to the internal table structure
- ▶ Is not case sensitive
- ▶ Is not used for the column label (COUNT. will be displayed as the column label regardless of the name you provide)

```
*-----------------------------------------------------------------
FORM zf_build_layout USING ls_layout TYPE lvc_s_layo.

  ls_layout-zebra       = 'X'.
  ls_layout-cwidth_opt  = 'X'.
  ls_layout-totals_bef  = 'X'.
  ls_layout-grid_title  = gv_title.

  ls_layout-countfname  = 'Count'.

ENDFORM.
```

Figure 6.29: Field to be used for icon-driven record counts (CF)

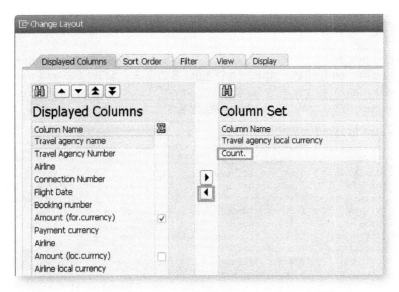

Figure 6.30: Count field is also available in change layout (CF)

Instead of using the button dropdown, the user can click the CHANGE LAYOUT button (Figure 6.30) to display this new count subtotal which is hidden on initial display.

If the user of the report applies filtering criteria after displaying the data, the count column will update to reflect the number of records matching the filter (Figure 6.31).

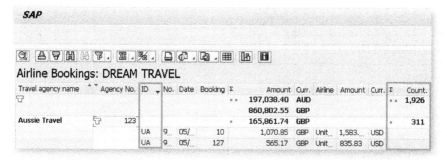

Figure 6.31: Record counts after user filter action, detail (CF)

For the field catalog count technique, you make three changes:

1. Add a new integer field at the end of the internal table structure (Figure 6.28)

2. Add the field to the field catalog

3. Populate the count field for each record in the internal table with '1'

If you have already added the COUNTFNAME line of code to the layout while coding the first technique (Figure 6.29), comment it or delete it now. You don't need two columns of record counts.

Add the new count field to the field catalog as shown in Figure 6.32. Because this field was not selected from an existing database table, you won't be able to reference an existing table and field from the data dictionary. Supply short, medium, and long texts to avoid displaying a blank column heading. Pass 'I' (integer) in the internal data type structure component INTTYP. Add the familiar DO_SUM line so that the record counts display immediately at the group levels predefined in the sort table.

```
*_____
FORM zf_build_fieldcatalog USING lt_fieldcat TYPE lvc_t_fcat.

  DATA: ls_fieldcat TYPE lvc_s_fcat.    "single row

  CLEAR ls_fieldcat.
  ls_fieldcat-fieldname = 'NAME'.
  ls_fieldcat-ref_table = 'STRAVELAG'.
  APPEND ls_fieldcat TO lt_fieldcat.

** adding counter field at the end of the fieldcatalog
  CLEAR ls_fieldcat.
  ls_fieldcat-fieldname = 'COUNT'.
  ls_fieldcat-do_sum    = 'X'.
  ls_fieldcat-inttype   = 'I'.
  ls_fieldcat-scrtext_l = 'RecCount'.    "up to 40 chars
  ls_fieldcat-scrtext_m = 'RecCount'.    "up to 20 chars
  ls_fieldcat-scrtext_s = 'RecCount'.    "up to 10 chars
  APPEND ls_fieldcat TO lt_fieldcat.

ENDFORM.
```

Figure 6.32: Adding a record count to the field catalog (CF)

Unlike the first technique, this technique requires that we populate the COUNT field with '1' for every record. You can do that, without looping through the internal table, by using a MODIFY/TRANSPORTING command (Figure 6.33). The GS_OUTPUT structure is based on local type LTY_OUTPUT (Figure 3.3), but was not referenced until now.

The report with record totals provided using the second technique appears in Figure 6.34.

When the detail records are exposed, you can see the '1' that you populated on each table row (Figure 6.35). Compare this to the detail records in Figure 6.31.

```
DESCRIBE TABLE gt_output LINES gv_lines.
IF gv_lines NE 0.                       "data was retrieved

  CLEAR gs_output.
  gs_output-count = 1.

  MODIFY gt_output FROM gs_output
    TRANSPORTING count WHERE NOT agencynum IS INITIAL.

  SORT gt_output BY agencynum
                    carrid
                    connid
                    fldate
                    bookid.
  PERFORM zf_build_layout       USING gs_layout.
  PERFORM zf_build_fieldcatalog USING gt_fieldcat[].
  PERFORM zf_build_sort         USING gt_sort[].

  CALL SCREEN 9100.
ELSE.
  MESSAGE ID '00' TYPE 'I' NUMBER 001 WITH 'No data retrieved'(013).
  RETURN.
ENDIF.
```

Figure 6.33: Populating the count field in the internal table (CF)

SAP

Airline Bookings: DREAM TRAVEL

Travel agency name		Agency No.	ID No.	Date	Booking	Σ	Amount	Curr.	Airline Amount	Curr.	Σ RecCount
						◾◾	1,028,775.04	AUD			◾◾ 10,262
							4,364,153.15	GBP			
Aussie Travel		123				◾	836,886.68	GBP			◾ 1,662
Ben McCloskey Ltd.		107				◾	856,941.48	GBP			◾ 1,662
Hot Socks Travel		102				◾	1,028,775.04	AUD			◾ 1,665
Kangeroos		109				◾	981,205.58	GBP			◾ 1,949
Super Agency		112				◾	848,529.40	GBP			◾ 1,661
The Ultimate Answer		295				◾	840,590.01	GBP			◾ 1,663

Figure 6.34: Record counts display immediately (CF)

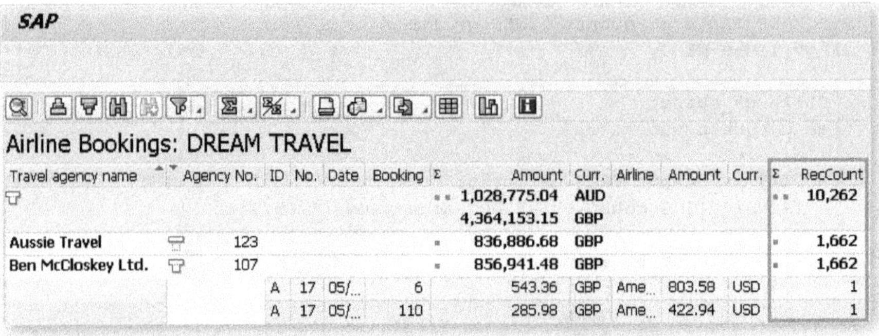

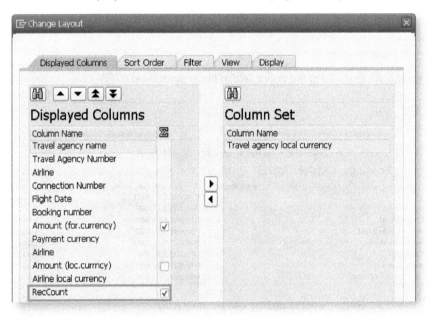

Figure 6.35: Detail records show count of 1 (CF)

COUNT no longer appears on the dropdown list next to the TOTAL button. The CHANGE LAYOUT pop-up reflects the label you provided and shows it in the list of displayed and summed columns (Figure 6.36).

Figure 6.36: Record count is visible in change layout (CF)

6.4   Handling ALV report layout variants

So far, you have used a number of techniques to present the ALV report output in exactly the format required for a particular training scenario requirement: a particular summarization, visible counts, a predefined column order, a hidden column, zebra-striped records, etc.

Once the output is displayed, users can use the standard ALV *application toolbar* to change the appearance and can save their changes to an ALV *report layout variant* for re-use. This is one of the strengths of the SAP List Viewer: the flexibility it provides the user to re-format data layout without additional coding.

For the training scenario, let's imagine that the person running the report for the owner of the travel agencies known collectively as Dream Travel has created a layout that she uses for a quarterly export of the data to Microsoft Excel (Figure 6.37). The cell merge and subtotals are absent from this layout.

Airline Bookings: DREAM TRAVEL Q

Trvl agcy	Agency No.	Carrier	No.	Flight Date	Booking Σ	Amount	Curr.	Airline	Amount	Curr.	Σ RecCount
						Σ 1,028,775.04	AUD				Σ 10,262
						4,364,153.15	GBP				
Aussie Travel	123	AA	17	05/25/2011	113	243.09	GBP	American Airlines	359.50	USD	1
Aussie Travel	123	AA	17	05/25/2011	230	285.98	GBP	American Airlines	422.94	USD	1
Aussie Travel	123	AA	17	05/25/2011	265	271.68	GBP	American Airlines	401.79	USD	1

Figure 6.37: Custom variant with no cell merge, no subtotals (FM, CF)

Instead of requiring her to choose the desired layout **after** initial display of the data, we will provide a parameter on the selection screen that will allow her to override our default layout with this quarterly export layout (Figure 6.38).

Travel Agency Number	102	to	
Airline		to	
Flight Date		to	

Subtotals

⦿ By Agency

◯ By Agency, then Airline

ALV Report Layout (optional)

| Layout | /QUARTERLY |

Figure 6.38: Layout variant (FM, CF)

Because much of the coding for handling report layout variants is the same for both ALV techniques covered here, we'll only distinguish between the two at the very end (Chapter 6.4.1 and Chapter 6.4.2).

To start, add parameter P_VARI at the end of the selection screen definition (Figure 6.39). It is shown within a new block labelled "ALV Report Layout (optional)", but it can be defined without being part of an on-screen block.

```
* ALV Report Layout parameter
SELECTION-SCREEN BEGIN OF BLOCK b2 WITH FRAME TITLE text-006.
PARAMETERS:       p_vari TYPE disvariant-variant.
SELECTION-SCREEN END OF BLOCK b2.
```

Figure 6.39: Selection screen parameter for layout variant (FM, CF)

Edit, save, and activate the associated selection text (Figure 6.40) and text symbol (Figure 6.41).

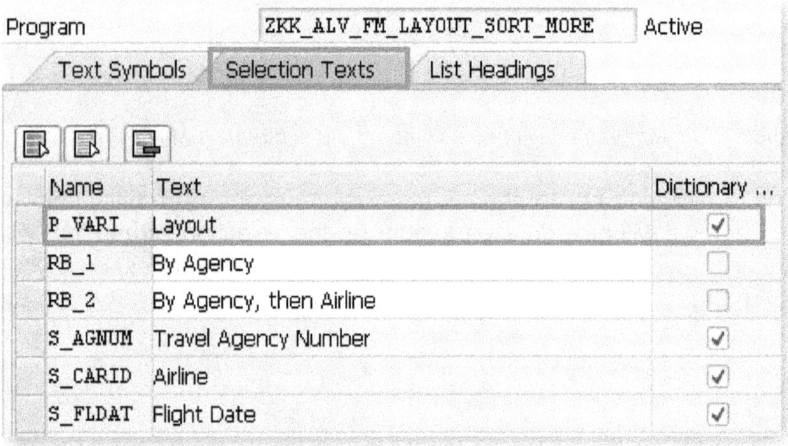

Program	ZKK_ALV_FM_LAYOUT_SORT_MORE	Active

Text Symbols	Selection Texts	List Headings

Name	Text	Dictionary ...
P_VARI	Layout	✓
RB_1	By Agency	☐
RB_2	By Agency, then Airline	☐
S_AGNUM	Travel Agency Number	✓
S_CARID	Airline	✓
S_FLDAT	Flight Date	✓

Figure 6.40: Text element for the new parameter (FM, CF)

The default text for P_VARI is "Layout" (Figure 6.40). If you prefer a different label, omit the checkmark in the dictionary column and provide your own text.

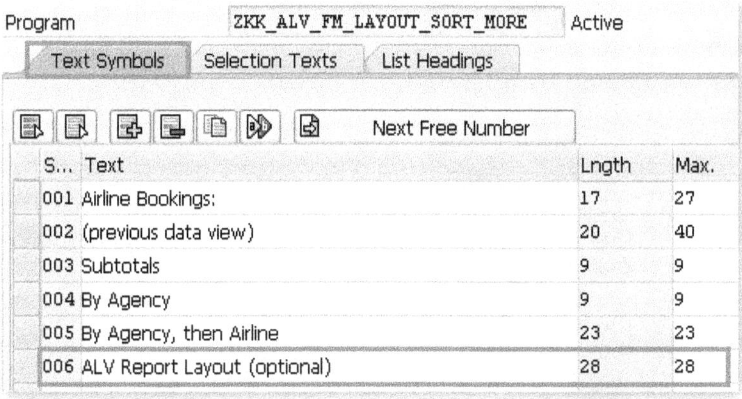

Program	ZKK_ALV_FM_LAYOUT_SORT_MORE	Active

Text Symbols	Selection Texts	List Headings

🖳 🖳 🖳 🖳 🖺 ⏩ 🖺   Next Free Number

S...	Text	Lngth	Max.
001	Airline Bookings:	17	27
002	(previous data view)	20	40
003	Subtotals	9	9
004	By Agency	9	9
005	By Agency, then Airline	23	23
006	ALV Report Layout (optional)	28	28

Figure 6.41: Text symbol for the new block's frame title (FM, CF)

New variables and structures must be added to the data declarations area (Figure 6.42).

```
* for management of layout variants
DATA: gs_variant        TYPE disvariant,    "passed in ALV function call
      gs_variant_temp  TYPE disvariant,    "user-specified layout variant
      gv_save          TYPE c,
      gv_exit          TYPE c.
```

Figure 6.42: Data declarations for handling of layout variant (FM, CF)

Let's look more closely at the structure DISVARIANT (Figure 6.43) upon which we've based P_VARI, GS_VARIANT, and GS_VARIANT_TEMP. The only two components of the structure DISVARIANT that you will be filling and passing in the ALV call are REPORT and VARIANT.

When the DISVARIANT structure is passed with VARIANT blank, the ALV report will display the default layout you programmed. When passed with a valid user-specified layout name in VARIANT, the ALV report will display as previously modified and saved under that variant name.

Structure	DISVARIANT			Active	
Short Description	Layout (External Use)				

Attributes	Components	Entry help/check	Currency/quantity fields

Predefined Type   1 / 7

Component	Data Type	Length	Deci...	Short Description
REPORT	CHAR	40	0	ABAP Program Name
HANDLE	CHAR	4	0	Mgt. ID for repeated calls from the same program
LOG_GROUP	CHAR	4	0	Logical group name
USERNAME	CHAR	12	0	User name for user-specific storage
VARIANT	CHAR	12	0	Layout
TEXT	CHAR	40	0	Description for layout
DEPENDVARS	CHAR	10	0	Dependent variant entry vector

Figure 6.43: Disvariant structure components (FM, CF)

When adding parameters and select-options to a selection screen, it is a best practice to provide these features:

▶ Validation of the user-provided value(s)

▶ Input help (F4 function key)

▶ Help (F1 function key)

Many features are provided automatically when we reference ABAP data dictionary objects such as DISVARIANT and SBOOK-CARRID. Without our having to write additional code, the user can use the F1 function key on the selection screen fields ("Travel Agency Number" and "Airline") to see their definitions and metadata.

We didn't take time earlier to add selection screen validation of user-provided values for "Travel Agency Number" or "Airline", but we'll do so for the new parameter P_VARI. We'll also add code to display a list of available layout variants when the user presses the F4 function key or clicks the POSSIBLE ENTRIES button next to the LAYOUT input field (Figure 6.44).

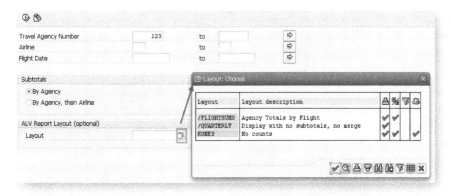

Figure 6.44: List of possible entries for the layout (FM, CF)

Global vs. user-specific report layouts

 Layouts that are global and available to all users must be prefaced by a slash (/) when named. Layouts that are available only to the user who created them have no leading slash in their names. The values that we pass in the GV_SAVE variable can vary throughout the program, depending upon our need.

X indicates cross-user (global) layouts.

U indicates user-specific layouts.

A indicates cross-user (global) and user-specific layouts.

First, the validation logic. Add this code for P_VARI (Figure 6.45) to your program, after the empty INITIALIZATION event and before the START-OF-SELECTION event. If you wish, you can create and call a subroutine containing this logic rather than coding it directly in the AT SELECTION SCREEN event.

131

```
AT SELECTION-SCREEN ON p_vari.
* if the user provided a report layout variant name, verify it exists
  IF NOT p_vari IS INITIAL.
    CLEAR gs_variant_temp.
    gs_variant_temp-report  = syst-repid.
    gs_variant_temp-variant = p_vari.
    gv_save = 'A'.                          "check All variant types

    CALL FUNCTION 'REUSE_ALV_VARIANT_EXISTENCE'
      EXPORTING
        i_save        = gv_save
      CHANGING
        cs_variant    = gs_variant_temp
      EXCEPTIONS
        wrong_input   = 1
        not_found     = 2
        program_error = 3
        OTHERS        = 4.
    IF sy-subrc <> 0.
*     user will need to correct before proceeding
      MESSAGE ID '00' TYPE 'W' NUMBER 001
      WITH 'ALV Report Layout variant was not found'(007).
    ENDIF.
  ENDIF.
```

Figure 6.45: Validation logic for the layout parameter (FM, CF)

If the user has proposed an alternate layout using the P_VARI parameter, pass the report name and the variant name to SAP function module RE-USE_ALV_VARIANT_EXISTENCE (Figure 6.45). If the parameter value is found, the return code (SY-SUBRC) is 0 and no further action is taken. If the parameter value is not found, you want to display a status line message informing the user that the layout variant was not found. (Remember to add text symbols for custom messages by double-clicking on the message text and using forward navigation to save and activate them.)

Next, the input help (F4 function key). Following the validation logic you just added, add the code shown in Figure 6.46.

To display a list of all variants available, pass the GS_VARIANT structure to SAP function module REUSE_ALV_VARIANT_F4 with only the report name specified (Figure 6.46).

```
AT SELECTION-SCREEN ON VALUE-REQUEST FOR p_vari.    "pick-list
  CLEAR: gs_variant, gs_variant_temp, gv_exit.
  gs_variant-report = syst-repid.
  gv_save           = 'A'.                "list all variants
  CALL FUNCTION 'REUSE_ALV_VARIANT_F4'
    EXPORTING
      is_variant    = gs_variant          "default/blank
      i_save        = gv_save
    IMPORTING
      e_exit        = gv_exit             "X for no choice made
      es_variant    = gs_variant_temp     "user's choice
    EXCEPTIONS
      not_found     = 1
      program_error = 2
      others        = 3.
  IF sy-subrc <> 0.
    MESSAGE ID '00' TYPE 'I' NUMBER 001
    WITH 'No ALV Report Layout variants have been created' (009).
  ELSE.
    IF gv_exit <> 'X'.
*       display the user's F4 choice on the selection screen
      p_vari = gs_variant_temp-variant.
    ELSE.
*       do nothing, user opted out of the value-request process.
    ENDIF.
  ENDIF.
```

Figure 6.46: Input help for the layout parameter (FM, CF)

The function module displays the list, then passes the name of the user-selected variant back in the structure we've called GS_VARIANT_TEMP.

The code following the function module call (Figure 6.46) addresses three scenarios:

▶ No layouts were found for this program—display informational pop-up message to the user

▶ The user selected a layout from the possible entries list—move that layout name to the selection screen parameter

▶ The user exited the possible entries list without selecting a layout (GV_EXIT = 'X')—take no action

Use of "not released" SAP function modules

 Both of the function modules used here (RE-USE_ALV_VARIANT_EXISTENCE and REUSE_ALV_VARIANT _F4) have been released by SAP for customer develop-ment. Two similar function modules (LVC_VARIANT _EXISTENCE_CHECK and LVC_VARIANT_F4) are "not re-leased" and are subject to change or removal without warning. The release status is shown on every function module's attributes tab. Given the choice of using a released or a "not released" function module in your development, it is better to use the released function module.

The layout parameter handling within the selection screen is complete so you can now populate the structure to be passed in the ALV call. In Chapter 4.6 you added a subroutine ZF_START to contain one-time activi-ties such as customizing the title text. That subroutine is where you will add the report layout variant information to the GS_VARIANT structure (Figure 6.47).

```
FORM zf_start.
* populate the structure that passes an ALV Report Layout variant
  CLEAR gs_variant.
  gs_variant-report = syst-repid.
  IF NOT p_vari IS INITIAL.
*   user-specified ALV layout variant validated AT SELECTION-SCREEN
    gs_variant-variant = p_vari.
  ELSE.
*   no user-specified ALV layout variant, pass blank for default layout
  ENDIF.
  gv_save          = 'A'.          "allows global and user-specific saves
```

Figure 6.47: Populate the structure passed in the ALV call (FM, CF)

Authority-check for ALV report layout saving

 User authorization to save global, user-specific, or no ALV layouts is often granted within security roles using security objects such as S_ALV_LAYO or S_ALV_LAYR. For the ALV call in our example program, we will pass 'A' in the GV_SAVE variable to allow saving of all layout types. Another approach would be to fill GV_SAVE based on the results of an AUTHORITY-CHECK. For instance, you might fill GV_SAVE with 'A' when the authority-check return code (SY-SUBRC) is 0, otherwise fill GV_SAVE with 'U'.

A allows saving of global and user-specific layouts.

U allows saving of only user-specific layouts.

X allows saving of only global layouts.

Leaving the field blank prevents any saving of layouts.

6.4.1   Function module

Two lines need to be added to the ALV call (Figure 6.48):

1. GV_SAVE: to pass the level of layout saving authorization the user will have after display of the ALV report

2. GS_VARIANT: to pass either the user-specified layout name or a blank for the default layout

```
*-------------------------------------------------------------
FORM zf_display_alv.

   CALL FUNCTION 'REUSE_ALV_GRID_DISPLAY'
      EXPORTING
         i_callback_program = sy-repid
         is_layout          = gs_layout
         it_fieldcat        = gt_fieldcat[]
         it_sort            = gt_sort[]
         i_save             = gv_save
         is_variant         = gs_variant
      TABLES
         t_outtab           = gt_output
      EXCEPTIONS
         program_error      = 1
         OTHERS             = 2 .
```

Figure 6.48: ALV call with layout variant information (FM)

6.4.2   ALV control framework

Two lines need to be added to the ALV call (Figure 6.49):

1.   GV_SAVE: to pass the level of layout saving authorization the user will have after display of the ALV report

2.   GS_VARIANT: to pass either the user-specified layout name or a blank for the default layout

```
   CALL METHOD grid1->set_table_for_first_display
      EXPORTING
         i_structure_name = 'LTY_OUTPUT'
         is_variant       = gs_variant
         i_save           = gv_save
         is_layout        = gs_layout
      CHANGING
         it_fieldcatalog  = gt_fieldcat
         it_sort          = gt_sort
         it_outtab        = gt_output.
```

Figure 6.49: ALV call with layout variant information (CF)

6.5   Adding a top_of_page event and a logo

SAP provides logic for various SAP List Viewer *events* such as US-
ER_COMMAND, CALLER_EXIT, and TOP_OF_PAGE. In this chapter, we'll add
header text and a logo using the TOP_OF_PAGE event.

> ### Screen space trade-offs
>
>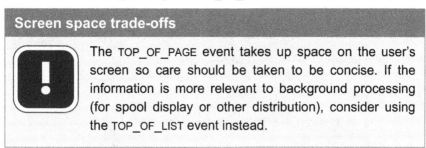
> The TOP_OF_PAGE event takes up space on the user's
> screen so care should be taken to be concise. If the
> information is more relevant to background processing
> (for spool display or other distribution), consider using
> the TOP_OF_LIST event instead.

6.5.1   Function module

When done, the header will appear between the toolbar and the column
headings (Figure 6.50).

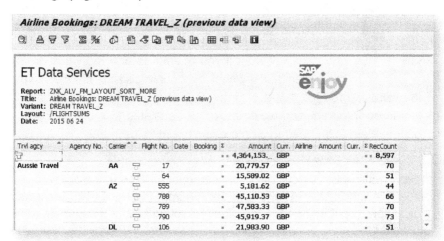

Figure 6.50: Custom header text with logo (FM)

Two tables and a constant need to be declared (Figure 6.51):

1. GT_TOP_TEXT: for the lines of text

2. GT_EVENTS: for the list of events

3. GC_FORMNAME_TOP: containing the name of the subroutine containing our custom top_of_page logic

```
DATA: gs_output    TYPE lty_output,
      gt_output    TYPE STANDARD TABLE OF lty_output,
      gt_sort      TYPE slis_t_sortinfo_alv,
      gt_fieldcat  TYPE slis_t_fieldcat_alv,
      gs_layout    TYPE slis_layout_alv,
      gt_top_text  TYPE slis_t_listheader,
      gt_events    TYPE slis_t_event.

CONSTANTS: gc_formname_top TYPE slis_formname VALUE 'ZF_TOP_OF_PAGE'.
```

Figure 6.51: Data declarations for top_of_page event (FM)

No need to create numbered text symbol for constants

 Constants are hard-coded values listed in the data area of the program for transparency and maintainability. The value is used as is within the program. (Forward navigation does not work if you attempt to add the value as a numbered text symbol by double-clicking it.) Because the value ZF_TOP_OF_PAGE in Figure 6.51 is the name of the subroutine in our program and would never be translated to a different language, there is no need to create a numbered text symbol.

Next, create the ZF_TOP_OF_PAGE subroutine (Figure 6.52). You can place this subroutine anywhere in the program that facilitates a chronological flow. (I put it ahead of the other subroutines coded so far, immediately after the main program logic.) You'll pass an SAP-provided logo and a table of text, not yet populated, to function module REUSE_ALV _COMMENTARY_WRITE.

Add two PERFORM statements to the main program logic area, before the ALV call subroutine (Figure 6.53).

```
************ End of main program logic ****************************
*-----------------------------------------------------------------
FORM zf_top_of_page.          "does not need a corresponding PERFORM
  CALL FUNCTION 'REUSE_ALV_COMMENTARY_WRITE'
    EXPORTING
      i_logo               = 'ENJOYSAP_LOGO'
      it_list_commentary = gt_top_text.
ENDFORM.
```

Figure 6.52: Top_of_page subroutine (FM)

```
************ Start of main program logic **********************

  PERFORM zf_build_layout USING gs_layout.
  PERFORM zf_build_fieldcatalog USING gt_fieldcat[].
  PERFORM zf_build_sort_table USING gt_sort[].

  PERFORM zf_build_event_table USING gt_events[].

  PERFORM zf_build_top_text_table USING gt_top_text[].

  PERFORM zf_display_alv.
```

Figure 6.53: Main program section with two new subroutine calls (FM)

The first of the two new subroutines is ZF_BUILD_EVENT_TABLE (Figure 6.54). In it, you retrieve a table of standard events using function module REUSE_ALV_EVENTS_GET.

```
*-----------------------------------------------------------------
FORM zf_build_event_table USING lt_events type slis_t_event.

  DATA: ls_event TYPE slis_alv_event.

  CALL FUNCTION 'REUSE_ALV_EVENTS_GET'
    EXPORTING
      I_LIST_TYPE = 4                "for REUSE_ALV_GRID_DISPLAY
    IMPORTING
      ET_EVENTS   = lt_events.

  READ TABLE lt_events WITH KEY name =  slis_ev_top_of_page
    INTO ls_event.
  IF sy-subrc = 0.
    MOVE gc_formname_top to ls_event-form.
    MODIFY lt_events FROM ls_event INDEX sy-tabix.
  ENDIF.
ENDFORM.
```

Figure 6.54: Retrieve and modify the events table (FM)

The I_LIST_TYPE parameter value in the function call should match the technique used to display the ALV output (Table 6.1). Since this program calls REUSE_ALV_GRID_DISPLAY, retrieve the events for list type 4.

List type	Function module called for ALV display	ALV type
0	REUSE_ALV_LIST_DISPLAY	simple list
1	REUSE_ALV_HIERSEQ_LIST_DISPLAY	hierarchical-sequential list
2	REUSE_ALV_BLOCK_LIST_APPEND	simple block list
3	REUSE_ALV_BLOCK_LIST_HS_APPEND	hierarchical-sequential block list
4	REUSE_ALV_GRID_DISPLAY	grid

Table 6.1: List types for events retrieval (FM)

The retrieved table of events contains a blank field (FORM) for the name of your subroutine. The new ZF_BUILD_EVENT_TABLE subroutine (Figure 6.54) adds the ZF_TOP_OF_PAGE constant to the LT_EVENTS table (Figure 6.55).

Now, create subroutine ZF_BUILD_TOP_TEXT_TABLE (Figure 6.56 and Figure 6.57) to populate the table of text lines to be output at the top of the screen (Figure 6.50)

Use TYP = 'H' for bold larger font text strings (up to 60 characters).

Use TYP = 'S' for standard detail lines that consist of two parts:

1. Key: a smaller bold description like "Report:" or "Date:" (up to 10 characters)

2. Info: a non-bold text (up to 60 characters)

Tables	Table Contents		

Table   LT_EVENTS

Attributes   Standard [18x2(120)]

Insert Column ⊞

Row	NAME [C(30)]	FORM [C(30)]
1	CALLER_EXIT	
2	USER_COMMAND	
3	TOP_OF_PAGE	ZF_TOP_OF_PAGE
4	TOP_OF_COVERPAGE	
5	END_OF_COVERPAGE	
6	FOREIGN_TOP_OF_PAGE	
7	FOREIGN_END_OF_PAGE	
8	PF_STATUS_SET	
9	LIST_MODIFY	
10	TOP_OF_LIST	
11	END_OF_PAGE	
12	END_OF_LIST	
13	AFTER_LINE_OUTPUT	
14	BEFORE_LINE_OUTPUT	
15	REPREP_SEL_MODIFY	
16	SUBTOTAL_TEXT	
17	GROUPLEVEL_CHANGE	
18	CONTEXT_MENU	

Figure 6.55: Events table with subroutine name populated (FM)

```
*-----------------------------------------------------------------
FORM zf_build_top_text_table USING lt_top_text TYPE slis_t_listheader.
* typ is 1 char, key is 20 chars, info is 60 chars
  DATA: ls_textline TYPE slis_listheader,
        lv_date(10) TYPE c.

  CLEAR ls_textline.
  ls_textline-typ  = 'H'.                        "header, bold
* ls_textline-key  (not applicable for H lines)
  ls_textline-info = 'ET Data Services'(010).
  APPEND ls_textline TO lt_top_text.

  CLEAR ls_textline.
  ls_textline-typ  = 'S'.                        "standard line
  ls_textline-key  = 'Report:'(011).
  ls_textline-info = sy-repid.
  APPEND ls_textline TO lt_top_text.

  CLEAR ls_textline.
  ls_textline-typ  = 'S'.                        "standard line
  ls_textline-KEY  = 'Title:'(012).
  ls_textline-info = gv_title.
  APPEND ls_textline TO lt_top_text.

  CLEAR ls_textline.
  ls_textline-typ  = 'S'.                        "standard line
  ls_textline-KEY  = 'Variant:'(013).
  ls_textline-info = sy-slset.
  APPEND ls_textline TO lt_top_text.
```

Figure 6.56: Texts for top_of_page section, part 1 (FM)

Create numbered text symbols for explicit texts such as "Report:" and "Date:". Use system values (REPID, SLSET, DATUM, etc.) instead of hard-coding, where possible (Figure 6.57).

The last step is modification of the ALV function call to include the new events table (Figure 6.58).

The report displays as shown in Figure 6.50.

```
  CLEAR ls_textline.
  ls_textline-typ  = 'S'.                          "standard line
  ls_textline-KEY  = 'Layout:'(014).
  ls_textline-info = p_vari.
  APPEND ls_textline TO lt_top_text.

* format sy-datum YYYYMMDD as YYYY MM DD, then append to table
  CLEAR lv_date.
  lv_date+0(4) = sy-datum+0(4).
  lv_date+5(2) = sy-datum+4(2).
  lv_date+8(2) = sy-datum+6(2).
  CLEAR ls_textline.
  ls_textline-typ  = 'S'.                          "standard line
  ls_textline-key  = 'Date:'(015).
  ls_textline-info = lv_date.
  APPEND ls_textline TO lt_top_text.
ENDFORM.
```

Figure 6.57: Texts for top_of_page section, part 2 (FM)

```
*-------------------------------------------------------------------
FORM zf_display_alv.

  CALL FUNCTION 'REUSE_ALV_GRID_DISPLAY'
    EXPORTING
      i_callback_program = sy-repid
      is_layout          = gs_layout
      it_fieldcat        = gt_fieldcat[]
      it_sort            = gt_sort[]
      i_save             = gv_save
      is_variant         = gs_variant
      it_events          = gt_events[]
    TABLES
      t_outtab           = gt_output
    EXCEPTIONS
      program_error      = 1
      OTHERS             = 2.
```

Figure 6.58: ALV function call with events table (FM)

143

Check appearance and behavior in other formats

When adding new functionality to a program, it is wise to check the appearance and behavior in other ALV output formats available to users. It will allow you to speak knowledgeably if asked and can help you avoid surprises such as the one described in Chapter 7.1: the actual variant name replaced by an alias like &00000N when run in background from transaction code se38.

Click the button to generate "Excel in place" to view the TOP_OF_PAGE layout in that format (Figure 6.59, window is not maximized in this figure).

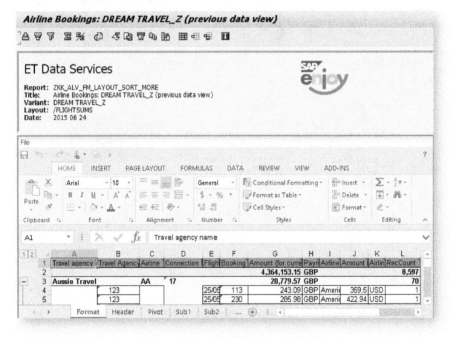

Figure 6.59: Top_of_page event with "Excel in place" (FM)

6.5.2 ALV control framework

When done, the custom container will have been split into an HTML section for the header and an ALV grid section (Figure 6.60). The HTML section on top uses *dynamic document* functionality, including a table of items that can be displayed without borders (as shown) or with borders.

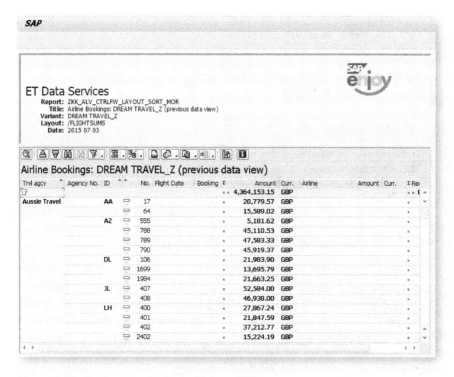

Figure 6.60: Custom header text with logo (CF)

Several additional data declarations are needed (Figure 6.61), including a splitter container.

```
DATA: gv_lines            TYPE I,
      gv_title            TYPE syst-TITLE,
      ok_code             LIKE sy-ucomm,
      g_container         TYPE scrfname VALUE 'ZKK_ALV_CTRLFW_9100_CONT1',
      grid1               TYPE REF TO cl_gui_alv_grid,
      g_custom_container  TYPE REF TO cl_gui_custom_container,
      g_dyndoc_id         TYPE REF TO cl_dd_document,
      g_splitter          TYPE REF TO cl_gui_splitter_container,
      g_parent_header     TYPE REF TO cl_gui_container,
      g_parent_report     TYPE REF TO cl_gui_container.
```

Figure 6.61: Data declarations for the top_of_page event (CF)

An event handler class must be defined and implemented with a method for the TOP_OF_PAGE event (Figure 6.62).

```
* * * * * * * *
CLASS lcl_event_handler DEFINITION.
  PUBLIC SECTION.
  METHODS:
    top_of_page   FOR EVENT top_of_page OF cl_gui_alv_grid
      IMPORTING e_dyndoc_id.
  ENDCLASS.
* * * * * * * *
DATA: g_event_handler   TYPE REF TO lcl_event_handler.
* * * * * * * *
CLASS lcl_event_handler IMPLEMENTATION.
  METHOD top_of_page.
    PERFORM zf_top_of_page USING e_dyndoc_id.
  ENDMETHOD.
ENDCLASS.
```

Figure 6.62: Top_of_page method in handler class (CF)

The revised ZM_STATUS_9100 module (Figure 6.63) begins and ends as it did before, but contains logic to split the custom container into two rows (top and bottom). If two side-by-side sections were desired, you would indicate that in the CREATE OBJECT G_SPLITTER command by exporting rows = 1 and columns = 2.

In the two GET_CONTAINER method calls, you provide names for the top and bottom portions of the splitter container, G_PARENT_HEADER and G_PARENT_REPORT.

Set_row_height

 Once you have populated the HTML header section using the dynamic document logic in the TOP_OF_PAGE subroutine and you have displayed it, you may find that the default header window is too tall or too short (vertical scroll bar present). You can use the SET_ROW_HEIGHT method to provide a more pleasing initial display (Figure 6.63). The user will still be able to resize the two sections using a drag-and-drop technique, if desired.

```
*--------------------------------------------------------------
MODULE zm_status_9100 OUTPUT.
  SET PF-STATUS 'MAIN9100'.
  IF g_custom_container IS INITIAL.
    CREATE OBJECT g_custom_container
      EXPORTING
        container_name = g_container.

* Split the custom container into 2 sections
    CREATE OBJECT g_splitter
      EXPORTING
        parent  = g_custom_container
        ROWS    = 2                    "top + ALV = 2
        columns = 1.                   "full-width = 1
*    First container is for HTML header from top_of_page
    CALL METHOD g_splitter->get_container
      EXPORTING
        row    = 1
        column = 1
      RECEIVING
        container = g_parent_header.
    CALL METHOD g_splitter->set_row_height
      EXPORTING
        ID     = 1         "top container (header)
        height = 30.       "adjust, as needed
*    Second container is for ALV grid
    CALL METHOD g_splitter->get_container
      EXPORTING
        row    = 2
        column = 1
      RECEIVING
        container = g_parent_report.
```

Figure 6.63: Splitter_container provides two sections (CF)

Continuing with the ZM_STATUS_9100 changes, change the CREATE OB-JECT GRID1 command from G_CUSTOM_CONTAINER to the new destination of the report output: G_PARENT_REPORT (Figure 6.64) and add the additional logic shown. Notice the references to GRID1, the object of the SET_TABLE_FOR_FIRST_DISPLAY method call.

```
* Align the ALV grid and the top_of_page event with grid1
  CREATE OBJECT grid1
    EXPORTING
      i_parent = g_parent_report.

  CREATE OBJECT g_event_handler.
  SET HANDLER g_event_handler->top_of_page FOR grid1.

* Dynamic document that will contain the HTML content for header
  CREATE OBJECT g_dyndoc_id
    EXPORTING
      style = 'ALV_GRID'.

  CALL METHOD grid1->list_processing_events
    EXPORTING
      i_event_name = 'TOP_OF_PAGE'
      i_dyndoc_id  = g_dyndoc_id.

  CALL METHOD grid1->set_table_for_first_display
    EXPORTING
      i_structure_name = 'LTY_OUTPUT'
      is_variant       = gs_variant
      i_save           = gv_save
      is_layout        = gs_layout
    CHANGING
      it_fieldcatalog  = gt_fieldcat
      it_sort          = gt_sort
      it_outtab        = gt_output.
  ENDIF.
ENDMODULE.
```

Figure 6.64: Dynamic document and top_of_page (CF)

Next, create the ZF_TOP_OF_PAGE subroutine (Figure 6.65). You can place this subroutine anywhere in the program. (I put it ahead of the other subroutines coded so far, immediately after the main program logic.) Declare the local data items shown, then initialize G_DYNDOC_ID by calling the INITIALIZE_DOCUMENT method of class CL_DD_DOCUMENT.

An overall header text "ET Data Services" and the EnjoySAP logo will be the first items displayed with a horizontal gap between them (Figure 6.65).

148

```
*-----------------------------------------------------------------
FORM zf_top_of_page USING lo_dyndoc_id TYPE REF TO cl_dd_document.
  DATA: lt_tab    TYPE REF TO cl_dd_table_element,
        lv_col1   TYPE REF TO cl_dd_area,          "label, bold
        lv_col2   TYPE REF TO cl_dd_area,          "space
        lv_col3   TYPE REF TO cl_dd_area,          "value
        lv_text(255) TYPE C.

  CALL METHOD lo_dyndoc_id->initialize_document.

* output the header and logo
  CALL METHOD lo_dyndoc_id->add_text
    EXPORTING
      TEXT          = 'ET Data Services'(014)
      sap_style     = cl_dd_area=>heading
      sap_color     = cl_dd_area=>list_heading_int
      sap_fontsize  = cl_dd_area=>medium
      sap_emphasis  = cl_dd_area=>strong
      style_class   = space.

  CALL METHOD lo_dyndoc_id->add_gap
    EXPORTING width = 120.

  CALL METHOD lo_dyndoc_id->add_picture
    EXPORTING picture_id = 'ENJOYSAP_LOGO'.
```

Figure 6.65: Top_of_page logic, part 1 (CF)

How to view dynamic document formatting options

 To view the many text formatting options available, display class CL_DD_AREA using transaction code se24, then click on the attributes tab. The values are listed in the attributes column, and the usage is found in the description column. A few frequently used values are shown in Table 6.2.

149

method	parameter	values
set_column_style	sap_emphasis	STRONG NORMAL
set_column_style	sap_align	LEFT CENTER RIGHT
set_column_style	sap_valign	TOP CENTER BOTTOM
set_column_style	sap_color	LIST_KEY KEY
add_text	sap_style	HEADING TABLE_HEADING KEY SUCCESS WARNING
add_text	sap_fontsize	LARGE MEDIUM SMALL
add_text	sap_emphasis	STRONG (bold) EMPHASIS (italic)

Table 6.2: Text formatting examples (CF)

Because the remainder of the header information consists of several rows of labels and values, a tabular approach works well (Figure 6.66). The table column width percentages are relative to the table width, not to the entire screen width, and do not need to be exact.

Use 20% for the labels in column 1 and 78% for the values in column 3. Define an empty column of 2% for column 2 to improve readability. If you wish, you can use the SET_COLUMN_STYLE method for column 1 to bold the labels and right-align the colons (Figure 6.66).

```
* create a table and divide it into columns for remaining header info
  CALL METHOD lo_dyndoc_id->add_table
    EXPORTING
      no_of_columns = 3
      border        = '0'    "0 for none, 1 for cell borders
    IMPORTING
      TABLE         = lt_tab.
  CALL METHOD lt_tab->add_column          "column 1 for labels
    EXPORTING
      width = '20%'
    IMPORTING
      column = lv_col1.
  CALL METHOD lt_tab->add_column          "column 2 for spacing
    EXPORTING
      width = '2%'
    IMPORTING
      column = lv_col2.
  CALL METHOD lt_tab->add_column          "column 3 for values
    EXPORTING
      width = '78%'
    IMPORTING
      column = lv_col3.
* Right-align and bold the labels in column 1 of the table
* (For values in column 3, defaults will suffice.)
  CALL METHOD lt_tab->set_column_style
    EXPORTING
      col_no       = 1
      sap_emphasis = 'STRONG'
      sap_align    = 'RIGHT'.
```

Figure 6.66: Top_of_page logic, part 2 (CF)

Add the header information in columns 1 and 3 of the table (Figure 6.67). The variable LV_TEXT (Figure 6.65) is used each time to ensure that the data is consistent with the format required for the ADD_TEXT method.

```
*  ---------- line 1 of table ---------------------------------
   CALL METHOD lv_col1->add_text              "label in col 1
     EXPORTING TEXT = 'Report:'(007).

   CLEAR lv_text.
   lv_text = sy-repid.
   CALL METHOD lv_col3->add_text                "value in col 3
     EXPORTING TEXT = lv_text.

   CALL METHOD lt_tab->new_row.     "use new_row for table fill
*  ---------- line 2 of table ---------------------------------
   CALL METHOD lv_col1->add_text              "label in col 1
     EXPORTING TEXT = 'Title:'(008).

   CLEAR lv_text.
   lv_text = gv_title.
   CALL METHOD lv_col3->add_text                "value in col 3
     EXPORTING TEXT = lv_text.

   CALL METHOD lt_tab->new_row.     "use new_row for table fill
*  ---------- line 3 of table ---------------------------------
   CALL METHOD lv_col1->add_text              "label in col 1
     EXPORTING TEXT = 'Variant:'(009).

   CLEAR lv_text.
   lv_text = sy-slset.
   CALL METHOD lv_col3->add_text                "value in col 3
     EXPORTING TEXT = lv_text.

   CALL METHOD lt_tab->new_row.     "use new_row for table fill
```

Figure 6.67: Top_of_page logic, part 3 (CF)

New_line vs. new_row for dynamic document creation

 Use NEW_LINE to insert space between elements of the dynamic document (not needed in this program). Within a table, use NEW_ROW to start the new row (Figure 6.67 and Figure 6.68).

Two more rows of text are added to the header table (Figure 6.68). Create numbered text symbols for explicit texts like "Report:" and "Date:". Use system values (REPID, SLSET, DATUM, etc.) instead of hard-coding, where possible.

```
* --------- line 4 of table ------------------------------------
  CALL METHOD lv_col1->add_text            "label in col 1
    EXPORTING TEXT = 'Layout:'(010).

  CLEAR lv_text.
  lv_text = p_vari.
  CALL METHOD lv_col3->add_text            "value in col 3
    EXPORTING TEXT = lv_text.

  CALL METHOD lt_tab->new_row.      "use new_row for table fill
* --------- line 5 of table ------------------------------------
  CALL METHOD lv_col1->add_text            "label in col 1
    EXPORTING TEXT = 'Date:'(011).

* format sy-datum YYYYMMDD as YYYY MM DD, then append to table
  CLEAR lv_text.
  lv_text+0(4) = sy-datum+0(4).
  lv_text+5(2) = sy-datum+4(2).
  lv_text+8(2) = sy-datum+6(2).
  CALL METHOD lv_col3->add_text            "value in col 3
    EXPORTING TEXT = lv_text.
* ------------------------------------------------------------
```

Figure 6.68: Top_of_page logic, part 4 (CF)

The final part of the ZF_TOP_OF_PAGE logic is the calling of two methods: MERGE_DOCUMENT and DISPLAY_DOCUMENT (Figure 6.69).

```
  CALL METHOD lo_dyndoc_id->merge_document.

  CALL METHOD lo_dyndoc_id->display_document
    EXPORTING
      reuse_control = 'X'
      parent        = g_parent_header
    EXCEPTIONS
      html_display_error = 1.
  IF sy-subrc <> 0.        "status line message
    MESSAGE ID '00' TYPE 'I' NUMBER 001
      WITH 'ALV Header section output error, top_of_page'(012).
  ENDIF.
ENDFORM.
```

Figure 6.69: Top_of_page logic, part 5 (CF)

6.6 Adding hotspot logic

It is possible to configure ALV columns or rows as *hotspots* and execute custom logic when the user clicks on them. Hotspots and *user command* logic are overlapping concepts. Hotspots are used to trigger user command logic when the user clicks on a predefined area of the data output.

For the training scenario, let's provide three hotspots in the ALV output.

- ▶ Travel agency name—display agency master data from table STRAVELAG
- ▶ Agency number—display agency master data from table STRAVELAG
- ▶ Flight number—display connection master data from table SPFLI

Hotspot for transaction calls

 A hotspot can be used to call a transaction code when the user clicks on it. In the hotspot logic, set one or more parameter IDs based on field content from the clicked record: set parameter id 'xxx' field value. Next, call the transaction: call transaction 'tcode' and skip first screen. Include the with authority-check clause on the call statement, if appropriate.

6.6.1 Function module

When detail records are displayed, the underline that indicates a hotspot is visible in the detail row (Figure 6.70).

When summarized data is displayed, it may be necessary to use the EXPAND SELECTION button to expose a hotspot (Figure 6.71).

A pop-up window will be used to display the master data record retrieved from table STRAVELAG (Figure 6.72).

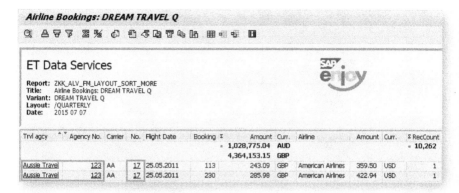

Figure 6.70: Hotspots on detail output (FM)

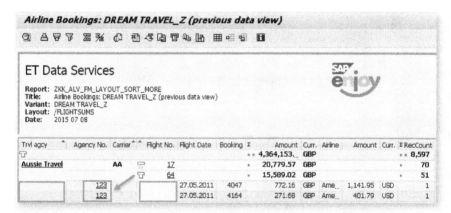

Figure 6.71: Hotspots on summarized output (FM)

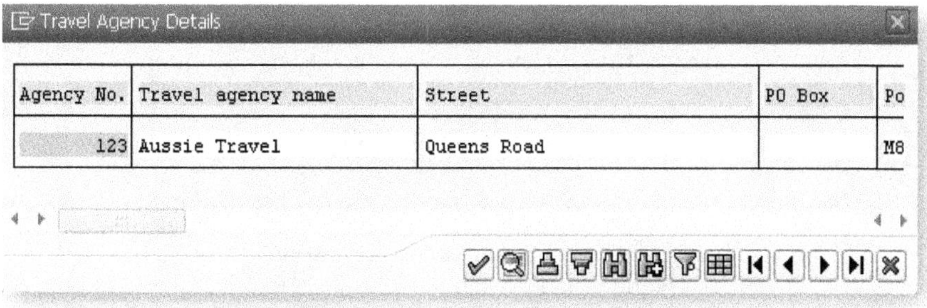

Figure 6.72: Travel agency data from stravelag in pop-up (FM)

A pop-up window will be used to display the master data record(s) retrieved from table SPFLI (Figure 6.73).

155

ID	No.	Ctr	Depart. city	Depart	Ctr	Arrival city	Apt	FlghtTime	D
AA	64	US	SAN FRANCISCO	SFO	US	NEW YORK	JFK	5:21	0

Figure 6.73: Flight data from spfli in pop-up (FM)

A new constant is needed for the events table population (Figure 6.74). To review a previous event-handling exercise, see Chapter 6.5 (TOP_OF _PAGE event).

```
CONSTANTS: gc_formname_top TYPE slis_formname VALUE 'ZF_TOP_OF_PAGE',
           gc_formname_com TYPE slis_formname VALUE 'ZF_USER_COMMAND'.
```

Figure 6.74: Data for hotspot (user_command) event (FM)

```
*-------------------------------------------------------------
FORM zf_build_event_table USING lt_events TYPE slis_t_event.
  DATA: ls_event TYPE slis_alv_event.

  CALL FUNCTION 'REUSE_ALV_EVENTS_GET'
    EXPORTING
      i_list_type = 4                    "for REUSE_ALV_GRID_DISPLAY
    IMPORTING
      et_events   = lt_events.

  READ TABLE lt_events WITH KEY name = slis_ev_user_command
    INTO ls_event.
  IF sy-subrc = 0.
    MOVE gc_formname_com TO ls_event-form.
    MODIFY lt_events FROM ls_event INDEX sy-tabix.
  ENDIF.

  READ TABLE lt_events WITH KEY name = slis_ev_top_of_page
    INTO ls_event.
  IF sy-subrc = 0.
    MOVE gc_formname_top TO ls_event-form.
    MODIFY lt_events FROM ls_event INDEX sy-tabix.
  ENDIF.
ENDFORM.
```

Figure 6.75: Inclusion of user_command subroutine name in events table (FM)

In the ZF_BUILD_EVENT_TABLE subroutine, add the constant for the new subroutine ZF_USER_COMMAND to the LT_EVENTS table (Figure 6.75).

The LT_EVENTS table will include ZF_USER_COMMAND in the FORM field after execution of ZF_BUILD_EVENT_TABLE (Figure 6.76).

Tables	Table Contents	

Table	LT_EVENTS
Attributes	Standard [18x2(120)]
Insert Column	

Row	NAME [C(30)]	FORM [C(30)]
1	CALLER_EXIT	
2	USER_COMMAND	ZF_USER_COMMAND
3	TOP_OF_PAGE	ZF_TOP_OF_PAGE
4	TOP_OF_COVERPAGE	
5	END_OF_COVERPAGE	
6	FOREIGN_TOP_OF_PAGE	
7	FOREIGN_END_OF_PAGE	
8	PF_STATUS_SET	
9	LIST_MODIFY	
10	TOP_OF_LIST	
11	END_OF_PAGE	
12	END_OF_LIST	
13	AFTER_LINE_OUTPUT	
14	BEFORE_LINE_OUTPUT	
15	REPREP_SEL_MODIFY	
16	SUBTOTAL_TEXT	
17	GROUPLEVEL_CHANGE	
18	CONTEXT_MENU	

Figure 6.76: Subroutine name added to events table (FM)

I_callback_user_command vs. events table

Instead of populating the subroutine names in the events table (Figure 6.76), you can pass them directly to the REUSE_ALV_GRID_DISPLAY function module by using the optional parameters: I_CALLBACK_USER_COMMAND and I_CALLBACK_TOP_OF_PAGE. In Chapter 6.8.1, you'll use the I_CALLBACK_PF_STATUS_SET parameter to pass the subroutine name instead of using the events table. Both approaches are fine.

Create a new subroutine called ZF_USER_COMMAND with two parameters based on SY-UCOMM and SLIS_SELFIELD (Figure 6.77). SY-UCOMM contains '&IC1' when the user clicks a hotspot.

The SLIS_SELFIELD structure contains information about where the user clicked; for instance, the field name, the value in the field, etc. (Figure 6.80).

Slis_selfield-tabindex problematic with summarized output

 For summarized output reports generated with the REUSE_ALV_GRID_DISPLAY function module, the SLIS_ SELFIELD-TABINDEX value is sometimes 0 instead of the row number of the desired data record. As a result, the index cannot be used reliably in a READ statement to obtain the values in other fields on the row clicked. A work-around for this limitation is used for the flight number hotspot (Figure 6.78).

In the ZF_USER_COMMAND subroutine, define the local data items shown (Figure 6.77). Add an IF statement to immediately leave the subroutine if the user clicked somewhere in a hotspot column that didn't populate the VALUE component of the SLIS_SELFIELD structure.

Using CASE statements allows for easy expansion over time and further modularization. The first CASE statement evaluates the UCOMM value and provides logic for hotspots (&IC1). The second CASE statement evaluates the field that was clicked and provides logic for displaying data using function module REUSE_ALV_POPUP_TO_SELECT.

Because there is a one-to-one relationship between the agency name, the agency number, and the master data record being retrieved from table STRAVELAG, the pop-up returns an identical single record regardless of which of those two hotspots was clicked (Figure 6.72).

Two SELECT statements are shown for the single record retrieval (Figure 6.77):

- ▶ SELECT SINGLE...: (syntax for retrieval from STRAVELAG using key field AGENCYNUM)
- ▶ SELECT... UP TO 1 ROWS. ENDSELECT.: (syntax for retrieval from STRAVELAG using non-key field NAME)

Use of asterisk wildcard in select statements

 For the training scenario hotspot logic, you will be retrieving and displaying all the fields of the requested master data record. It is acceptable to use the SELECT * and SELECT SINGLE * syntax for this. Follow your employer's or client's standards for SELECT statements for other situations.

```
FORM zf_user_command USING lv_ucomm      LIKE sy-ucomm
                            ls_selfield TYPE slis_selfield.
  DATA: ls_stravelag    TYPE stravelag,
        lt_stravelag    TYPE TABLE OF stravelag,
        lt_spfli        TYPE TABLE OF spfli,
        lt_output_temp TYPE TABLE OF lty_output.

* do not display popup if user clicks where no identifiable data value
  IF ls_selfield-value IS INITIAL.
    RETURN.
  ENDIF.

  CASE lv_ucomm.
    WHEN '&IC1'.                     "hotspot was clicked
      CASE ls_selfield-fieldname.
        WHEN 'AGENCYNUM'
          OR 'NAME'.                 "display STRAVELAG details
          CLEAR: ls_stravelag, lt_stravelag.
          IF ls_selfield-fieldname = 'AGENCYNUM'.
            SELECT SINGLE * FROM stravelag       "table key
                   INTO ls_stravelag
                   WHERE agencynum = ls_selfield-value.
          ELSE.                      "NAME
            SELECT * FROM stravelag UP TO 1 ROWS  "not table key
                   INTO ls_stravelag
                   WHERE name = ls_selfield-value.
            ENDSELECT.
          ENDIF.
          APPEND ls_stravelag TO lt_stravelag.
          CALL FUNCTION 'REUSE_ALV_POPUP_TO_SELECT'
            EXPORTING
              i_title          = 'Travel Agency Details'(017)
              i_selection      = ' '           "display only
              i_tabname        = '1'
              i_structure_name = 'STRAVELAG'
            TABLES
              t_outtab         = lt_stravelag
            EXCEPTIONS
              program_error    = 1
              others           = 2.
          IF sy-subrc <> 0.
            MESSAGE ID '00' TYPE 'I' NUMBER 001 WITH 'Popup error'(018).
            RETURN.
          ENDIF.
```

Figure 6.77: Hotspot logic, part 1 (FM)

For the flight number hotspot (CONNID), you need to know the airline (CARRID) on the row that the user clicked in order to retrieve the specific master data record. From the warning box above, you know that SLIS_SELFIELD-TABINDEX is not a reliable way to identify the clicked row in a summarized data display created with the REUSE_ALV_GRID_DISPLAY function module. However, the number of instances in our training database in which the same flight number has been used by multiple airlines is few to none, making a work-around suitable (Figure 6.78). We will code for multiples with the awareness that rarely will more than one record appear in the pop-up window (Figure 6.73).

```
      WHEN 'CONNID'.    "display SPFLI details, code for more than 1
           CLEAR: lt_spfli.
* will display all selected carriers that use connection ID clicked
           lt_output_temp[] = gt_output[].
           DELETE lt_output_temp WHERE connid <> ls_selfield-value.
           IF lt_output_temp[] IS INITIAL.
* unlikely, but verify table has content prior to FOR ALL ENTRIES
                RETURN.
           ENDIF.
           SORT lt_output_temp BY carrid connid.
           DELETE ADJACENT DUPLICATES FROM lt_output_temp
             COMPARING carrid connid.
           SELECT * FROM spfli
             INTO TABLE lt_spfli
             FOR ALL ENTRIES IN lt_output_temp
               WHERE carrid = lt_output_temp-carrid
                 AND connid = lt_output_temp-connid.
           CALL FUNCTION 'REUSE_ALV_POPUP_TO_SELECT'
             EXPORTING
               i_title         = 'Connection Details (All Airlines)'(019)
               i_selection     = ' '              "display only
               i_tabname       = '1'
               i_structure_name = 'SPFLI'
             TABLES
               t_outtab        = lt_spfli
             EXCEPTIONS
               program_error   = 1
               others          = 2.
           IF sy-subrc <> 0.
              MESSAGE ID '00' TYPE 'I' NUMBER 001 WITH 'Popup error'(018).
              RETURN.
           ENDIF.
      ENDCASE.
  ENDCASE.
ENDFORM.
```

Figure 6.78: Hotspot logic, part 2 (FM)

We can narrow the airlines to be included in our pop-up by starting with the data selected by the user from the selection screen (GT_OUTPUT).

Delete the records from a **copy** of that table (LT_OUTPUT_TEMP) where the flight numbers (CONNID) don't match the hotspot value passed to the subroutine. Sort and then delete adjacent duplicates to reduce the copied table to one record per airline/flight number combination. Select the relevant master data record(s) from table SPFLI, then display them using the REUSE_ALV_POPUP_TO_SELECT function module (Figure 6.78).

To enable hotspots, fill the HOTSPOT field of the field catalog with X in the ZF_BUILD_FIELDCATALOG subroutine (Figure 6.79).

```
FORM zf_build_fieldcatalog USING lt_fieldcat TYPE slis_t_fieldcat_alv.

  DATA: ls_fieldcat TYPE slis_fieldcat_alv.
  CLEAR lt_fieldcat.

  CLEAR ls_fieldcat.
  ls_fieldcat-fieldname     = 'NAME'.
  ls_fieldcat-ref_fieldname = 'NAME'.
  ls_fieldcat-ref_tabname   = 'STRAVELAG'.
  ls_fieldcat-hotspot       = 'X'.
  APPEND ls_fieldcat TO lt_fieldcat.

  CLEAR ls_fieldcat.
  ls_fieldcat-fieldname     = 'AGENCYNUM'.
  ls_fieldcat-ref_fieldname = 'AGENCYNUM'.
  ls_fieldcat-ref_tabname   = 'STRAVELAG'.
  ls_fieldcat-hotspot       = 'X'.
  APPEND ls_fieldcat TO lt_fieldcat.

  CLEAR ls_fieldcat.
  ls_fieldcat-fieldname     = 'CURRENCY'.
  ls_fieldcat-ref_fieldname = 'CURRENCY'.
  ls_fieldcat-ref_tabname   = 'STRAVELAG'.
  ls_fieldcat-no_out        = 'X'.            "hide field
  APPEND ls_fieldcat TO lt_fieldcat.

  CLEAR ls_fieldcat.
  ls_fieldcat-fieldname     = 'CARRID'.
  ls_fieldcat-ref_fieldname = 'CARRID'.
  ls_fieldcat-ref_tabname   = 'SBOOK'.
  APPEND ls_fieldcat TO lt_fieldcat.

  CLEAR ls_fieldcat.
  ls_fieldcat-fieldname     = 'CONNID'.
  ls_fieldcat-ref_fieldname = 'CONNID'.
  ls_fieldcat-ref_tabname   = 'SBOOK'.
  ls_fieldcat-hotspot       = 'X'.
  APPEND ls_fieldcat TO lt_fieldcat.
```

Figure 6.79: Field catalog additions for three hotspots (FM)

161

Alternative approach using fieldcat-key and layout-key_hotspot

Instead of using the field catalog HOTSPOT functionality (Figure 6.79), you can combine the field catalog option KEY with the layout option KEY_HOTSPOT.

The full structure of SLIS_SELFIELD is shown in Figure 6.80.

Structures	Fld.list				
Struct.	LS_SELFIELD				
Struc. Type	Structure: flat, not ...				
Exp. Component	Val	al.		C...	Technical Type
TABNAME		1		✎	C(30)
TABINDEX		2		✎	I(4)
SUMINDEX		0		✎	I(4)
ENDSUM				✎	C(1)
SEL_TAB_FIELD		1-AGENCYNUM		✎	C(60)
VALUE		123		✎	C(60)
BEFORE_ACTION				✎	C(1)
AFTER_ACTION				✎	C(1)
REFRESH				✎	C(1)
IGNORE_MULTI				✎	C(1)
COL_STABLE				✎	C(1)
ROW_STABLE				✎	C(1)
EXIT				✎	C(1)
FIELDNAME		AGENCYNUM		✎	C(30)
GROUPLEVEL		0		✎	I(4)
COLLECT_FROM		0		✎	I(4)
COLLECT_TO		0		✎	I(4)

Problematic with summarized ALV data

Figure 6.80: Slis_selfield structure used with hotspot (FM)

6.6.2 ALV control framework

When detail records are displayed, the underline that indicates a hotspot is visible in the detail row (Figure 6.81).

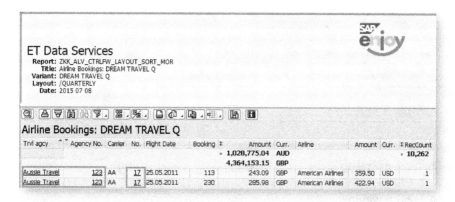

Figure 6.81: Hotspots on detail output (CF)

When summarized data is displayed, it may be necessary to use the EXPAND SELECTION button to expose a hotspot (Figure 6.82). Using your program, if the user clicks on a hotspot cell in a detail line (even if cell merging prevents the display of the value there), the desired action will occur. If the user clicks on a sub-total line, a pop-up message will appear advising them to click a detail line cell. Other behavior can also be coded.

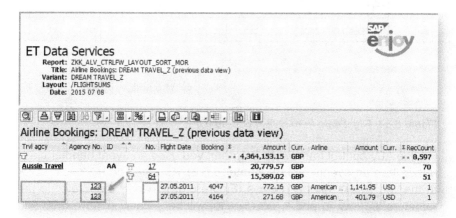

Figure 6.82: Hotspots on summarized output (CF)

A pop-up window will be used to display the master data record retrieved from table STRAVELAG (Figure 6.83).

Travel Agency Details
Agency No.
Travel agency name
Street
PO Box
Po
123
Aussie Travel
Queens Road
M8

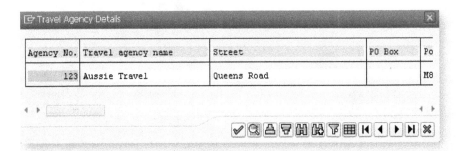

Figure 6.83: Travel agency data from stravelag in pop-up (CF)

A pop-up window will be used to display the master data record retrieved from table SPFLI (Figure 6.84). SAP's CL_GUI_ALV_GRID class provides more information than does the SLIS_SELFIELD structure (Figure 6.80) we used in the function module version of this program (Chapter 6.6.1). Since we can identify the specific detail row clicked by the user, we can return a single record in the pop-up by using multiple fields from the record.

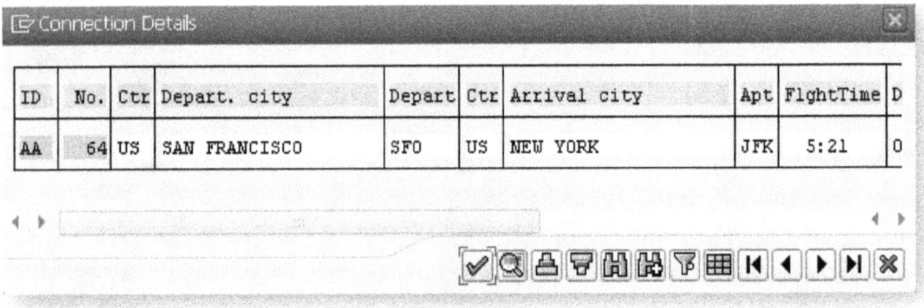

Connection Details
ID
No.
Ctr
Depart. city
Depart
Ctr
Arrival city
Apt
FlghtTime
D
AA
64
US
SAN FRANCISCO
SFO
US
NEW YORK
JFK
5:21
0

Figure 6.84: Flight data from spfli in pop-up (CF)

For the ALV control framework program, you used an event handler class rather than an events table (Chapter 6.5.2). Add method HOTSPOT_CLICK to the LCL_EVENT_HANDLER class (Figure 6.85). Two of the available parameters, E_ROW_ID and E_COLUMN_ID, will be suitable (Figure 6.90 and Figure 6.91).

In method HOTSPOT_CLICK (Figure 6.85), we evaluate whether the user has clicked on a summary line (where E_ROW_ID-ROWTYPE has content) or a detail line (where E_ROW_ID-ROWTYPE is initial).

Check need for subroutine call prior to calling it

 Whenever possible, evaluate whether conditions have been met for any subroutine call prior to calling it rather than inside the subroutine itself. For the ALV control framework technique (Figure 6.85), E_ROW_ID-ROWTYPE is checked prior to performing ZF_HOTSTPOT_CLICK. For the function module technique (Figure 6.77), the SLIS_SELFIELD-VALUE evaluation has to be done inside ZF_USER_COMMAND because the developer does not expressly call the subroutine and has no opportunity to evaluate before it is executed.

Continuing with method HOTSPOT_CLICK (Figure 6.85), if the user has clicked on a hotspot cell on a detail line (E_ROW_ID-ROWTYPE is initial), use the INDEX value from E_ROW_ID to read the output table. Pass the retrieved record and the name of the field clicked to a new subroutine called ZF_HOTSTPOT_CLICK.

Writing code in the method vs. in a called subroutine

 You can code the TOP_OF_PAGE and HOTSPOT_CLICK logic entirely in the respective method, but to improve readability and simplify support where the code is lengthy, developers sometimes move it to a subroutine as we've done with ZF_TOP_OF_PAGE and ZF_HOTSPOT _CLICK in the ALV control framework program. Follow your employer's or client's standard if provided.

```
********
CLASS lcl_event_handler DEFINITION.
  PUBLIC SECTION.
  METHODS:
    top_of_page   FOR EVENT top_of_page   OF cl_gui_alv_grid
      IMPORTING e_dyndoc_id,
      hotspot_click FOR EVENT hotspot_click OF cl_gui_alv_grid
        IMPORTING e_row_id
                  e_column_id.
ENDCLASS.
********
DATA: g_event_handler   TYPE REF TO lcl_event_handler.
********
CLASS lcl_event_handler IMPLEMENTATION.
  METHOD top_of_page.
    PERFORM zf_top_of_page USING e_dyndoc_id.
  ENDMETHOD.
  METHOD hotspot_click.
    IF e_row_id-rowtype IS INITIAL.  "blank rowtype = detail line
      READ TABLE gt_output INTO gs_output INDEX e_row_id-INDEX.
      IF sy-subrc = 0.
        PERFORM zf_hotspot_click USING gs_output
                                       e_column_id-fieldname.
      ENDIF.
    ELSE.                            "summarized line
      MESSAGE ID '00' TYPE 'I' NUMBER 001
        WITH 'Hotspot available. Click cell on detail line.'(017).
    ENDIF.
  ENDMETHOD.
ENDCLASS.
```

Figure 6.85: Hotspot_click method added to handler class (CF)

The SET HANDLER command for the new event must be added to module ZM_STATUS_9100 (Figure 6.86).

```
    CREATE OBJECT g_event_handler.
    SET HANDLER g_event_handler->top_of_page   FOR grid1.
    SET HANDLER g_event_handler->hotspot_click FOR grid1.
```

Figure 6.86: Hotspot_click aligned with ALV grid (CF)

Next, create the ZF_HOTSPOT_CLICK subroutine called from method HOT-STPOT_CLICK (Figure 6.87). The two parameters provide the output table detail record retrieved in method HOTSPOT_CLICK and the fieldname from E_COLUMN_ID. Define the local data structures and the tables needed for the REUSE_ALV_POPUP_TO_SELECT function module. Using CASE statements for the LS_FIELDNAME evaluation allows for easy expansion over time and further modularization.

Because there is a one-to-one relationship between the agency name, the agency number, and the master data record being retrieved from table STRAVELAG, the pop-up will return an identical single record regardless of which of those two hotspots was clicked (Figure 6.83). Since the key for the table read (STRAVELAG-AGENCYNUM) is available in the record passed in LS_OUTPUT, use the SELECT SINGLE syntax (Figure 6.87).

```
FORM zf_hotspot_click USING ls_output    TYPE lty_output
                            ls_fieldname TYPE lvc_s_col-fieldname.

  DATA: ls_stravelag   TYPE stravelag,
        lt_stravelag   TYPE TABLE OF stravelag,
        ls_spfli       TYPE spfli,
        lt_spfli       TYPE TABLE OF spfli.

  CASE ls_fieldname.
    WHEN 'AGENCYNUM'
      OR 'NAME'.                    "display STRAVELAG details
      CLEAR: ls_stravelag, lt_stravelag.
      SELECT SINGLE * FROM stravelag          "table key
        INTO ls_stravelag
        WHERE agencynum = ls_output-agencynum.
      APPEND ls_stravelag TO lt_stravelag.
      CALL FUNCTION 'REUSE_ALV_POPUP_TO_SELECT'
      EXPORTING
        i_title          = 'Travel Agency Details'(020)
        i_selection      = ' '          "display only
        i_tabname        = '1'
        i_structure_name = 'STRAVELAG'
      TABLES
        t_outtab         = lt_stravelag
      EXCEPTIONS
        program_error    = 1
        OTHERS           = 2.
      IF sy-subrc <> 0.
        MESSAGE ID '00' TYPE 'I' NUMBER 001 WITH 'Popup error'(018).
      ENDIF.
```

Figure 6.87: Hotspot_click logic, part 1 (CF)

For the flight number hotspot (CONNID), use both of the SPFLI table key fields (CARRID, CONNID) in the record passed in LS_OUTPUT for the SELECT SINGLE retrieval (Figure 6.88) before displaying the master data record to the user (Figure 6.84).

```
WHEN 'CONNID'.                    "display SPFLI details
   CLEAR: ls_spfli, lt_spfli.
   SELECT SINGLE * FROM spfli
     INTO ls_spfli
     WHERE carrid = ls_output-carrid
       AND connid = ls_output-connid.
   APPEND ls_spfli TO lt_spfli.
   CALL FUNCTION 'REUSE_ALV_POPUP_TO_SELECT'
   EXPORTING
     i_title           = 'Connection Details' (019)
     i_selection       = ' '          "display only
     i_tabname         = '1'
     i_structure_name  = 'SPFLI'
   TABLES
     t_outtab          = lt_spfli
   EXCEPTIONS
     program_error     = 1
     OTHERS            = 2.
   IF sy-subrc <> 0.
     MESSAGE ID '00' TYPE 'I' NUMBER 001 WITH 'Popup error' (018).
   ENDIF.
 ENDCASE.
ENDFORM.
```

Figure 6.88: Hotspot_click logic, part 2 (CF)

To enable the hotspots, fill the HOTSPOT field of the field catalog with X in the ZF_BUILD_FIELDCATALOG subroutine (Figure 6.89).

The CL_GUI_ALV_GRID structure E_COLUMN_ID contains the fieldname for the hotspot (Figure 6.90).

The CL_GUI_ALV_GRID structure E_ROW_ID contains a blank rowtype when the hotspot field is on a detail line. The index value can be used to retrieve the entire output record clicked even if the user has filtered or resorted the data after initial display (Figure 6.91).

```
*-------------------------------------------------------------------
FORM zf_build_fieldcatalog USING lt_fieldcat TYPE lvc_t_fcat.

  DATA: ls_fieldcat TYPE lvc_s_fcat.        "single row

  CLEAR ls_fieldcat.
  ls_fieldcat-fieldname = 'NAME'.
  ls_fieldcat-ref_table = 'STRAVELAG'.
  ls_fieldcat-hotspot   = 'X'.
  APPEND ls_fieldcat TO lt_fieldcat.

  CLEAR ls_fieldcat.
  ls_fieldcat-fieldname = 'AGENCYNUM'.
  ls_fieldcat-ref_table = 'STRAVELAG'.
  ls_fieldcat-hotspot   = 'X'.
  APPEND ls_fieldcat TO lt_fieldcat.

  CLEAR ls_fieldcat.
  ls_fieldcat-fieldname = 'CURRENCY'.
  ls_fieldcat-ref_table = 'STRAVELAG'.
  ls_fieldcat-no_out    = 'X'.              "hide field
  APPEND ls_fieldcat TO lt_fieldcat.

  CLEAR ls_fieldcat.
  ls_fieldcat-fieldname = 'CARRID'.
  ls_fieldcat-ref_table = 'SBOOK'.
  APPEND ls_fieldcat TO lt_fieldcat.

  CLEAR ls_fieldcat.
  ls_fieldcat-fieldname = 'CONNID'.
  ls_fieldcat-ref_table = 'SBOOK'.
  ls_fieldcat-hotspot   = 'X'.
  APPEND ls_fieldcat TO lt_fieldcat.
```

Figure 6.89: Field catalog additions for three hotspots (CF)

Structures	Fld.list	
Struct.	E_COLUMN_ID	
Struc. Type	Structure: flat, charlike(66)	
Exp. Component	Val...	Val.
FIELDNAME		CONNID
HIERLEVEL		

Figure 6.90: Fieldname identifies the cell clicked (CF)

169

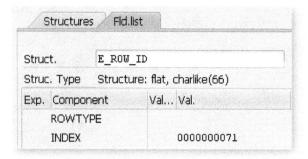

Figure 6.91: Index for blank rowtype matches detail in table (CF)

When the E_ROW_ID-ROWTYPE is non-blank, the index cannot be used to retrieve a detail record (Figure 6.92).

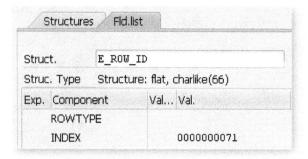

Figure 6.92: Index for summary line rowtype not suitable for table read for detail record (CF)

6.7 Excluding buttons from the ALV application toolbar

On occasion, you are asked to remove buttons from the standard ALV application toolbar. This can be done easily. (In Chapter 6.8, you will see how to add toolbar buttons—a more complex activity in programs using an ALV function module technique.)

6.7.1 Function module

Two buttons have been identified for removal in the training scenario: ABC ANALYSIS and GRAPHIC (Figure 6.93).

Figure 6.93: Standard toolbar showing unneeded buttons (FM)

Identifying button function codes

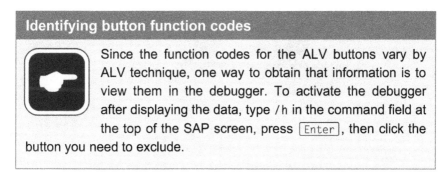

Since the function codes for the ALV buttons vary by ALV technique, one way to obtain that information is to view them in the debugger. To activate the debugger after displaying the data, type / h in the command field at the top of the SAP screen, press Enter, then click the button you need to exclude.

After the coding changes, the two buttons will no longer appear (Figure 6.94).

Figure 6.94: Buttons no longer visible (FM)

A new table must be declared (Figure 6.95). Table type SLIS_T_EXTAB is based on structure SLIS_EXTAB which contains a single field called FCODE.

```
DATA: gs_output    TYPE lty_output,
      gt_output    TYPE STANDARD TABLE OF lty_output,
      gt_sort      TYPE slis_t_sortinfo_alv,
      gt_fieldcat  TYPE slis_t_fieldcat_alv,
      gs_layout    TYPE slis_layout_alv,
      gt_top_text  TYPE slis_t_listheader,
      gt_events    TYPE slis_t_event,
      gt_exclude   TYPE slis_t_extab.
```

Figure 6.95: Table for function codes to be excluded from display (FM)

Add a new PERFORM statement to the main program logic area to popu-late the new table (Figure 6.96).

```
************* Start of main program logic *********************
  PERFORM zf_build_layout USING gs_layout.
  PERFORM zf_build_fieldcatalog USING gt_fieldcat[].
  PERFORM zf_build_sort_table USING gt_sort[].
  PERFORM zf_build_event_table USING gt_events[].
  PERFORM zf_build_top_text_table USING gt_top_text[].

  PERFORM zf_build_exclude_table USING gt_exclude[].

  PERFORM zf_display_alv.
************* End of main program logic *********************
```

Figure 6.96: Build table of excluded function codes (FM)

Add the function code of each button to be excluded to the FCODE field of the new table (Figure 6.97).

```
*-------------------------------------------------------------
FORM zf_build_exclude_table USING lt_exclude type slis_t_extab.

  DATA: ls_exclude TYPE slis_extab.

  ls_exclude-fcode = '&ABC'.
  APPEND ls_exclude TO lt_exclude.
  ls_exclude-fcode = '&GRAPH'.
  APPEND ls_exclude TO lt_exclude.

ENDFORM.
```

Figure 6.97: Population of function codes in the table (FM)

Add the table to the function module call (Figure 6.98).

```
FORM zf_display_alv.

  CALL FUNCTION 'REUSE_ALV_GRID_DISPLAY'
    EXPORTING
      i_callback_program = sy-repid
      is_layout          = gs_layout
      it_fieldcat        = gt_fieldcat[]
      it_excluding       = gt_exclude[]
      it_sort            = gt_sort[]
      i_save             = gv_save
      is_variant         = gs_variant
      it_events          = gt_events[]
    TABLES
      t_outtab           = gt_output
    EXCEPTIONS
      program_error      = 1
      OTHERS             = 2 .
```

Figure 6.98: Exclusion table is passed in the ALV call (FM)

6.7.2 ALV control framework

One button (DISPLAY GRAPHIC) will be removed for this training scenario (Figure 6.99).

Figure 6.99: Standard toolbar showing unneeded button (CF)

173

Two ways to identify cl_gui_alv_grid function codes

 One way to identify the function code for an ALV button is to step through the code in the debugger after clicking the button. Another way is to check the attributes tab of the CL_GUI_ALV_GRID class (using transaction code se24 or double-clicking CL_GUI_ALV_GRID in the program). Choose from the list attributes that have an "Associated Type" of UI_FUNC; these typically have names beginning with MC_FC.

After the coding changes, the button will no longer appear (Figure 6.100).

Figure 6.100: Button no longer visible (CF)

A new table is declared (Figure 6.101) based on UI_FUNCTIONS. It contains a single field called UI_FUNC.

```
DATA: gs_layout    TYPE lvc_s_layo,              "layout params
      gs_output    TYPE lty_output,             "local structure (line)
      gt_output    TYPE STANDARD TABLE OF lty_output,
      gt_sort      TYPE lvc_t_sort,
      gt_fieldcat  TYPE lvc_t_fcat,              "table
      gt_exclude   TYPE ui_functions.
```

Figure 6.101: Table for function codes to be excluded from the display (CF)

Add a new PERFORM statement to the main program logic area to populate the new table (Figure 6.102).

```
PERFORM zf_build_layout        USING gs_layout.
PERFORM zf_build_fieldcatalog  USING gt_fieldcat[].
PERFORM zf_build_sort          USING gt_sort[].
PERFORM zf_build_exclude_table USING gt_exclude[].
CALL SCREEN 9100.
```

Figure 6.102: Build table of excluded functions (CF)

Add the function code of each button to be excluded to the table using the associated attribute name from class CL_GUI_ALV_GRID (Figure 6.103). The function value for "Display Graphic" is MC_FC_GRAPH.

```
*----------------------------------------------------------------
FORM zf_build_exclude_table USING lt_exclude TYPE ui_functions.

  DATA: ls_exclude TYPE ui_func.

  ls_exclude = cl_gui_alv_grid=>MC_FC_GRAPH.
  APPEND ls_exclude TO lt_exclude.

ENDFORM.
```

Figure 6.103: Exclusion table populated (CF)

Add the table to the method call (Figure 6.104).

```
CALL METHOD grid1->set_table_for_first_display
  EXPORTING
    i_structure_name    = 'LTY_OUTPUT'
    is_variant          = gs_variant
    i_save              = gv_save
    is_layout           = gs_layout
    it_toolbar_excluding = gt_exclude
  CHANGING
    it_fieldcatalog     = gt_fieldcat
    it_sort             = gt_sort
    it_outtab           = gt_output.
```

Figure 6.104: Exclusion table is passed in the ALV call (CF)

6.8   Adding buttons to the ALV application toolbar

Adding buttons to the ALV application toolbar is a bit more complex than excluding them (Chapter 6.7), especially if you are using the RE-USE_ALV_GRID_DISPLAY function module technique, since that requires copying and modifying the default GUI status.

Another difference between the ALV control framework and the ALV function module techniques is apparent in this chapter. In the ALV function module program, the hotspot logic and the custom button logic share the ZF_USER_COMMAND subroutine. In the ALV control framework program, the hotspot logic is in the HOTSPOT_CLICK method while the custom button logic is in the USER_COMMAND method (coupled with a TOOLBAR_ADD method).

Copy your program before continuing

This is a good time to copy your in-progress program(s), making the next changes in a copy. Save and activate, as usual. An error during the GUI status change exercise (only relevant for the ALV function module program example) could put your in-progress program at risk.

In the training scenario, we have identified a need to add a button with an icon image to the ALV application toolbar. It will use the icon named ICON_ANNOTATION with a text label that reads "Edit Comment". When the user hovers the mouse over the new button, the pop-up instruction will say "Add note to record". The function code will be 'NOTE', and the buttons that were previously excluded (Chapter 6.7) will remain hidden.

How to display a list of all icons

To see all the icons that SAP provides, use transaction code se38 or sa38 to run the program called SHOWICON (Figure 6.105). For the ALV control framework, you will provide the icon name in the TOOLBAR event. For the REUSE_ALV_GRID_DISPLAY program, you will provide the icon name during the customization of the GUI status.

Display Icons in Lists

Icon	Icon name	Comment	Lngth	Printab.	internal	B
	ICON_ALV_VARIANTS	Layouts	2		LZ VARIAN	2
	ICON_ALV_VARIANT_CHOOSE	Choose Layout	2		DM VARCHO	2
	ICON_ALV_VARIANT_SAVE	Save Layout	2		DN VARSAV	2
	ICON_ANNOTATION	Note; remark	2	✓	OJ B_ANNO	1
	ICON_ANY_DOCUMENT	Unknown document class	2		09 ANYDOC	A

Figure 6.105: SHOWICON program shows each icon with its image

Logic for the new button will be added in Chapter 8 so, for now, a place-holder comment will be shown.

6.8.1 Function module

After making these changes, the toolbar will display with the new EDIT COMMENT button and without the ABC ANALYSIS and GRAPHIC buttons (Figure 6.106).

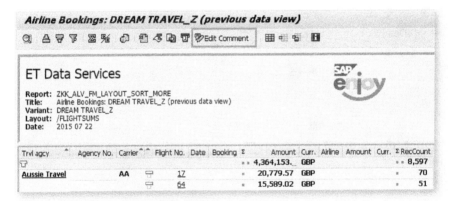

Figure 6.106: New toolbar button (FM)

Before making source code changes in the function module program, you need to replace the existing GUI status of your program with a full copy to be modified. There are a lot of steps, but it is not complicated. (By copying an existing status, you can add a button and avoid having to re-create all the buttons formerly available.)

How to identify the default GUI status

 Numerous GUI statuses can be copied to replace the default in your program, but if you want to continue with the same set of buttons used so far, you can obtain the details (the program name and GUI status name) using the ABAP debugger. To do this, display your ALV as usual, type /h in the command line, then click on any button in the ALV application toolbar. Write down the program name at the top of the debugger screen. Display the value in SY-PFKEY and write that down, as well—it is the name of the default GUI status used in your program (Figure 6.107).

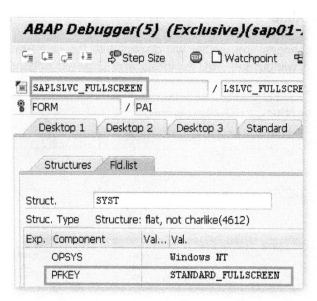

Figure 6.107: Program name and GUI status name (FM)

Type the program name and status name into the selection screen of transaction code se41 (Menu Painter), then click on the COPY STATUS button (Figure 6.108). You can also do this from other transaction codes such as se80 (object navigator).

In the pop-up window, provide your program name and a new name for the status (Figure 6.109), then click the COPY button.

Figure 6.108: Copy the current GUI status, part 1 (FM)

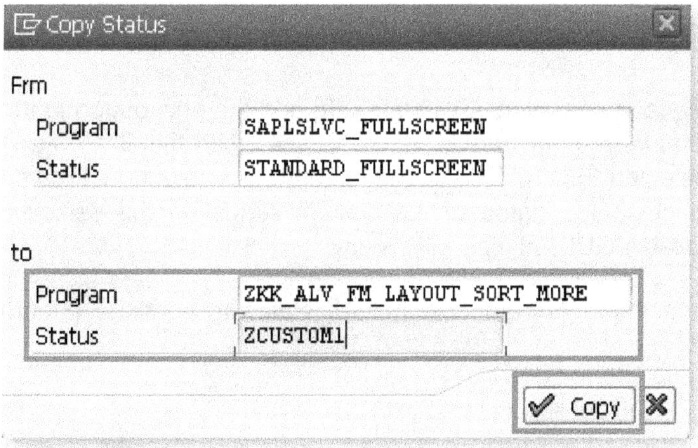

Figure 6.109: Copy the current GUI status, part 2 (FM)

No changes are needed on the informational pop-up so click the COPY button again (Figure 6.110).

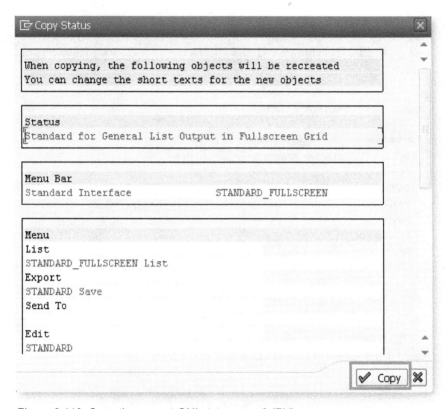

Figure 6.110: Copy the current GUI status, part 3 (FM)

Save and activate your custom GUI status. To add the new button to the custom GUI status, re-start transaction code se41 with the STATUS LIST radio button selected (Figure 6.111). Click on the CHANGE button. (You do not need to include the name of the custom status on the selection screen; all available GUI statuses will display.)

Double-click the name of your custom GUI status to continue (Figure 6.112).

Figure 6.111: Add button to custom GUI status, part 1 (FM)

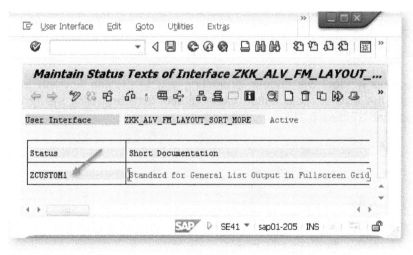

Figure 6.112: Add button to custom GUI status, part 2 (FM)

Click on the EXPAND button next to "Application Toolbar", then put your cursor in an unused cell. Click the ADD button on the toolbar, then type the function code chosen earlier: NOTE (Figure 6.113).

Figure 6.113: Add button to custom GUI status, part 3 (FM)

A pop-up window will appear, prompting you to provide function text. Retain the default radio button value (Static Text) and click the green checkmark (Figure 6.114).

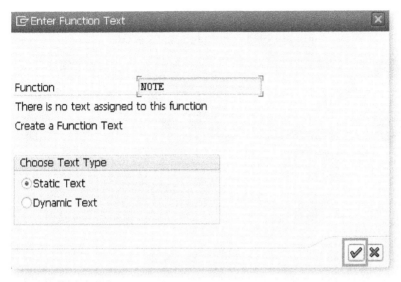

Figure 6.114: Add button to custom GUI status, part 4 (FM)

Provide the values shown, then click the green checkmark (Figure 6.115). (You can complete the function text, the icon name, or both as shown.)

▶ FUNCTION TEXT: Label visible on the button itself

▶ ICON NAME: Official icon name from the showicon program (Figure 6.105)

▶ INFO. TEXT: Instructional information that appears when mouse hovers over the button

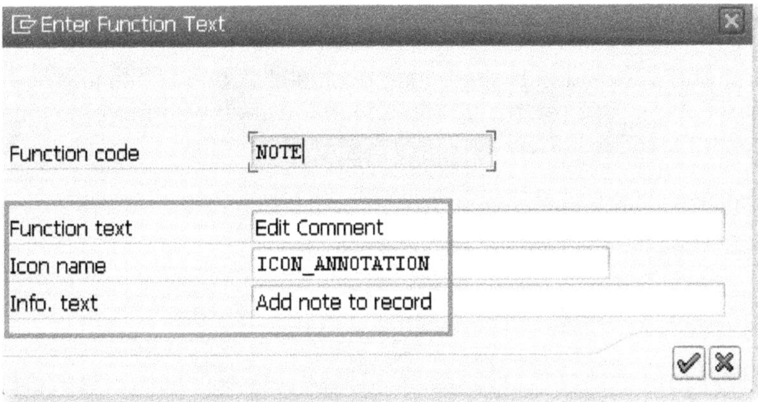

Figure 6.115: Add button to custom GUI status, part 5 (FM)

In the pop-up window, choose any of the function keys presented as available, then click the green checkmark (Figure 6.116).

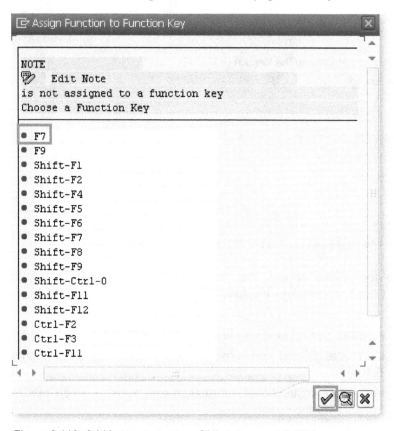

Figure 6.116: Add button to custom GUI status, part 6 (FM)

In order to add a text label to the button double-click on the cell just added (Figure 6.117). This returns you to an input screen with more options including the "Icon Text" input field.

Add the text for the button in the ICON TEXT field and click on the green checkmark (Figure 6.118).

Figure 6.117: Add button to custom GUI status, part 7 (FM)

Function Attributes

Function Code	NOTE
Functional Type	☐ Application Function
Switch	

Reaction ▼

Static Function Texts

Function Text	Edit Comment
Icon Name	ICON_ANNOTATION
Icon Text	Edit Comment
Info. Text	Add note to record
Fastpath	

✓ Change Text Type ✕

Figure 6.118: Add button to custom GUI status, part 8 (FM)

Save and activate, then exit transaction code se41 (Figure 6.119).

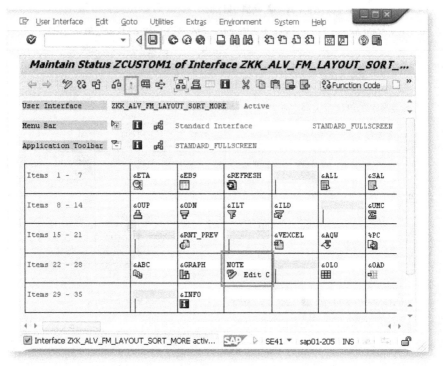

Figure 6.119: Add button to custom GUI status, part 9 (FM)

Now change the source code to add logic for the new button in the custom GUI status. For variety, we'll use a callback parameter (I_CALLBACK_PF_STATUS_SET) this time instead of repeating the events table approach used for the TOP_OF_PAGE (Chapter 6.5.1) and HOTSPOT (Chapter 6.6.1) logic. Either approach is fine.

Define a constant with the name of the subroutine that will set the GUI status. Because the SET PF-STATUS command has a built-in excluding clause, you can delete the GT_EXCLUDE table from the data area (Figure 6.120).

```
DATA: gs_output    TYPE lty_output,
      gt_output    TYPE STANDARD TABLE OF lty_output,
      gt_sort      TYPE slis_t_sortinfo_alv,
      gt_fieldcat  TYPE slis_t_fieldcat_alv,
      gs_layout    TYPE slis_layout_alv,
      gt_top_text  TYPE slis_t_listheader,
      gt_events    TYPE slis_t_event.
*     gt_exclude   TYPE slis_t_extab.            "delete, no longer needed

CONSTANTS: gc_formname_top TYPE slis_formname VALUE 'ZF_TOP_OF_PAGE',
           gc_formname_com TYPE slis_formname VALUE 'ZF_USER_COMMAND',
           gc_formname_pf  TYPE slis_formname VALUE 'ZF_SET_PFSTATUS'.
```

Figure 6.120: Data changes for button addition (FM)

The content of ZF_BUILD_EXCLUDE_TABLE will be moved from its own sub-routine to the new ZF_SET_PFSTATUS. subroutine so the explicit PERFORM statement can be deleted (Figure 6.121).

```
************* Start of main program logic ***********************
   PERFORM zf_build_layout USING gs_layout.
   PERFORM zf_build_fieldcatalog USING gt_fieldcat[].
   PERFORM zf_build_sort_table USING gt_sort[].
   PERFORM zf_build_event_table USING gt_events[].
   PERFORM zf_build_top_text_table USING gt_top_text[].

**  PERFORM zf_build_exclude_table USING gt_exclude[].       "delete

   PERFORM zf_display_alv.
************* End of main program logic ***********************
```

Figure 6.121: Delete the perform statement of the excluding table build (FM)

Create a new subroutine called ZF_SET_PFSTATUS (Figure 6.122). The name must match the constant you declared (Figure 6.120). Copy the content from ZF_BUILD_EXCLUDE_TABLE into the new ZF_SET_PFSTATUS subroutine, then add the SET PF-STATUS command with your custom GUI status ZCUSTOM1.

(Each time the ZF_SET_PFSTATUS subroutine is executed, SAP's standard table of function-codes-to-be-excluded is presented anew. The function codes that you want to exclude from the ALV application toolbar must be re-appended to the SAP list on every pass.)

187

```
*-----------------------------------------------------------------
FORM zf_set_pfstatus USING lt_exclude TYPE slis_t_extab.
  DATA: ls_exclude TYPE slis_extab.

* add to the exclude table pre-populated by SAP on each pass
  ls_exclude-fcode = '&ABC'.
  APPEND ls_exclude TO lt_exclude.
  ls_exclude-fcode = '&GRAPH'.
  APPEND ls_exclude TO lt_exclude.

  SET PF-STATUS 'ZCUSTOM1' EXCLUDING lt_exclude.

ENDFORM.
```

Figure 6.122: New subroutine to update the table of buttons to be excluded and set the custom GUI status (FM)

Now that you have moved the logic from the ZF_BUILD_EXCLUDE_TABLE subroutine to the ZF_SET_PFSTATUS subroutine, delete ZF_BUILD_EXCLUDE _TABLE (Figure 6.123).

```
*-----------------------------------------------------------------
*FORM zf_build_exclude_table USING lt_exclude type slis_t_extab.
* logic moved to zf_set_pfstatus
*   DATA: ls_exclude TYPE slis_extab.
*   ls_exclude-fcode = '&ABC'.
*   APPEND ls_exclude TO lt_exclude.
*   ls_exclude-fcode = '&GRAPH'.
*   APPEND ls_exclude TO lt_exclude.
*ENDFORM.
```

Figure 6.123: Delete the former subroutine (FM)

The logic to execute when the user clicks the new button on the ALV application toolbar (function code = NOTE) will be added to the existing ZF_USER_COMMAND subroutine in Chapter 8.3.1. A placeholder can be added now (Figure 6.124).

The final changes are made in the REUSE_ALV_GRID_DISPLAY call (Figure 6.125). Add the constant containing the name of the ZF_SET_PFSTATUS subroutine and remove the exclude table reference since the exclude table is now being passed via the I_CALLBACK_PF_STATUS_SET parameter.

```
*------------------------------------------------------------
FORM zf_user_command USING lv_ucomm      LIKE sy-ucomm
                           ls_selfield TYPE slis_selfield.
  DATA: ls_stravelag    TYPE stravelag,
        lt_stravelag    TYPE TABLE OF stravelag,
        lt_spfli        TYPE TABLE OF spfli,
        lt_output_temp TYPE TABLE OF lty_output.

* do nothing if user clicks where no identifiable data value
  IF ls_selfield-value IS INITIAL.
    RETURN.
  ENDIF.


  CASE lv_ucomm.
    WHEN 'NOTE'.                    "toolbar button clicked
*       logic will be added here later

    WHEN '&IC1'.                    "hotspot was clicked
      CASE ls_selfield-fieldname.
        WHEN 'AGENCYNUM'
          OR 'NAME'.               "display STRAVELAG details
```

Figure 6.124: Placeholder for new button logic (FM)

```
*------------------------------------------------------------
FORM zf_display_alv.

  CALL FUNCTION 'REUSE_ALV_GRID_DISPLAY'
    EXPORTING
      i_callback_program       = sy-repid
      i_callback_pf_status_set = gc_formname_pf
      is_layout                = gs_layout
      it_fieldcat              = gt_fieldcat[]
*     it_excluding             = gt_exclude[]    "delete, not needed
      it_sort                  = gt_sort[]
      i_save                   = gv_save
      is_variant               = gs_variant
      it_events                = gt_events[]
    TABLES
      t_outtab                 = gt_output
    EXCEPTIONS
      program_error            = 1
      OTHERS                   = 2.
```

Figure 6.125: Two changes for the function module call (FM)

189

6.8.2   ALV control framework

After making these changes, the toolbar will display with the new EDIT COMMENT button and without the GRAPHIC button (Figure 6.126).

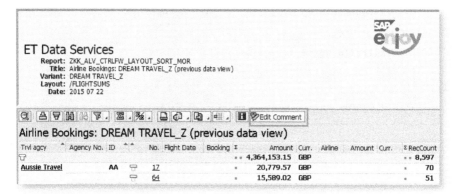

Figure 6.126: New application toolbar button (CF)

Two events are associated with the additional button on the ALV application toolbar: TOOLBAR and USER_COMMAND (Figure 6.127). (The method names I used are TOOLBAR_ADD and USER_COMMAND_ALV, but you can choose other names, if you wish.)

```
* * * * * * * *
CLASS lcl_event_handler DEFINITION.
  PUBLIC SECTION.
  METHODS:
    toolbar_add       FOR EVENT toolbar       OF cl_gui_alv_grid
      IMPORTING e_object
                e_interactive,
    user_command_alv FOR EVENT user_command  OF cl_gui_alv_grid
      IMPORTING e_ucomm,
    top_of_page       FOR EVENT top_of_page   OF cl_gui_alv_grid
      IMPORTING e_dyndoc_id,
    hotspot_click     FOR EVENT hotspot_click OF cl_gui_alv_grid
      IMPORTING e_row_id
                e_column_id.
  ENDCLASS.
* * * * * * * *
DATA: g_event_handler   TYPE REF TO lcl_event_handler.
* * * * * * * *
```

Figure 6.127: Two new events (CF)

For each of these methods, you can call a separate subroutine (Figure 6.128) or you can write the code directly in the method implementation.

```
* * * * * * * *
CLASS lcl_event_handler IMPLEMENTATION.
  METHOD toolbar_add.
    PERFORM zf_toolbar_add USING e_object.
  ENDMETHOD.

  METHOD user_command_alv.
    PERFORM zf_user_command_alv USING e_ucomm.
  ENDMETHOD.

  METHOD top_of_page.
    PERFORM zf_top_of_page USING e_dyndoc_id.
  ENDMETHOD.

  METHOD hotspot_click.
    IF e_row_id-rowtype IS INITIAL.  "blank rowtype = detail line
      READ TABLE gt_output INTO gs_output INDEX e_row_id-index.
      IF sy-subrc = 0.
        PERFORM zf_hotspot_click USING gs_output
                                       e_column_id-fieldname.
      ENDIF.
    ELSE.                            "summarized line
      MESSAGE ID '00' TYPE 'I' NUMBER 001
        WITH 'Hotspot available. Click cell on detail line.'(017).
    ENDIF.
  ENDMETHOD.
ENDCLASS.
```

Figure 6.128: Two new methods for new button (CF)

In ZF_TOOLBAR_ADD, set the attributes of the new button (Figure 6.129). The BUTN_TYPE values include:

▶ 0: Button (normal)
▶ 1: Menu and default button
▶ 2: Menu
▶ 3: Separator
▶ 4: Radio button
▶ 5: Checkbox
▶ 6: Menu entry

```
*---------------------------------------------------------------
FORM zf_toolbar_add USING lo_object
              TYPE REF TO cl_alv_event_toolbar_set.

  DATA: ls_toolbar TYPE stb_button.
  CLEAR ls_toolbar.
  ls_toolbar-function  = 'NOTE'.              "own fcode for logic
  ls_toolbar-icon      = icon_annotation.     "from ICON include
  ls_toolbar-quickinfo = 'Add note to record'.
  ls_toolbar-butn_type = 0.                   "basic button, not menu
  ls_toolbar-disabled  = ' '.
  ls_toolbar-text      = 'Edit Comment'.      "label on button
  APPEND ls_toolbar TO lo_object->mt_toolbar.
ENDFORM.
```

Figure 6.129: New subroutine with toolbar button details (CF)

The logic to execute when the user clicks the new button on the ALV application toolbar (function code = NOTE) will be added to the existing ZF_USER_COMMAND_ALV subroutine in Chapter 8.3.2. A placeholder can be added now (Figure 6.130).

```
*---------------------------------------------------------------
FORM zf_user_command_alv USING lv_ucomm TYPE sy-ucomm.

  CASE lv_ucomm.
    WHEN 'NOTE'.
*      logic will be added here later
  ENDCASE.
ENDFORM.
```

Figure 6.130: New subroutine for user command logic (CF)

zf_user_command_alv and zm_user_command_9100

 Don't be confused by the two similarly named sections of code in this example program. The PAI module called ZM_USER_COMMAND_9100 manages the top row of function keys we configured as BACK, EXIT, and CANCEL in Figure 3.26. The new subroutine ZF_USER_COMMAND _ALV will contain logic related to the ALV application toolbar buttons.

The final changes are made in the ZM_STATUS_9100 module (Figure 6.131): Setting handlers for the new TOOLBAR and USER_COMMAND events, calling the SET_TOOLBAR_INTERACTIVE method.

```
CREATE OBJECT g_event_handler.

SET HANDLER g_event_handler->toolbar_add        FOR grid1.
SET HANDLER g_event_handler->user_command_alv   FOR grid1.

SET HANDLER g_event_handler->top_of_page        FOR grid1.
SET HANDLER g_event_handler->hotspot_click      FOR grid1.

CALL METHOD grid1->set_toolbar_interactive.
```

Figure 6.131: Zm_status_9100 module changes (CF)

No change is needed for the ZF_BUILD_EXCLUDE_TABLE subroutine (Figure 6.103). The exclude table will continue to be passed to the SET _TABLE_FOR_FIRST_DISPLAY method for the removal of the DISPLAY GRAPHIC button from the ALV application toolbar.

6.9   Summary

In this chapter you learned how to customize the ALV output to meet a number of requirements you may encounter.

Key points:

► Hiding columns

► Displaying sub-totals immediately

► Providing record counts using a layout structure technique and a field catalog technique

► Handling report layout variants from the selection screen including validation, on-value-request lookup logic, and variant-saving authorization concepts

► Using TOP_OF_PAGE, USER_COMMAND, HOTSPOT_CLICK, and TOOLBAR events

► Displaying top_of_page content (text and logo), including use of a splitter container to divide the screen and use of dynamic document functionality to output report parameters

► Customizing the ALV application toolbar by removing or adding buttons, including how to copy and modify the default GUI status for the function module technique

In Chapter 7, you'll see examples of code that can be used in ALV and non-ALV programs.

In Chapter 8, you'll add edit capability to an ALV to support small volumes of data changes.

7 Solving challenges with handy features applicable to many program types

The information in this chapter may be useful for solving challenges you face. With adaptations, the concepts can be applied to a wide range of program types, not just SAP List Viewer programs.

7.1 Retrieving the variant name during transaction code se38 background execution

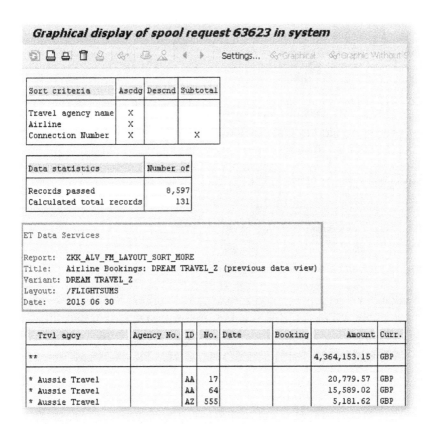

Figure 7.1: Actual variant name in background top_of_page

In Chapter 6.5, you added a top_of_page event to display text and a logo at the top of the screen (Figure 6.50 and Figure 6.60). If you were to run the program with the same variant in background using transaction code sm36 (Schedule Background Job), the top_of_page output in the print spool would look like Figure 7.1. The background output matches the foreground output, without the logo.

Sometimes, though, developers execute programs in the background from transaction code se38, sending the report to the spool. It is helpful in those cases to have a record of the variant that generated the report. Unfortunately, a variant alias is substituted in the SY-SLSET field when run that way (Figure 7.2).

```
ET Data Services

Report:   ZKK_ALV_FM_LAYOUT_SORT_MORE
Title:    Airline Bookings: &0000000000002
Variant: &0000000000002
Layout:   /FLIGHTSUMS
Date:     2015 06 24
```

Figure 7.2: Alias for variant name during se38 > background

If you need a solution to this problem (that only impacts those making a transaction code se38 switch from foreground to background mode), one work-around is to store the variant name in a selection screen parameter field (Figure 7.3). (It is hidden from view using NO_DISPLAY because it requires no user interaction.)

```
PARAMETERS:     p_slset TYPE sy-slset NO-DISPLAY.   "for SE38 > backgrnd
```

Figure 7.3: Hidden parameter to hold the variant name

After adding the parameter, add a new global variable (Figure 7.4). Use of this variable will reduce the number of IF statements and simplify the code.

```
DATA: gv_lines TYPE i,
      gv_title TYPE syst-title,
      gv_slset TYPE syst-slset.
```

Figure 7.4: Variable to hold the variant name

Add the AT SELECTION-SCREEN OUTPUT logic shown in Figure 7.5. This logic is executed multiple times while the user or developer interacts online (in foreground mode) with the selection screen. Each time, it moves the variant name from the SY-SLSET system field to the new hidden parameter field. The IF statement prevents the alias from overwriting the actual variant name stored in P_SLSET during the final pass through the AT SELECTION-SCREEN OUTPUT logic when switching from foreground to background mode.

```
AT SELECTION-SCREEN OUTPUT.
  IF sy-batch = 'X'.
    RETURN.            "avoid overlay by &0000 name with se38 > bkgrnd
  ENDIF.
  p_slset = sy-slset.
```

Figure 7.5: Populate hidden parameter

Add an IF statement to the ZF_START subroutine coded earlier (Figure 7.6). (Subroutine ZF_START executes for both foreground and background runs.) If the hidden parameter field has been filled, move it to the new variable. If not, move the SY-SLSET value to the new variable. Modify the title logic in ZF_START to use GV_SLSET instead of SY-SLSET (Figure 7.6).

```
*-----------------------------------------------------------------
FORM zf_start.
* save the variant name from either the pseudo-parameter filled in
*    AT SELECTION-SCREEN OUTPUT or from system variable
  IF NOT p_slset IS INITIAL.
    gv_slset = p_slset.            "foreground, SE38 > background
  ELSE.
    gv_slset = sy-slset.           "SM36 background
  ENDIF.

* fill title variable using variant variable from above
  CONCATENATE 'Airline Bookings:'(001)
              gv_slset
  INTO gv_title SEPARATED BY space.
  IF gv_slset CS '_Z'.
    CONCATENATE gv_title
                '(previous data view)'(002)
    INTO gv_title SEPARATED BY space.
  ENDIF.
```

Figure 7.6: Populate the new variable and modify the title build

Another place that requires a change from SY-SLSET to the new variable GV_SLSET is in the subroutine ZF_BUILD_TOP_TEXT_TABLE (Figure 7.7). Adapt this for other top_of_page text fill techniques.

197

```
CLEAR ls_textline.
ls_textline-typ  = 'S'.                    "standard line
ls_textline-key  = 'Variant:' (013).
ls_textline-info = gv_slset.
APPEND ls_textline TO lt_top_text.
```

Figure 7.7: Pass the variable to the text table for top_of_page (FM)

With these changes, you will see the actual variant name rather than the alias in your configured top_of_page header for all methods of execution.

7.2   Modifying the selection screen for different user groups

An ABAP selection screen can be modified dynamically to accommodate more than one user group: one with display authorization and one with change authorization.

Approaches might include checking standard or custom authorization objects or creating separate transaction codes for each group.

This chapter describes how to use a MODIF ID to hide or disable (gray out) a selection screen element.

Using the editable ALV exercise from Chapter 8.2 as a starting point, a MODIF ID called ZKK has been declared (Figure 7.8) for the checkbox parameter called P_EDIT. An authority-check can be executed to fill variable GV_EDIT_FLAG for evaluation in the AT SELECTION-SCREEN OUTPUT logic. (ZF_AUTHORITY_CHECK content is not shown for this example.)

In the example (Figure 7.8), if the user has display authorization, the selection screen will be modified to hide the selection screen elements aligned with the MODIF ID (Figure 7.9).

```
SELECTION-SCREEN BEGIN OF LINE.
PARAMETERS:    p_edit   AS CHECKBOX DEFAULT ' '  MODIF ID zkk.
* text-100 contains "Display in edit mode for comment changes"
SELECTION-SCREEN COMMENT 5(40) text-100 FOR FIELD p_edit.
SELECTION-SCREEN END OF LINE.

INITIALIZATION.
  PERFORM zf_authority_check USING gv_edit_flag.

AT SELECTION-SCREEN OUTPUT.
  IF gv_edit_flag = ' '.                   "no edit authority
*   alternative to edit_flag IF could be sy-tcode = display-only tcode
    LOOP AT SCREEN.
      CHECK screen-group1 = 'ZKK'.
      screen-active = '0'.                "hide the edit checkbox param
*     screen-input = '0'.                 "visible, but greyed-out
      MODIFY SCREEN.
    ENDLOOP.
  ENDIF.
```

Figure 7.8: MODIF ID example

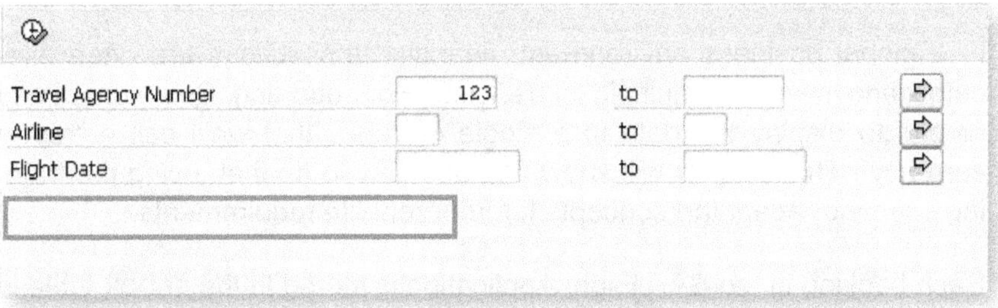

Figure 7.9: Screen-active = 0 hides the field

If the user has change authorization, no modification of the selection screen is needed. The user will still have the option of specifying edit mode or non-edit mode using the P_EDIT checkbox (Figure 8.3).

A few of the choices available to you when changing the selection screen using LOOP AT SCREEN:

▶ SCREEN-ACTIVE = 0 hides the field (Figure 7.9)

▶ SCREEN-INPUT = 0 disables (grays out) the field without hiding it (Figure 7.10)

Figure 7.10: Screen-input = 0 grays out the field without hiding

Another option: If separate transaction codes, managed through security roles, have been created for the edit users and for the display-only users, the IF statement in AT SELECTION-SCREEN OUTPUT can be written instead to evaluate which transaction code (SY-TCODE) was being run by the user.

7.3 Converting all currency values to a user-specified "report currency"

In a global business environment, financial transactions are often executed and saved in multiple currencies. For reporting, it is sometimes helpful to display the data in a single currency that we'll call a "report currency". This chapter will show you one way to do that, using the training scenario. Adapt the concepts for your real-life requirements.

Each booking in the SAP Flight Application is stored in the SBOOK table in foreign currency (matching the travel agency's currency) and local currency (matching the airline's currency). In the training scenario, the owner of Dream Travel is based in Great Britain, but had recently acquired an Australia-based agency called Hot Socks Travel. When records are summed, the ALV provides a separate total for each currency—here shown in Australian dollars and British pounds (Figure 7.11).

Agency No.	Travel agency name	Curr.	ID	No.	Flight Date	Book. no.	Σ Amount (for.currency)	Curr.	Airline	Amount	Curr.
							1,028,775.04	AUD			
							4,364,153.15	GBP			
	Aussie Travel						836,886.68	GBP			
	Ben McCloskey Ltd.						856,941.48	GBP			
	Hot Socks Travel						1,028,775.04	AUD			
	Kangeroos						981,205.58	GBP			
	Super Agency						848,529.40	GBP			
	The Ultimate Answer						840,590.01	GBP			
295		GBP	AA	17	05/25/2011	24	543.36	GBP	American Airlines	803.58	USD
295		GBP	AA	17	05/25/2011	83	285.98	GBP	American Airlines	422.94	USD
295		GBP	AA	17	05/25/2011	124	257.39	GBP	American Airlines	380.65	USD

Figure 7.11: ALV grid before conversion to a single currency

The report would be more useful to the Dream Travel owner if all the records were reported in a single currency (GBP, British pounds) for easier comparison of agency performance (Figure 7.12).

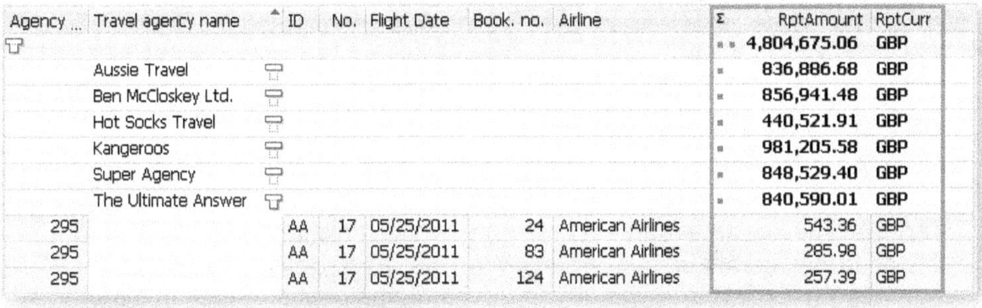

Agency	Travel agency name	ID	No.	Flight Date	Book. no.	Airline	Σ	RptAmount	RptCurr
							■ ■	4,804,675.06	GBP
	Aussie Travel						■	836,886.68	GBP
	Ben McCloskey Ltd.						■	856,941.48	GBP
	Hot Socks Travel						■	440,521.91	GBP
	Kangeroos						■	981,205.58	GBP
	Super Agency						■	848,529.40	GBP
	The Ultimate Answer						■	840,590.01	GBP
295		AA	17	05/25/2011	24	American Airlines		543.36	GBP
295		AA	17	05/25/2011	83	American Airlines		285.98	GBP
295		AA	17	05/25/2011	124	American Airlines		257.39	GBP

Figure 7.12: ALV grid after conversion to a single currency

The selection screen block provides enough information for a user to understand how and when to use the "Report Currency" parameter (Figure 7.13).

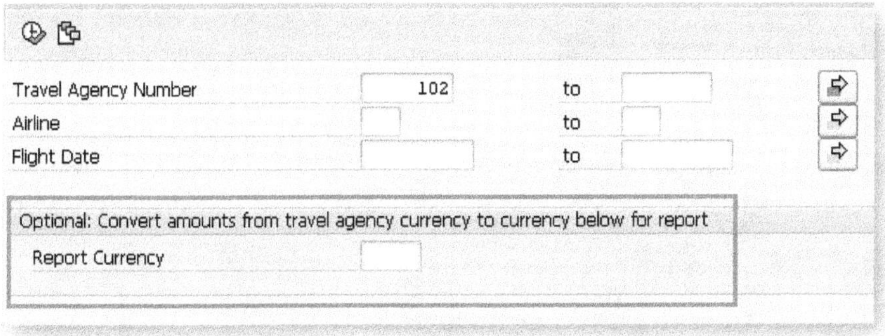

Travel Agency Number	102	to
Airline		to
Flight Date		to

Optional: Convert amounts from travel agency currency to currency below for report

Report Currency

Figure 7.13: Parameter on selection screen

The frame title "Optional: Convert amounts from travel agency currency to currency below for report" has been saved as text symbol TEXT-002 (Figure 7.14). The parameter label "Report Currency" has been saved as a selection text.

```
SELECT-OPTIONS: s_agnum FOR stravelag-agencynum DEFAULT '123',
                s_carid FOR sbook-carrid,
                s_fldat FOR sbook-fldate.
```

```
SELECTION-SCREEN SKIP.
SELECTION-SCREEN BEGIN OF BLOCK b1 WITH FRAME TITLE TEXT-002.
PARAMETERS:     p_curr  TYPE tcurc-waers.
SELECTION-SCREEN END OF BLOCK b1.
```

Figure 7.14: Selection screen block for new parameter

The SAP master data table that stores all valid currencies is TCURC and the code values are stored in field WAERS. By specifying type TCURC-WAERS for the P_CURR parameter, the F4 input help and F1 help functionality are enabled (Figure 7.14).

Currency exchange rates change often and financial postings are time specific. To ensure that our conversions use the conversion rate that was in effect at the time of the booking, ORDER_DATE will be retrieved from SBOOK for each record (Figure 7.15). Add RPTCURAM and RPTCURKEY to the local type LTY_OUTPUT. The table type TT_OUTPUT is defined for use later (Figure 7.18).

```
TYPES: BEGIN OF lty_output,
         agencynum  TYPE stravelag-agencynum, "agency number
         name       TYPE stravelag-name,      "agency name
         currency   TYPE stravelag-currency,  "agency currency
         carrid     TYPE sbook-carrid,        "booked carrier
         connid     TYPE sbook-connid,        "booked connection
         fldate     TYPE sbook-fldate,        "booked date
         bookid     TYPE sbook-bookid,        "booking ID
         forcuram   TYPE sbook-forcuram,      "price in foreign currency
         forcurkey  TYPE sbook-forcurkey,     "foreign currency key
         carrname   TYPE scarr-carrname,      "carrier name
         loccuram   TYPE sbook-loccuram,      "price in airline curr
         loccurkey  TYPE sbook-loccurkey,     "local currency of airline
         order_date TYPE sbook-order_date,    "transaction date
         rptcuram   TYPE sbook-forcuram,      "amount in report curr
         rptcurkey  TYPE sbook-forcurkey,     "report currency
       END OF lty_output.
```

```
TYPES: tt_output   TYPE STANDARD TABLE OF lty_output.
```

Figure 7.15: Data additions for currency conversion logic

By adding the new retrieved field ORDER_DATE before the non-selected fields RPTCURAM and RPTCURKEY (Figure 7.15), it is possible to continue using the efficient SELECT statement already in place (Figure 7.16). The

202

new subroutine ZF_FILL_REPORT_CURRENCY is only executed when a report currency has been requested using the P_CURR parameter.

```
START-OF-SELECTION.                      "retrieve data
  SELECT stravelag~agencynum stravelag~name stravelag~currency
         sbook~carrid sbook~connid sbook~fldate sbook~bookid
         sbook~forcuram sbook~forcurkey
         scarr~carrname
         sbook~loccuram sbook~loccurkey
         sbook~order_date
    FROM stravelag join sbook
                   on stravelag~agencynum = sbook~agencynum
                   join scarr
                   on sbook~carrid        = scarr~carrid
    INTO TABLE gt_output
       WHERE stravelag~agencynum IN s_agnum
         AND sbook~carrid        IN s_carid
         AND sbook~fldate        IN s_fldat.

  DESCRIBE TABLE gt_output LINES gv_lines.
  IF gv_lines NE 0.                       "data was retrieved

    IF NOT p_curr IS INITIAL.
      PERFORM zf_fill_report_currency CHANGING gt_output[].
    ENDIF.

    SORT gt_output BY agencynum
                      carrid
                      connid
                      fldate
                      bookid.
  ELSE.
    MESSAGE ID '00' TYPE 'I' NUMBER 001 WITH 'No data retrieved'.
    RETURN.
  ENDIF.
```

Figure 7.16: Inclusion of transaction date and parameter-driven logic

The three new output fields are only applicable when the user requests that amounts be converted to a report currency. The fields can be added at the end of the existing field catalog using an IF statement (Figure 7.17). ORDER_DATE will be included in the ALV report for troubleshooting, but will be hidden using the NO_OUT field catalog setting. Depending upon user preference and requirements, you can hide the five other fields related to currency (CURRENCY, FORCURAM, FORCURKEY, LOCCURAM, and LOCCURKEY) using a MODIFY statement. (The field catalog fieldnames shown are for SLIS_FIELDCAT_ALV. Adjust these when using other field catalog structures such as LVC_S_FCAT.)

```
IF NOT p_curr IS INITIAL.
  CLEAR ls_fieldcat.
  ls_fieldcat-fieldname     = 'ORDER_DATE'.
  ls_fieldcat-ref_fieldname = 'ORDER_DATE'.
  ls_fieldcat-ref_tabname   = 'SBOOK'.
  ls_fieldcat-no_out        = 'X'.
  APPEND ls_fieldcat TO lt_fieldcat.

  CLEAR ls_fieldcat.
  ls_fieldcat-fieldname   = 'RPTCURAM'.
  ls_fieldcat-cfieldname  = 'RPTCURKEY'.    "currency key here
  ls_fieldcat-ctabname    = 'GT_OUTPUT'.
  ls_fieldcat-seltext_l   = 'RptAmount'.    "up to 40 chars
  ls_fieldcat-seltext_m   = 'RptAmount'.    "up to 20 chars
  ls_fieldcat-seltext_s   = 'RptAmount'.    "up to 10 chars
  APPEND ls_fieldcat TO lt_fieldcat.

  CLEAR ls_fieldcat.
  ls_fieldcat-fieldname     = 'RPTCURKEY'.
  ls_fieldcat-seltext_l     = 'RptCurr'.    "up to 40 chars
  ls_fieldcat-seltext_m     = 'RptCurr'.    "up to 20 chars
  ls_fieldcat-seltext_s     = 'RptCurr'.    "up to 10 chars
  ls_fieldcat-ref_fieldname = 'TCURC'.
  ls_fieldcat-ref_tabname   = 'WAERS'.
  APPEND ls_fieldcat TO lt_fieldcat.

  CLEAR ls_fieldcat.
  ls_fieldcat-no_out = 'X'.                          "hide fields
  MODIFY lt_fieldcat FROM ls_fieldcat TRANSPORTING no_out
    WHERE fieldname = 'CURRENCY'
       OR fieldname = 'FORCURAM'
       OR fieldname = 'FORCURKEY'
       OR fieldname = 'LOCCURAM'
       OR fieldname = 'LOCCURKEY'.
ENDIF.
ENDFORM.
```

Figure 7.17: Field catalog changes for report currency

Always display the currency key for financial amounts

 Report users should always be able to tell the currency of all the amounts shown in a report. Cross-reference the currency key field using CFIELDNAME and display the field on the report.

Subroutine ZF_FILL_REPORT_CURRENCY uses function module CON-VERT_TO_LOCAL_CURRENCY (Figure 7.18) to convert the amounts using time-specific exchange rates from the TCURR table. Three outcomes are possible when looping through the table of retrieved data.

▶ The amount is already stored in the requested currency—move existing amount over to the new field.

▶ The amount needs to be converted to the requested currency and the conversion is successful—move converted amount to new field.

▶ The amount needs to be converted to the requested currency and the conversion fails—leave the new amount field initial and move "error" to the new currency key field.

```
FORM zf_fill_report_currency CHANGING lt_output TYPE tt_output.
  DATA: ls_output TYPE lty_output,
        lv_rptamt TYPE lty_output-rptcuram,
        lv_tabix  TYPE sy-tabix.

  LOOP AT lt_output into ls_output.
    lv_tabix = sy-tabix.
    IF ls_output-forcurkey = p_curr.
      ls_output-rptcuram  = ls_output-forcuram.
      ls_output-rptcurkey = p_curr.
    ELSE.
      CALL FUNCTION 'CONVERT_TO_LOCAL_CURRENCY'
        EXPORTING
          date              = ls_output-order_date
          foreign_amount    = ls_output-forcuram
          foreign_currency  = ls_output-forcurkey
          local_currency    = p_curr
          type_of_rate      = 'M'
          read_tcurr        = 'X'
        IMPORTING
          local_amount      = lv_rptamt
        EXCEPTIONS
          no_rate_found     = 1
          overflow          = 2
          no_factors_found  = 3
          no_spread_found   = 4
          derived_2_times   = 5
          others            = 6.
      IF sy-subrc = 0.
        ls_output-rptcuram  = lv_rptamt.
        ls_output-rptcurkey = p_curr.
      ELSE.
        ls_output-rptcurkey = 'error'(003).
      ENDIF.
    ENDIF.
    MODIFY lt_output FROM ls_output INDEX lv_tabix
      TRANSPORTING rptcuram rptcurkey.
  ENDLOOP.
ENDFORM.
```

Figure 7.18: Conversion to report currency has 3 possibilities

Type of rate for conversion function module

SAP uses exchange rate type M for many financial postings, but it is a good practice to verify during design that this is appropriate for the program you are coding.

If there is conversion failure on any record, other options include interrupting the program or populating the original amount into the new amount field with the original currency. In the case of conversion failure, you should not populate a zero amount aligned with the report currency because it may not be apparent to the user that some data failed to convert, especially when it is summarized. The approach shown here populates "error" into RPTCURKEY for greater visibility (Figure 7.19).

Agency No.	Trvl agcy	Airline	No.	Flight Date	Booking	Airline	Σ	RptAmount	RptCurr
							■	427,603.50	GBP
								0.00	error
102	Hot Socks Travel	AA	17	05/25/2011	12	American Airlines		281.70	GBP
102	Hot Socks Travel	AA	17	05/25/2011	52	American Airlines		444.80	GBP
102	Hot Socks Travel	AA	17	05/25/2011	82	American Airlines		0.00	error
102	Hot Socks Travel	AA	17	05/25/2011	104	American Airlines		133.44	GBP
102	Hot Socks Travel	AA	17	05/25/2011	240	American Airlines		148.27	GBP
102	Hot Socks Travel	AA	17	05/25/2011	293	American Airlines		140.85	GBP

Figure 7.19: Population of error to ensure it is not overlooked

Foreign vs. local parameters of this function module

The CONVERT_TO_LOCAL_CURRENCY function module can also be used to change the local currency amount LOCCURAM to the user-requested report currency. When working with these function module parameters, think of "foreign_" as source data and "local_" as target data, irrespective of how the fields are named in the data dictionary.

7.4   Summary

This chapter contains a few examples of challenges solved by using standard SAP functionality. The examples can be adapted for other program types, not just SAP List Viewer programs. You may or may not encounter these exact situations, but exposure to the examples may be helpful.

Key points:

- ▶ Replacing an SAP-generated alias with the actual transaction variant name in the top_of_page output
- ▶ Using MODIF ID to meet the needs of different user audiences using a shared program and to provide a selection screen tailored to each audience
- ▶ Converting transaction amounts to a single "report currency" specified by the user from the selection screen

8 Adding edit capability to an ALV program

In this chapter, you'll see how to enable editing for the user of an ALV report. Editing can be enabled across an entire grid or selectively. The edited content can be used to update database tables, but can also be used for applications that require no persistence of the data beyond a printout or an exported file (for example, for "what if" analysis). Editable ALV is not the best tool for performing large volume data updates, but may be appropriate for some applications.

This chapter will show you how to save modifications to a database table each time the user changes an editable cell. It is a merely an introduction to editable ALV and does not cover functionality such as multi-row updates or toggling between edit/display modes using the READY_FOR _INPUT method. Another technique used to create editable ALV reports uses REUSE_ALV_GRID_DISPLAY_LVC, a function module not released for customer use and not included in this book.

8.1 Training scenario

For the training scenario, we will address a new requirement to allow the user to add a brief comment to a detail record and save the comment to a custom table. Existing comments will be selected from the database table and displayed in the ALV report whenever it is run.

> **No authorization or desire to create a table for the exercise?**
>
> If you do not have authorization or a desire to create a table in the ABAP data dictionary for this exercise, you can still complete the exercises ahead. Omit the logic that updates the database table and use a function module such as POPUP_TO_DISPLAY_TEXT to simulate the logic flow.

The new table is called ZKKDEMO (Figure 8.1), maintainable using trans-action code sm30 in function group ZKKTEMP. Its key fields are the fields from our ALV local type that ensure a unique record: AGENCYNUM, CARRID, CONNID, FLDATE, and BOOKID. The field to hold a comment text is called ZCOMMENT, based on *data element* CHAR0128. Only one comment will be saved so there is no effective date or sequence number key field in the table to permit saving a series of comments.

Dictionary: Change Table

Field	Key	Ini...	Data element	Data Type	Length	Deci...	Short Description
MANDT	✓	✓	S_MANDT	CLNT	3	0	Client
AGENCYNUM	✓	✓	S_AGNCYNUM	NUMC	8	0	Travel Agency Number
CARRID	✓	✓	S_CARR_ID	CHAR	3	0	Airline Code
CONNID	✓	✓	S_CONN_ID	NUMC	4	0	Flight Connection Number
FLDATE	✓	✓	S_DATE	DATS	8	0	Flight date
BOOKID	✓	✓	S_BOOK_ID	NUMC	8	0	Booking number
ZCOMMENT	☐	☐	CHAR0128	CHAR	128	0	Character String - 128 User-Defined Characters

Transparent Table ZKKDEMO — Active
Short Description: Demo Table for SAP List Viewer Application
Attributes | Delivery and Maintenance | Fields | Entry help/check | Currency/Quantity Fields

Figure 8.1: New table to capture comments

Since the editing occurs at the detail level, and our in-progress program displays summarized levels, I've provided two examples in this chapter using different starting points for the data display: detail and summary (Table 8.1). Before proceeding with each one, make a copy of your exist-ing program (and its components), save, and activate.

For illustration, not by requirement, the first pair of exercises use a selec-tion screen parameter to indicate that the report should display with edit capability. The second pair of exercises use the EDIT COMMENT button created earlier (Chapter 6.8.1 and Chapter 6.8.2) to make the grid edita-ble. Depending upon requirements, many different approaches can be used.

Exercise	Copy from (starting point)	Copy to
8.2.1 (detail start)	Chapter 2 end: zkk_alv_fm	zkk_alv_fm_selscrn
8.2.2 (detail start)	Chapter 2 end: zkk_alv _ctrlfw	zkk_alv_ctrlfw_selscrn
8.3.1 (summary start)	Chapter 6 end: zkk_alv_fm_layout_sort _more	zkk_alv_fm_edit_button
8.3.2 (summary start)	Chapter 6 end: zkk_alv_ctrlfw_layout_sort _mor	zkk_alv_ctrlfw_edit_button

Table 8.1: Suggested starting points for next exercises

8.2 Enabling edit based on a selection screen checkbox

For this example, you are starting with an ALV program that already displays the detail data with no summing, no grouping, no subtotaling, and no cell-merging.

You'll provide a checkbox parameter on the selection screen. If the user leaves the checkbox blank, the report grid will be presented without edit functionality. To enable edit functionality, the user will click the checkbox before executing the report. (Chapter 7.2 shows how to modify a selection screen based on a user's authorization.)

Several activities are identical for both the function module and the ALV control framework technique, including syntax.

1. Add a checkbox parameter P_EDIT to the selection screen so the user can display the grid in edit mode (Figure 8.2).

2. Create a text symbol for the checkbox label (Figure 8.3).

3. Add the comment field to the local type lty_output (Figure 8.4).

```
SELECT-OPTIONS: s_agnum FOR stravelag-agencynum DEFAULT '123',
                s_carid FOR sbook-carrid,
                s_fldat FOR sbook-fldate.

SELECTION-SCREEN BEGIN OF LINE.
  PARAMETERS:     p_edit  AS CHECKBOX DEFAULT ' '.
* text-100 contains "Display in edit mode for comment changes"
  SELECTION-SCREEN COMMENT 5(40) TEXT-100 FOR FIELD p_edit.
SELECTION-SCREEN END OF LINE.
```

Figure 8.2: Checkbox for selection screen

After defining the new parameter in the selection screen, create a text symbol with "Display in edit mode for comment changes" (Figure 8.3). You can use forward navigation (by double-clicking on TEXT-100) to add this text, then save and activate.

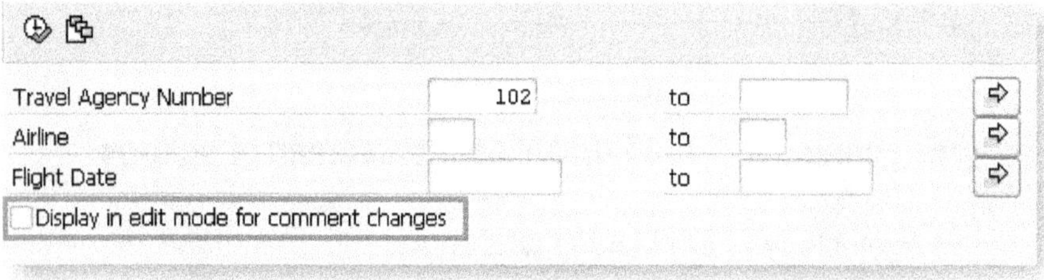

Figure 8.3: Selection screen with edit checkbox

If you will not be creating and updating the custom table for this exercise, you can use CHAR0128 as the type when you add the new field ZCOMMENT at the end of LTY_OUTPUT (Figure 8.4).

```
TYPES: BEGIN OF lty_output,
         agencynum TYPE stravelag-agencynum,  "agency number
         name      TYPE stravelag-name,       "agency name
         currency  TYPE stravelag-currency,   "agency currency
         carrid    TYPE sbook-carrid,         "booked carrier
         connid    TYPE sbook-connid,         "booked connection
         fldate    TYPE sbook-fldate,         "booked date
         bookid    TYPE sbook-bookid,         "booking ID
         forcuram  TYPE sbook-forcuram,       "price in foreign currency
         forcurkey TYPE sbook-forcurkey,      "foreign currency key
         carrname  TYPE scarr-carrname,       "carrier name
         loccuram  TYPE sbook-loccuram,       "price in airline curr
         loccurkey TYPE sbook-loccurkey,      "local currency of airline
         zcomment  TYPE zkkdemo-zcomment,     "or TYPE char0128
       END OF lty_output.
```

Figure 8.4: Comment field added to local type lty_output

212

Since the syntax varies for the remaining steps, continue with Chapter 8.2.1 for the function module program or Chapter 8.2.2 for the ALV control framework program.

8.2.1 Function module

By simply adding the new comment field to the field catalog table in this program with an EDIT value of X, (Figure 8.9), the user can display the ALV grid, can type text into the comment field, and can scroll through the grid with temporary retention of those comments within the internal table GT_OUTPUT. To do more than that, we need to decide whether our goal (the ZKKDEMO table update) is better served by grid-level or cell-level processing.

▶ Grid-level processing: &DATA_SAVE user command event, triggered by the user clicking on the SAVE (diskette) icon

▶ Cell-level processing: DATA_CHANGED event, triggered when the user moves the cursor away from an editable cell

With the grid-level approach, we would need to also decide whether to update all the comments (changed or not) to the ZKKDEMO table or whether to update the ZKKDEMO table selectively after comparing all the comments in the ALV grid to a copy of the ALV table as it was first displayed. (If comparing, we would need to overwrite our copy of the initial table to reflect the revised grid content for the next comparison-on-save—unless we force a program exit at the end of the &DATA_SAVE logic.)

With the cell-level approach, we can reduce some of the coding and complexity. The grid-level approach is suitable for some applications, but for the training scenario example, we will use the cell-level approach.

The data additions for the current program (Figure 8.5) include table type TT_OUTPUT based on type LTY_OUTPUT. This table type will be used in a new DATA_CHANGED event subroutine (Figure 8.12). The GT_EVENTS internal table first introduced in Chapter 6.5 reappears. An internal table and structure matching the database table ZKKDEMO are added for retrieval of existing comments. The GV_EDIT_FLAG variable will be used to communicate whether the user has chosen edit or display mode. Finally, to enable cell-level processing, declare structure GS_GLAY which will be passed in the ALV call using the I_GRID_SETTINGS parameter (Figure 8.16).

```
TYPES: tt_output TYPE STANDARD TABLE OF lty_output.

DATA: gs_output          TYPE lty_output,
      gt_output          TYPE STANDARD TABLE OF lty_output,
      gt_fieldcat        TYPE slis_t_fieldcat_alv,
      gt_events          TYPE slis_t_event,
      gt_zkkdemo         TYPE STANDARD TABLE OF zkkdemo,
      gs_zkkdemo         TYPE zkkdemo.

DATA: gv_lines      TYPE i,
      gv_edit_flag TYPE c,
      gs_glay      TYPE lvc_s_glay.
```

Figure 8.5: Data additions for edit exercise (FM)

To retrieve any existing comments from the ZKKDEMO table and display them in the ALV grid, you'll need to add logic after the population of GT_OUTPUT (Figure 8.6). The FOR ALL ENTRIES IN syntax can be used because you have first verified that GT_OUTPUT has lines of content.

If relevant records are retrieved into GT_ZKKDEMO, you loop through GT_ZKKDEMO to modify GT_OUTPUT. (GT_ZKKDEMO most likely has fewer records so is used for the LOOP statement.) If no relevant comments were retrieved from ZKKDEMO, no messaging is required (Figure 8.6).

After the data selection, you'll set two flags to match the selection screen checkbox value for P_EDIT: X for edit mode and blank for display mode (Figure 8.7). By populating the GV_EDIT_FLAG now, you can use it in other parts of the program, such as in ZF_BUILD_FIELDCATALOG, reducing the use of IF/ELSE/ENDIF logic there. The second flag being filled from the P_EDIT parameter is a component of the LVC_S_GLAY structure called EDT_CLL_CB (ALV control: Callback when leaving an edited cell).

```
DESCRIBE TABLE gt_output LINES gv_lines.
IF gv_lines NE 0.                          "data was retrieved
  SORT gt_output BY agencynum
                   carrid
                   connid
                   fldate
                   bookid.

    SELECT * FROM zkkdemo
      INTO TABLE gt_zkkdemo
      FOR ALL ENTRIES IN gt_output
      WHERE agencynum = gt_output-agencynum
        AND carrid    = gt_output-carrid
        AND connid    = gt_output-connid
        AND fldate    = gt_output-fldate
        AND bookid    = gt_output-bookid.
    IF sy-subrc = 0.                       "comments found
      SORT gt_zkkdemo BY agencynum
                         carrid
                         connid
                         fldate
                         bookid.
      LOOP AT gt_zkkdemo INTO gs_zkkdemo.   "smaller table
        READ TABLE gt_output INTO gs_output
          WITH KEY agencynum = gs_zkkdemo-agencynum
                   carrid    = gs_zkkdemo-carrid
                   connid    = gs_zkkdemo-connid
                   fldate    = gs_zkkdemo-fldate
                   bookid    = gs_zkkdemo-bookid.
        IF sy-subrc = 0.
          gs_output-zcomment = gs_zkkdemo-zcomment.
          MODIFY gt_output FROM gs_output INDEX sy-tabix
            TRANSPORTING zcomment.
        ENDIF.
      ENDLOOP.
    ENDIF.

ELSE.
  MESSAGE ID '00' TYPE 'I' NUMBER 001 WITH 'No data retrieved'(002).
  RETURN.
ENDIF.
```

Figure 8.6: Retrieval of comments from zkkdemo table (FM)

215

```
************* Start of main program logic *****************************
gv_edit_flag        = p_edit.           "X for edit, space for display
gs_glay-edt_cll_cb = p_edit.

PERFORM zf_build_event_table  USING gt_events[].
```
```
PERFORM zf_build_fieldcatalog USING gt_fieldcat[]
                                    gv_edit_flag.
PERFORM zf_display_alv.
```

Figure 8.7: Flag setting and additions (FM)

Update the USING parameter on the ZF_BUILD_FIELDCATALOG subroutine (Figure 8.8).

```
FORM zf_build_fieldcatalog USING lt_fieldcat  TYPE slis_t_fieldcat_alv
                                 lv_edit_flag TYPE c.
```

Figure 8.8: Use new flag when building the field catalog (FM)

Add the new ZCOMMENT field to the end of the field catalog table in ZF_BUILD_FIELDCATALOG (Figure 8.9). To provide a more meaningful label on the ALV, populate the DATATYPE, OUTPUTLEN, and SELTEXT values instead of providing a REF_TABNAME value of ZKKDEMO. The variable LV_EDIT_FLAG will manage the EDIT setting for this column based on how the P_EDIT parameter was set (X for edit, blank for display).

```
    CLEAR ls_fieldcat.
    ls_fieldcat-fieldname      = 'ZCOMMENT'.
    ls_fieldcat-outputlen      = 128.
    ls_fieldcat-seltext_l      = 'Comment'(001).    "up to 40 chars
    ls_fieldcat-seltext_m      = 'Comment'(001).    "up to 20 chars
    ls_fieldcat-seltext_s      = 'Comment'(001).    "up to 10 chars
    ls_fieldcat-datatype       = 'CHAR'.
    ls_fieldcat-edit           = lv_edit_flag.
    APPEND ls_fieldcat TO lt_fieldcat.
ENDFORM.
```

Figure 8.9: New field added to field catalog and edit value set (FM)

In Chapter 6.6.1, you saw that the subroutine names for some events can be passed to the REUSE_ALV_GRID_DISPLAY function module using an I_CALLBACK parameter and other event subroutine names can be passed using the events table. Since this program is not yet using any events and only one of the two events being added has an I_CALLBACK parameter (USER_COMMAND), add both events to the events table using a new subroutine called ZF_BUILD_EVENT_TABLE (Figure 8.10). This is the first of three new subroutines in this program related to event-handling.

```
*-----------------------------------------------------------------
FORM zf_build_event_table USING lt_events TYPE slis_t_event.

  DATA: ls_event TYPE slis_alv_event.

  CALL FUNCTION 'REUSE_ALV_EVENTS_GET'
    EXPORTING
      i_list_type = 4                    "for REUSE_ALV_GRID_DISPLAY
    IMPORTING
      et_events   = lt_events.

  READ TABLE lt_events WITH KEY name = slis_ev_user_command
    INTO ls_event.
  IF sy-subrc = 0.
    ls_event-form = 'ZF_USER_COMMAND'.
    MODIFY lt_events FROM ls_event INDEX sy-tabix.
  ENDIF.

* add incremental event to table for focus change functionality
  CLEAR ls_event.
  ls_event-name = slis_ev_data_changed.
  ls_event-form = 'ZF_DATA_CHANGED'.
  APPEND ls_event TO lt_events.
ENDFORM.
```

Figure 8.10: Populate two subroutine names in the event table (FM)

After the REUSE_ALV_EVENTS_GET function call (Figure 8.10), LT_EVENTS contains 18 records. In ZF_BUILD_EVENT_TABLE, populate your program's subroutine name for the provided event USER_COMMAND, then add a new record for event DATA_CHANGED. LT_EVENTS now contains 19 records (Figure 8.11), two of which will execute your custom code.

Tables	Table Contents	

Table	LT_EVENTS
Attributes	Standard [19x2(120)]
Insert Column	

Row	NAME [C(30)]	FORM [C(30)]
1	CALLER_EXIT	
2	USER_COMMAND	ZF_USER_COMMAND
3	TOP_OF_PAGE	
4	TOP_OF_COVERPAGE	
5	END_OF_COVERPAGE	
6	FOREIGN_TOP_OF_PAGE	
7	FOREIGN_END_OF_PAGE	
8	PF_STATUS_SET	
9	LIST_MODIFY	
10	TOP_OF_LIST	
11	END_OF_PAGE	
12	END_OF_LIST	
13	AFTER_LINE_OUTPUT	
14	BEFORE_LINE_OUTPUT	
15	REPREP_SEL_MODIFY	
16	SUBTOTAL_TEXT	
17	GROUPLEVEL_CHANGE	
18	CONTEXT_MENU	
19	DATA_CHANGED	ZF_DATA_CHANGED

Figure 8.11: Data_changed is an incremental event (FM)

lvc_s_glay-edt_cll_cb must be X for data_changed logic

With the function module technique, the DATA_CHANGED functionality is only accessible and triggered when LVC_S_GLAY-EDT_CLL_CB is set to X (Figure 8.7) and passed in the I_GRID_SETTINGS parameter in the ALV call (Figure 8.16).

Create another subroutine called ZF_DATA_CHANGED (Figure 8.12) to access the ABAP objects class CL_ALV_CHANGED_DATA_PROTOCOL. The FIELD-SYMBOL and ASSIGN statement are used to access the content of modified rows of the ALV. In our program, only single rows are modifiable so there will only be one row to process, the row whose comment field the user just left (Figure 8.13). Loop through <FT_OUTPUT> and populate a structure that matches the database table ZKKDEMO. Use the MODIFY command to write the work area record to table ZKKDEMO. (MODIFY will update an existing record or add a record if not found.)

```
*------------------------------------------------------------
FORM zf_data_changed USING lo_data_changed
                     TYPE REF TO cl_alv_changed_data_protocol.

  DATA: ls_output  TYPE lty_output,
        ls_zkkdemo TYPE zkkdemo.

  FIELD-SYMBOLS: <ft_output> TYPE tt_output.

  ASSIGN lo_data_changed->mp_mod_rows->* TO <ft_output>.

  LOOP AT <ft_output> INTO ls_output.
    CLEAR ls_zkkdemo.
    ls_zkkdemo-agencynum = ls_output-agencynum.
    ls_zkkdemo-carrid    = ls_output-carrid.
    ls_zkkdemo-connid    = ls_output-connid.
    ls_zkkdemo-fldate    = ls_output-fldate.
    ls_zkkdemo-bookid    = ls_output-bookid.
    ls_zkkdemo-zcomment  = ls_output-zcomment.

    MODIFY zkkdemo FROM ls_zkkdemo.
*   MODIFY will update an existing record or insert a new record
    IF sy-subrc NE 0.
      MESSAGE ID '00' TYPE 'I' NUMBER 001
        WITH 'The comment was not saved to table ZKKDEMO.'(004).
    ENDIF.
  ENDLOOP.
ENDFORM.
```

Figure 8.12: Data_changed subroutine called when cell focus changes (FM)

The record layout of <FT_OUTPUT> matches LTY_OUTPUT with the exception of a first field called ROW (Figure 8.13).

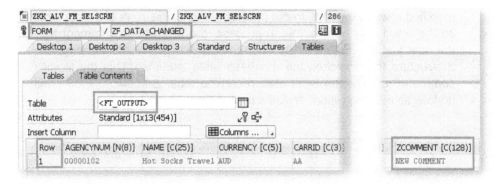

Figure 8.13: User-modified row in debugger (FM)

Refresher on previous FM exercise with user_command

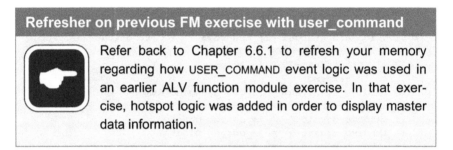

Refer back to Chapter 6.6.1 to refresh your memory regarding how USER_COMMAND event logic was used in an earlier ALV function module exercise. In that exercise, hotspot logic was added in order to display master data information.

The SAVE button is enabled on screen when we run the program in edit mode, so in the training scenario, we will provide a pop-up message to inform the user that changes were saved if they click it.

Create a third subroutine called ZF_USER_COMMAND (Figure 8.14) using the standard parameters of SY-UCOMM and SLIS_SELFIELD. Add a CASE statement that includes the LV_UCOMM value &DATA_SAVE. Call the function module POPUP_TO_CONFIRM to inform the user that the comments have been saved and give the option to continue or leave the program (Figure 8.15). (With proper error-handling in the ZF_DATA_CHANGED subroutine, any table update errors should have been communicated already.)

If the user clicks EXIT, the LEAVE PROGRAM command executes. If the user clicks CONTINUE, the user remains where they were in the grid (Figure 8.15).

```
*-----------------------------------------------------------------
FORM zf_user_command USING lv_ucomm    LIKE sy-ucomm
                            ls_selfield TYPE slis_selfield.
  DATA: lv_answer TYPE c.

  CASE lv_ucomm.
    WHEN '&IC1'.                    "double-click
*     for illustration, do nothing

    WHEN '&DATA_SAVE'.              "user clicked Save icon
      CALL FUNCTION 'POPUP_TO_CONFIRM'
        EXPORTING
          titlebar             =
            'Comments Saved to the ZKKDEMO Table'(007)
          text_question        =
            'Do you want to exit the program or continue working?'(008)
          text_button_1        = 'Exit'(009)
          text_button_2        = 'Continue'(010)
          default_button       = '1'
          display_cancel_button = ' '
        IMPORTING
          answer               = lv_answer.
      IF lv_answer = '1'.
        LEAVE PROGRAM.
      ENDIF.
  ENDCASE.
ENDFORM.
```

Figure 8.14: User command with save button logic (FM)

Figure 8.15: User command pop-up for &data_save action (FM)

The final change is to pass the GS_GLAY structure and the events table to the ALV call (Figure 8.16).

```
*-------------------------------------------------------------------
FORM zf_display_alv.

  CALL FUNCTION 'REUSE_ALV_GRID_DISPLAY'
    EXPORTING
      i_callback_program    = sy-repid
      it_fieldcat           = gt_fieldcat[]
      i_grid_settings       = gs_glay
      it_events             = gt_events[]
    TABLES
      t_outtab              = gt_output
    EXCEPTIONS
      program_error         = 1
      OTHERS                = 2.
```

Figure 8.16: ALV call with i_grid_settings structure passed (FM)

In edit mode, the ALV grid displays with these changes: SAVE button enabled, new REFRESH button on the ALV application toolbar, row selection column added, and editable field(s) ready for input (Figure 8.17). None of the buttons need to be excluded from display for our application.

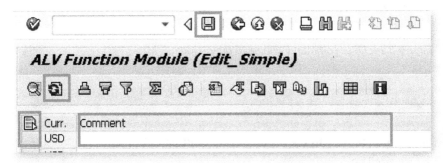

Figure 8.17: Screen changes due to use of lvc_s_glay (FM)

8.2.2 ALV control framework

The additions below will permit the user to make changes to the COMMENT cells in the ALV grid and update the ZKKDEMO database table as each record is changed.

For this exercise, start from a simple earlier version of the ALV control framework program (Table 8.1), then incorporate some new logic as well as add back some features that you used in Chapter 6 in other programs.

The data additions for the current program (Figure 8.18) include table type TT_OUTPUT based on type LTY_OUTPUT. This table type will be used in a new DATA_CHANGED method (Figure 8.24). The GT_EXCLUDE internal table first introduced in Chapter 6.7 reappears. An internal table and structure matching the database table ZKKDEMO are added for retrieval of existing comments. The GV_EDIT_FLAG variable will be used to communicate whether the user has chosen edit or display mode.

```
TYPES: tt_output TYPE STANDARD TABLE OF lty_output.

DATA: gs_output    TYPE lty_output,            "local structure (line)
      gt_output    TYPE STANDARD TABLE OF lty_output,
      gt_fieldcat  TYPE lvc_t_fcat,            "table
      gt_exclude   TYPE ui_functions,
      gt_zkkdemo   TYPE STANDARD TABLE of zkkdemo,
      gs_zkkdemo   TYPE zkkdemo.

DATA: gv_lines            TYPE i,
      gv_edit_flag        TYPE c,
      ok_code             LIKE sy-ucomm,
      g_container         TYPE scrfname VALUE 'ZKK_ALV_CTRLFW_9100_CONT1',
      grid1               TYPE REF TO cl_gui_alv_grid,
      g_custom_container  TYPE REF TO cl_gui_custom_container.
```

Figure 8.18: Data additions for edit exercise (CF)

To retrieve any existing comments from the ZKKDEMO table and display them in the ALV grid, you'll need to add logic after the population of GT_OUTPUT (Figure 8.19). The FOR ALL ENTRIES IN syntax can be used because you have first verified that GT_OUTPUT has lines of content.

If relevant records are retrieved into GT_ZKKDEMO, you loop through GT_ZKKDEMO to modify GT_OUTPUT. (GT_ZKKDEMO most likely has fewer records so is used as the loop driver.) If no relevant comments were retrieved from ZKKDEMO, no messages will be displayed (Figure 8.19).

```
DESCRIBE TABLE gt_output LINES gv_lines.
IF gv_lines NE 0.                          "data was retrieved
  SORT gt_output BY agencynum
                    carrid
                    connid
                    fldate
                    bookid.

  SELECT * FROM zkkdemo
    INTO TABLE gt_zkkdemo
    FOR ALL ENTRIES IN gt_output
    WHERE agencynum = gt_output-agencynum
      AND carrid    = gt_output-carrid
      AND connid    = gt_output-connid
      AND fldate    = gt_output-fldate
      AND bookid    = gt_output-bookid.
  IF sy-subrc = 0.                          "comments found
    SORT gt_zkkdemo BY agencynum
                       carrid
                       connid
                       fldate
                       bookid.
    LOOP AT gt_zkkdemo INTO gs_zkkdemo.     "smaller table
      READ TABLE gt_output INTO gs_output
        WITH KEY agencynum = gs_zkkdemo-agencynum
                 carrid    = gs_zkkdemo-carrid
                 connid    = gs_zkkdemo-connid
                 fldate    = gs_zkkdemo-fldate
                 bookid    = gs_zkkdemo-bookid.
      IF sy-subrc = 0.
        gs_output-zcomment = gs_zkkdemo-zcomment.
        MODIFY gt_output FROM gs_output INDEX sy-tabix
          TRANSPORTING zcomment.
      ENDIF.
    ENDLOOP.
  ENDIF.
ENDIF.
```

Figure 8.19: Retrieval of comments from zkkdemo table (CF)

After the data selection, set a flag to match the selection screen check-box value for P_EDIT. X for edit mode and blank for display mode (Figure 8.20). By populating the GV_EDIT_FLAG now, you can use it in other parts of the program, such as in ZF_BUILD_FIELDCATALOG, reducing the use of IF/ELSE/ENDIF logic there. Add a PERFORM statement for new subroutine ZF_BUILD_EXCLUDE_TABLE.

```
gv_edit_flag        = p_edit.

PERFORM zf_build_fieldcatalog USING gt_fieldcat[]
                              gv_edit_flag.
PERFORM zf_build_exclude_table USING gt_exclude[].

  CALL SCREEN 9100.
ELSE.
  MESSAGE ID '00' TYPE 'I' NUMBER 001 WITH 'No data retrieved'(001).
  RETURN.
ENDIF.
```

Figure 8.20: Flag setting and additions (CF)

The USING parameter will need to be updated on the ZF_BUILD _FIELDCATALOG subroutine (Figure 8.21).

```
FORM zf_build_fieldcatalog USING lt_fieldcat  TYPE lvc_t_fcat
                              lv_edit_flag TYPE c.
```

Figure 8.21: Use new flag when building the field catalog (CF)

Add the new ZCOMMENT field to the end of the field catalog table in ZF_BUILD_FIELDCATALOG (Figure 8.22). To provide a more meaningful label on the ALV column than the one associated with CHAR0128, popu-late the OUTPUTLEN, DATATYPE, and COLTEXT values instead of providing a REF_TABLE value of ZKKDEMO. The variable LV_EDIT_FLAG manages the EDIT setting for this column based on how the P_EDIT parameter was set (X for edit, blank for display).

```
CLEAR ls_fieldcat.
ls_fieldcat-fieldname = 'ZCOMMENT'.
ls_fieldcat-outputlen = 128.
ls_fieldcat-datatype  = 'CHAR'.
ls_fieldcat-coltext   = 'Comment'.
ls_fieldcat-edit      = lv_edit_flag.
APPEND ls_fieldcat TO lt_fieldcat.
ENDFORM.
```

Figure 8.22: New field added to field catalog and edit value set (CF)

Instead of an events table, we'll use the ALV control framework's event handler to provide logic for the event DATA_CHANGED (Figure 8.23). Eve-rything we need is present in the ER_DATA_CHANGED object.

```
********
CLASS lcl_event_handler DEFINITION.
  PUBLIC SECTION.
  METHODS:
    data_changed FOR EVENT data_changed OF cl_gui_alv_grid
      IMPORTING er_data_changed.
ENDCLASS.
********
DATA: g_event_handler    TYPE REF TO lcl_event_handler.
********
```

Figure 8.23: Method to handle data_changed event, part 1 (CF)

In method DATA_CHANGED (Figure 8.24), process the information about the row just edited by looping through the field symbol <FT_OUTPUT> to populate a structure that matches the database table ZKKDEMO. Use the MODIFY command to write the record to table ZKKDEMO. (MODIFY will update an existing record or add a record if not found.) In this program, the DATA_CHANGED event will be triggered when the user changes an editable COMMENT cell (Figure 8.29) so there will be only one row to process at a time.

At the end of the DATA_CHANGED method (Figure 8.24) is an example of how to populate and display a message using the ADD_PROTOCOL_ENTRY and DISPLAY_PROTOCOL methods. (In Figure 8.24, all the logic is typed into the method implementation. If you prefer, you can call a subroutine containing the processing logic.)

The record layout of <FT_OUTPUT> matches LTY_OUTPUT with the exception of the first field called ROW (Figure 8.25).

In edit mode, the ALV grid displays with these changes: row selection column added, editable field(s) ready for input, and new application toolbar buttons appear (Figure 8.26).

- ▶ CHECK ENTRIES and REFRESH buttons
- ▶ Cell-focused buttons: CUT, COPY TEXT, INSERT, and UNDO
- ▶ Row-focused buttons: APPEND ROW, INSERT ROW, DELETE ROW, and DUPLICATE ROW

```
********
CLASS lcl_event_handler IMPLEMENTATION.
  METHOD data_changed.
*    triggered by Check Entries, Refresh icons, and user leaving cell
      DATA: ls_output  TYPE lty_output,
            ls_zkkdemo TYPE zkkdemo,
            ls_modif   TYPE lvc_s_modi.

      FIELD-SYMBOLS: <ft_output> TYPE tt_output.

      ASSIGN er_data_changed->mp_mod_rows->* TO <ft_output>.
      LOOP AT <ft_output> INTO ls_output.
        CLEAR ls_zkkdemo.
        ls_zkkdemo-agencynum = ls_output-agencynum.
        ls_zkkdemo-carrid    = ls_output-carrid.
        ls_zkkdemo-connid    = ls_output-connid.
        ls_zkkdemo-fldate    = ls_output-fldate.
        ls_zkkdemo-bookid    = ls_output-bookid.
        ls_zkkdemo-zcomment  = ls_output-zcomment.

        MODIFY zkkdemo FROM ls_zkkdemo.
*       MODIFY will update an existing record or insert a new record
        IF sy-subrc NE 0.
          LOOP AT er_data_changed->mt_mod_cells INTO ls_modif.
            CALL METHOD er_data_changed->add_protocol_entry
              EXPORTING
                i_msgid = '00' i_msgno = '001'  i_msgty = 'W'
                i_msgv1 = 'The comment was not saved to table ZKKDEMO:'
                i_msgv2 = ls_modif-value
                i_fieldname = ls_modif-fieldname.
          ENDLOOP.
          CALL METHOD er_data_changed->display_protocol.
        ENDIF.
      ENDLOOP.
    ENDMETHOD.
ENDCLASS.
```

Figure 8.24: Method to handle data_changed event, part 2 (CF)

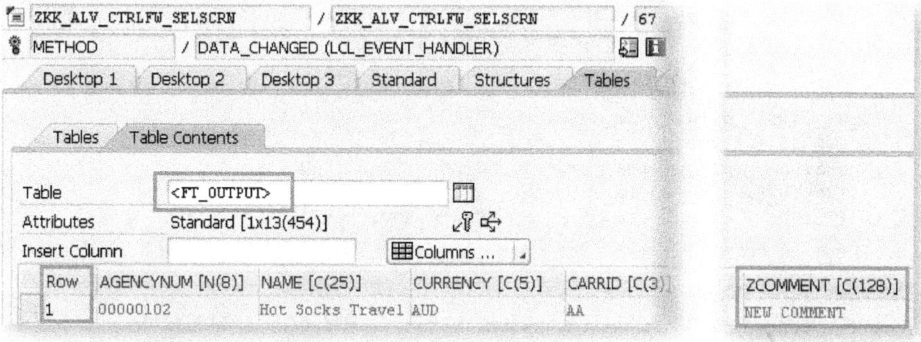

Figure 8.25: User-modified row in debugger (CF)

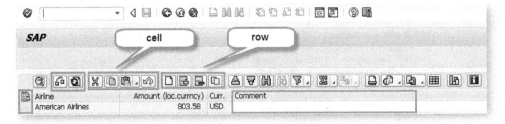

Figure 8.26: Screen changes including row edit buttons (CF)

Since this program will not be used to remove records from ZKKDEMO or to insert records, the row-focused buttons need to be excluded (Figure 8.27).

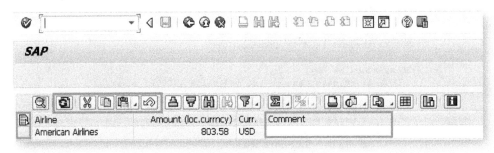

Figure 8.27: Toolbar without row edit buttons (CF)

Exactly as was done in Chapter 6.7.2, you can build a table of buttons to be omitted from the ALV application toolbar (Figure 8.28).

```
*-----------------------------------------------------------------
FORM zf_build_exclude_table USING lt_exclude TYPE ui_functions.
  DATA: ls_exclude TYPE ui_func.
* restrict user to changes, no row adds or deletes
  ls_exclude = cl_gui_alv_grid=>MC_FC_LOC_COPY_ROW.
  APPEND ls_exclude TO lt_exclude.
  ls_exclude = cl_gui_alv_grid=>MC_FC_LOC_DELETE_ROW.
  APPEND ls_exclude TO lt_exclude.
  ls_exclude = cl_gui_alv_grid=>MC_FC_LOC_APPEND_ROW.
  APPEND ls_exclude TO lt_exclude.
  ls_exclude = cl_gui_alv_grid=>MC_FC_LOC_INSERT_ROW.
  APPEND ls_exclude TO lt_exclude.
  ls_exclude = cl_gui_alv_grid=>MC_FC_LOC_MOVE_ROW.
  APPEND ls_exclude TO lt_exclude.

  SORT lt_exclude.
  DELETE ADJACENT DUPLICATES FROM lt_exclude COMPARING table_line.
ENDFORM.
```

Figure 8.28: Exclude row-focused toolbar buttons (CF)

The DATA_CHANGED event is triggered by default when the user clicks on the CHECK ENTRIES button or on the REFRESH button on the application toolbar. We can register other triggers, as well (Figure 8.29):

▶ MC_EVT_MODIFIED when cursor is moved from the modified cell

▶ MC_EVT_ENTER for user pressing ⌜Enter⌝ on keyboard

In module ZM_STATUS_9100, we have registered only the modified cell edit event (Figure 8.29). The final changes include creating the event handler object (because this program did not yet have event logic), setting the handler, and passing the table of toolbar functions to be excluded.

```
*---------------------------------------------------------------
MODULE zm_status_9100 OUTPUT.

  SET PF-STATUS 'MAIN9100'.
  IF g_custom_container IS INITIAL.
    CREATE OBJECT g_custom_container
      EXPORTING
        container_name = g_container.
    CREATE OBJECT grid1
      EXPORTING
        i_parent = g_custom_container.

    CALL METHOD grid1->register_edit_event
      EXPORTING
        i_event_id = cl_gui_alv_grid=>mc_evt_modified.   "cell leave
*   can repeat/replace previous method call with mc_evt_enter

    CREATE OBJECT g_event_handler.
    SET HANDLER g_event_handler->data_changed FOR grid1.

    CALL METHOD grid1->set_table_for_first_display
      EXPORTING
        i_structure_name    = 'LTY_OUTPUT'
        it_toolbar_excluding = gt_exclude
      CHANGING
        it_fieldcatalog     = gt_fieldcat
        it_outtab           = gt_output.
  ENDIF.

ENDMODULE.
```

Figure 8.29: Changes for ALV call (CF)

229

Enabling the save button in the ALV control framework programs

Unlike the function module versions of the edit programs in this chapter, the SAVE button is not enabled by default when using the ALV control framework technique. If you do wish to enable the SAVE button, use transaction code se80 to edit the GUI status, adding a label to the diskette function key (Figure 3.26). After saving and activating, add your custom logic within the CASE statement in the ZM_USER _COMMAND_9100 module (Figure 3.21).

8.3 Enabling edit using toolbar button

In Chapter 8.2, you started with a program that was already presenting ALV content at a detail level, then you added a parameter on the selection screen for the user to request an editable ALV output. Instead of making the ALV editable all the time for all users, you provided two modes, display or edit, driven by the selection screen checkbox.

In this chapter, the training scenario will start from a later version of the program (Table 8.1), a version with events, summarization on initial display, and a custom ALV application toolbar button (coded in Chapter 6.8). You'll add some of the logic used in Chapter 8.2 and new logic that will modify the output format after the user clicks on the EDIT COMMENT button. You'll again save comments to the ZKKDEMO database table each time the user leaves a modified cell.

Copying code sections from other programs

If you worked through the Chapter 8.2 exercises, you'll see opportunities to copy some code from those programs into this chapter's programs. Do this, but take care to re-number copied texts when they overlap existing text symbols in the destination program.

If you want to refresh your memory regarding the training scenario requirements, review Chapter 8.1.

8.3.1　Function module

If you have chosen not to create and update the custom table ZKKDEMO for this exercise, you can use CHAR0128 as the type when you add the new field ZCOMMENT at the end of LTY_OUTPUT (Figure 8.30). Other data additions include table type TT_OUTPUT based on type LTY_OUTPUT. This table type will be used in a new ZF_DATA_CHANGED subroutine (Figure 8.36). An internal table and structure matching the database table ZKK-DEMO are added for retrieval of existing comments. The GV_EDIT_FLAG variable will be used this time to indicate when the EDIT COMMENT button has been clicked so that the button can be excluded from the toolbar. Finally, to enable cell-level processing, declare structure GS_GLAY which will be passed in the ALV call using the I_GRID_SETTINGS parameter (Figure 8.43).

```
TYPES: BEGIN OF lty_output,
           agencynum TYPE stravelag-agencynum,   "agency number
           name      TYPE stravelag-name,        "agency name
           currency  TYPE stravelag-currency,    "agency currency
           carrid    TYPE sbook-carrid,          "booked carrier
           connid    TYPE sbook-connid,          "booked connection
           fldate    TYPE sbook-fldate,          "booked date
           bookid    TYPE sbook-bookid,          "booking ID
           forcuram  TYPE sbook-forcuram,        "price in foreign currency
           forcurkey TYPE sbook-forcurkey,       "foreign currency key
           carrname  TYPE scarr-carrname,        "carrier name
           loccuram  TYPE sbook-loccuram,        "price in airline curr
           loccurkey TYPE sbook-loccurkey,       "local currency of airline
           count     TYPE i,
           zcomment  TYPE zkkdemo-zcomment,      "or TYPE char0128
         END OF lty_output.

TYPES: tt_output TYPE STANDARD TABLE of lty_output.

DATA: gs_output     TYPE lty_output,
      gt_output     TYPE STANDARD TABLE OF lty_output,
      gt_sort       TYPE slis_t_sortinfo_alv,
      gt_fieldcat   TYPE slis_t_fieldcat_alv,
      gs_layout     TYPE slis_layout_alv,
      gt_top_text   TYPE slis_t_listheader,
      gt_events     TYPE slis_t_event,
      gs_glay       TYPE lvc_s_glay,
      gv_edit_flag  TYPE c,
      gt_zkkdemo    TYPE STANDARD TABLE OF zkkdemo,
      gs_zkkdemo    TYPE zkkdemo.
```

Figure 8.30: Data additions for edit exercise (FM)

To retrieve any existing comments from the ZKKDEMO table and display them in the ALV grid, you'll need to add logic after the population of

GT_OUTPUT (Figure 8.31). The FOR ALL ENTRIES IN syntax can be used because you have first verified that GT_OUPUT has content by evaluating the result of the DESCRIBE TABLE command.

If relevant records are retrieved into GT_ZKKDEMO, you loop through GT_ZKKDEMO to update GT_OUTPUT (Figure 8.31). (GT_ZKKDEMO is most likely the smaller of the two tables.) If no relevant comments were retrieved from ZKKDEMO, no messages will be displayed.

```
DESCRIBE TABLE gt_output LINES gv_lines.
IF gv_lines NE 0.                          "data was retrieved

  CLEAR gs_output.
  gs_output-count = 1.

  MODIFY gt_output FROM gs_output
    TRANSPORTING count WHERE NOT agencynum IS INITIAL.

  SORT gt_output BY agencynum
                    carrid
                    connid
                    fldate
                    bookid.

  SELECT * FROM zkkdemo
    INTO TABLE gt_zkkdemo
    FOR ALL ENTRIES IN gt_output
    WHERE agencynum = gt_output-agencynum
      AND carrid    = gt_output-carrid
      AND connid    = gt_output-connid
      AND fldate    = gt_output-fldate
      AND bookid    = gt_output-bookid.
  IF sy-subrc = 0.                          "comments found
    SORT gt_zkkdemo BY agencynum
                       carrid
                       connid
                       fldate
                       bookid.
    LOOP AT gt_zkkdemo INTO gs_zkkdemo.     "smaller table
      READ TABLE gt_output INTO gs_output
        WITH KEY agencynum = gs_zkkdemo-agencynum
                 carrid    = gs_zkkdemo-carrid
                 connid    = gs_zkkdemo-connid
                 fldate    = gs_zkkdemo-fldate
                 bookid    = gs_zkkdemo-bookid.
      IF sy-subrc = 0.
        gs_output-zcomment = gs_zkkdemo-zcomment.
        MODIFY gt_output FROM gs_output INDEX sy-tabix
          TRANSPORTING zcomment.
      ENDIF.
    ENDLOOP.
  ENDIF.
ENDIF.
```

Figure 8.31: Retrieval of comments from zkkdemo table (FM)

After the data selection, set two flags (Figure 8.32). The GV_EDIT_FLAG will be set to a blank space to signify that the user starts the report in display mode. Unlike the simpler edit program with the selection screen parameter (Chapter 8.2.1), this flag will not be used to influence layout, sort, or field catalog settings for initial display. It will only be used to indicate that the EDIT COMMENT button can be hidden after its first use.

The second flag is a component of the LVC_S_GLAY structure called EDT_CLL_CB (ALV control: Callback when leaving an edited cell). You can set it now and pass it to the ALV call in the I_GRID_SETTINGS parameter. Its effect won't be felt until at least one field in the field catalog has an EDIT value of X (Figure 8.32).

```
*************** Start of main program logic ***************************
gv_edit_flag        = ' '.            "start in display mode, X for edit
gs_glay-edt_cll_cb = 'X'.            "no effect until fieldcat-edit set

PERFORM zf_build_layout USING gs_layout.
PERFORM zf_build_fieldcatalog USING gt_fieldcat[].
PERFORM zf_build_sort_table USING gt_sort[].
PERFORM zf_build_event_table USING gt_events[].
PERFORM zf_build_top_text_table USING gt_top_text[].
PERFORM zf_display_alv.
```

Figure 8.32: Flag setting for cell edit awareness (FM)

The new ZCOMMENT field needs to be added to the end of the field catalog table in ZF_BUILD_FIELDCATALOG (Figure 8.33). To provide a more meaningful label on the ALV column than the one associated with CHAR0128, populate the DATATYPE, OUTPUTLEN, and SELTEXT values instead of providing a REF_TABNAME value of ZKKDEMO. Provide the EDIT parameter with a blank space value because the ALV grid will not be editable on initial display.

```
CLEAR ls_fieldcat.
ls_fieldcat-fieldname    = 'ZCOMMENT'.
ls_fieldcat-outputlen    = 128.
ls_fieldcat-seltext_l    = 'Comment' (020).    "up to 40 chars
ls_fieldcat-seltext_m    = 'Comment' (020).    "up to 20 chars
ls_fieldcat-seltext_s    = 'Comment' (020).    "up to 10 chars
ls_fieldcat-datatype     = 'CHAR'.
ls_fieldcat-edit         = ' '.                "display mode initially
APPEND ls_fieldcat TO lt_fieldcat.
ENDFORM.
```

Figure 8.33: New field added to field catalog with edit parameter set for display (FM)

In this in-progress program, event logic is coded in several subroutines whose names are passed to the REUSE-ALV_GRID_DISPLAY function module either via an i_callback parameter or the events table parameter (Table 8.2).

Event (FM)	Our setup	Activities handled
top_of_page	events table	text and logo
user_command	events table	hotspot pop-ups
		Save button (new)
		Edit Comment button (new)
data_changed (new)	events table	database table updates
pf_status	i_callback	button exclusions

Table 8.2: New event and several event revisions (FM)

Add the new event DATA_CHANGED to the events table using the ZF_BUILD_EVENT_TABLE subroutine (Figure 8.34). Because DATA_CHANGED is not one of the events retrieved by the REUSE_ALV_EVENTS_GET function call at the beginning of the subroutine, it will need to be appended as shown. To maintain consistency with the current program conventions, the subroutine name ZF_DATA_CHANGED can be declared as a constant such as GC_FORMNAME_CHG.

After the REUSE_ALV_EVENTS_GET function call (Figure 8.34), LT_EVENTS contains 18 records. In ZF_BUILD_EVENT_TABLE, populate your program's subroutine names for USER_COMMAND and TOP_OF_PAGE, then add a new record for event DATA_CHANGED. LT_EVENTS now contains 19 records (Figure 8.35), three of which will execute your custom code.

```
FORM zf_build_event_table USING lt_events TYPE slis_t_event.
  DATA: ls_event TYPE slis_alv_event.

  CALL FUNCTION 'REUSE_ALV_EVENTS_GET'
    EXPORTING
      i_list_type = 4                    "for REUSE_ALV_GRID_DISPLAY
    IMPORTING
      et_events   = lt_events.

  READ TABLE lt_events WITH KEY name = slis_ev_user_command
    INTO ls_event.
  IF sy-subrc = 0.
    MOVE gc_formname_com TO ls_event-form.
    MODIFY lt_events FROM ls_event INDEX sy-tabix.
  ENDIF.
  READ TABLE lt_events WITH KEY name = slis_ev_top_of_page
    INTO ls_event.
  IF sy-subrc = 0.
    MOVE gc_formname_top TO ls_event-form.
    MODIFY lt_events FROM ls_event INDEX sy-tabix.
  ENDIF.

* add incremental event to table for focus change functionality
  CLEAR ls_event.
  ls_event-name = slis_ev_data_changed.
  ls_event-FORM = 'ZF_DATA_CHANGED'.
  APPEND ls_event TO lt_events.
ENDFORM.
```

Figure 8.34: Add data_changed to existing event table (FM)

lvc_s_glay-edt_cll_cb must be X to use data_changed

With the function module technique, the DATA_CHANGED functionality is only accessible and triggered when LVC_S_GLAY-EDT_CLL_CB is set to X (Figure 8.32) and passed in the I_GRID_SETTINGS parameter in the ALV function module call (Figure 8.43).

Tables	Table Contents		

Table   LT_EVENTS

Attributes   Standard [19x2(120)]

Insert Column

Row	NAME [C(30)]	FORM [C(30)]
1	CALLER_EXIT	
2	USER_COMMAND	ZF_USER_COMMAND
3	TOP_OF_PAGE	ZF_TOP_OF_PAGE
4	TOP_OF_COVERPAGE	
5	END_OF_COVERPAGE	
6	FOREIGN_TOP_OF_PAGE	
7	FOREIGN_END_OF_PAGE	
8	PF_STATUS_SET	
9	LIST_MODIFY	
10	TOP_OF_LIST	
11	END_OF_PAGE	
12	END_OF_LIST	
13	AFTER_LINE_OUTPUT	
14	BEFORE_LINE_OUTPUT	
15	REPREP_SEL_MODIFY	
16	SUBTOTAL_TEXT	
17	GROUPLEVEL_CHANGE	
18	CONTEXT_MENU	
19	DATA_CHANGED	ZF_DATA_CHANGED

Figure 8.35: Data_changed is an incremental event (FM)

Create a new subroutine called ZF_DATA_CHANGED (Figure 8.36) to access the ABAP objects class CL_ALV_CHANGED_DATA_PROTOCOL. The FIELD-SYMBOL and ASSIGN statements are used to access the content of modified rows of the ALV. In our program, only single rows are modifiable so there will only be one row to process, the row whose comment field the user just changed (Figure 8.37). Loop through <FT_OUTPUT> and populate a structure that matches the database table ZKKDEMO. Use the MODIFY command to write the record to the database table ZKKDEMO. (MODIFY updates an existing record or adds a record if it is not found.)

```
*----------------------------------------------------------
FORM zf_data_changed USING lo_data_changed
        TYPE REF TO cl_alv_changed_data_protocol.

 DATA: ls_output  TYPE lty_output,
       ls_zkkdemo TYPE zkkdemo.

 FIELD-SYMBOLS: <ft_output> TYPE tt_output.

 ASSIGN lo_data_changed->mp_mod_rows->* TO <ft_output>.

 LOOP AT <ft_output> INTO ls_output.
   CLEAR ls_zkkdemo.
   ls_zkkdemo-agencynum = ls_output-agencynum.
   ls_zkkdemo-carrid    = ls_output-carrid.
   ls_zkkdemo-connid    = ls_output-connid.
   ls_zkkdemo-fldate    = ls_output-fldate.
   ls_zkkdemo-bookid    = ls_output-bookid.
   ls_zkkdemo-zcomment  = ls_output-zcomment.

   MODIFY zkkdemo FROM ls_zkkdemo.
*  MODIFY will update an existing record or insert a new record
   IF sy-subrc NE 0.
     MESSAGE ID '00' TYPE 'I' NUMBER 001
       WITH 'The comment was not saved to table ZKKDEMO.'(021).
   ENDIF.
 ENDLOOP.
ENDFORM.
```

Figure 8.36: Data_changed subroutine called when cell focus changes (FM)

The record layout of <FT_OUTPUT> matches LTY_OUTPUT with the exception of the first field called ROW (Figure 8.37).

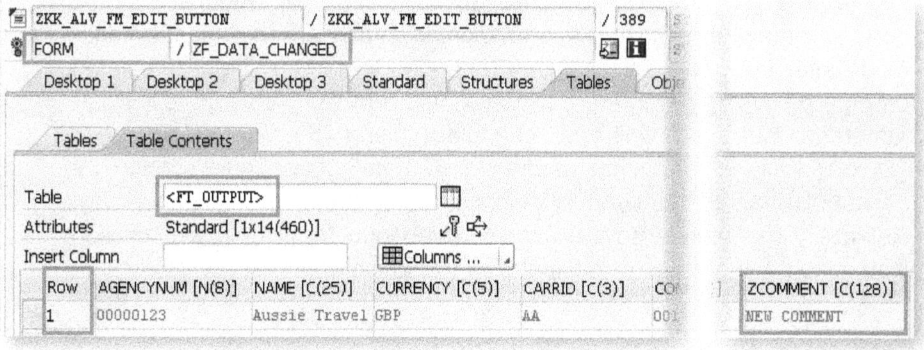

Figure 8.37: User-modified row in debugger (FM)

You may recall that we activated column width optimization in the layout structure of this program (Chapter 4.4). When this ALV grid is initially displayed, it is summarized. The COMMENT column has no content at a summary level so the narrow display is desirable (Figure 8.38). Unfortunately, when the user clicks on the EDIT COMMENT button to switch to a detail display, the Comment column does not widen. Fix that by respecifying the Comment field output length in ZF_USER_COMMAND (Figure 8.39).

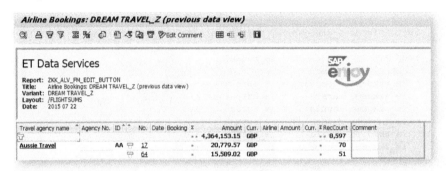

Figure 8.38: Default column width optimization is not a problem until switched to detail display (FM)

Edit the ZF_USER_COMMAND subroutine, adding the new local data declarations (Figure 8.39). The function code of the EDIT COMMENT toolbar button is NOTE (Figure 6.115) so add the WHEN 'NOTE' logic to the CASE statement. Set the GV_EDIT_FLAG to X, indicating that the user has switched to edit mode. For this exercise, code a one-time transition from display to edit mode. (If required, you can instead write code that allows the user to toggle back and forth between edit and display modes.)

The REUSE_ALV_GRID_LAYOUT_INFO_GET function call (Figure 8.39) is used to retrieve the current ALV settings. It returns any changes the user made after the grid was displayed (changes in sorting, filtering, column order, etc.). Many parameters are available, but limit retrieval to the parameters that you will be changing using the REUSE_ALV_GRID _LAYOUT_INFO_SET function module: field catalog and grid scroll. The LS_SCROLL values retrieved are applicable to the summarized display. Replace those values so the user can continue from their last position instead of having to scroll to it in the re-displayed detail list.

GRID or LIST versions of GET/SET function modules?

When using REUSE_ALV_GRID_DISPLAY for an ALV call, use REUSE_ALV_GRID_LAYOUT_INFO_GET/SET. When using REUSE_ALV_LIST_DISPLAY for an ALV call, use REUSE_ALV_LIST_LAYOUT_INFO_GET/SET.

"Layout" in these function module names

The GET/SET function modules described here can be used to access many properties of the ALV grid (layout, field catalog, sort, filter, variant, grid scroll, etc.) not just layout settings. The usage of the word "layout" in the function module name should not be taken literally. This varies from the ALV control framework program (Chapter 8.3.2) where separate method calls are used for each set of properties.

Three field catalog table settings will be populated and passed in the set function module: DO_SUM, OUTPUTLEN, and EDIT. To re-display the data at a detail level for editing, clear the field catalog DO_SUM setting on any fields set for summing, not just the ones set by the developer (Figure 8.39). On only the editable field ZCOMMENT, set the EDIT flag to X and the OUTPUTLEN to 128. By passing the output length again, you fix the too-narrow comment column, a result of optimization done for the initial summarized display (Figure 8.38).

Transporting and where clauses in the modify statement

Use the TRANSPORTING and WHERE clauses in your MODIFY statements to change only the particular fields you need to change. Other values will remain as they were.

The user's cursor position in the ALV grid when they clicked on the EDIT COMMENT button is available to us in the SLIS_SELFIELD structure. If they were on a detail line, you can move that detail row to the top of the re-displayed grid (Figure 8.39). Take care when transferring tabindex (row number) and fieldname from LS_SELFIELD to LS_SCROLL (a nested structure). The syntax to reach the lower level of the nested structure

LS_SCROLL requires two hyphens: LS_SCROLL-S_ROW_INFO-INDEX and LS_SCROLL-S_COL_INFO-FIELDNAME. (Note: if the user's cursor was on a summary line, the grid will re-display on the first record.)

```
FORM zf_user_command USING lv_ucomm      LIKE sy-ucomm
                            ls_selfield TYPE slis_selfield.
  DATA: ls_stravelag     TYPE stravelag,
        lt_stravelag     TYPE TABLE OF stravelag,
        lt_spfli         TYPE TABLE OF spfli,
        lt_output_temp TYPE TABLE OF lty_output.
  DATA: lt_fieldcat      TYPE slis_t_fieldcat_alv,
        ls_fieldcat      TYPE slis_fieldcat_alv,
        lv_answer        TYPE c,
        ls_scroll        TYPE lvc_s_scrl.          "nested structure

  CASE lv_ucomm.
    WHEN 'NOTE'.                       "toolbar button clicked
      gv_edit_flag = 'X'.             "flag to hide button after use
      CALL FUNCTION 'REUSE_ALV_GRID_LAYOUT_INFO_GET'
        IMPORTING
          ET_FIELDCAT               = lt_fieldcat
          ES_GRID_SCROLL            = ls_scroll
        EXCEPTIONS
          NO_INFOS                  = 1
          PROGRAM_ERROR             = 2
          OTHERS                    = 3.
      IF sy-subrc <> 0.
        MESSAGE ID '00' TYPE 'I' NUMBER 001
          WITH 'REUSE_ALV_GRID_LAYOUT_INFO_GET error' (027).
      ENDIF.

      ls_fieldcat-do_sum = ' '.
      MODIFY lt_fieldcat FROM ls_fieldcat TRANSPORTING do_sum
        WHERE do_sum = 'X'.              "any summed field
      ls_fieldcat-edit      = 'X'.
      ls_fieldcat-outputlen = 128.
      MODIFY lt_fieldcat FROM ls_fieldcat TRANSPORTING edit outputlen
        WHERE fieldname = 'ZCOMMENT'.

      clear ls_scroll.            "important to clear rowtype content
      ls_scroll-s_row_info-index     = ls_selfield-tabindex.
      ls_scroll-s_col_info-fieldname = ls_selfield-fieldname.

      CALL FUNCTION 'REUSE_ALV_GRID_LAYOUT_INFO_SET'
        EXPORTING
          IT_FIELDCAT               = lt_fieldcat
          IS_GRID_SCROLL            = ls_scroll.
      ls_selfield-col_stable = 'X'.
      ls_selfield-row_stable = 'X'.
      ls_selfield-refresh    = 'X'.
```

Figure 8.39: User command logic for edit button (FM)

The last two pieces of the WHEN 'NOTE' logic are the REUSE_ALV_GRID_LAYOUT_INFO_SET function call with the two parameters that we changed (field catalog and grid scroll) and the setting of the ROW_STABLE, COL_STABLE, and REFRESH fields of the SELFIELD structure (Figure 8.39).

It would be disruptive to inform the user every time they leave a comment cell that the change has been saved so that won't be done in the training scenario. Instead, you'll use the SAVE button (to provide a pop-up message to inform the user that changes were saved.

Add WHEN '&DATA_SAVE' logic to ZF_USER_COMMAND subroutine (Figure 8.40). Call the function module POPUP_TO_CONFIRM to inform the user that the comments have been saved and to give the option to continue or leave the program (Figure 8.41). (With proper error-handling in the ZF_DATA_CHANGED subroutine, any table update errors should have been communicated already.)

```
WHEN '&DATA_SAVE'.                      "user clicked Save icon
  CALL FUNCTION 'POPUP_TO_CONFIRM'
  EXPORTING
    TITLEBAR               =
    'Comments Saved to the ZKKDEMO Table' (022)
    text_question          =
    'Do you want to exit the program or continue working?' (023)
    text_button_1          = 'Exit' (024)
    text_button_2          = 'Continue' (025)
    default_button         = '1'
    display_cancel_button  = ' '
  IMPORTING
    answer                 = lv_answer.
  IF lv_answer = '1'.
    LEAVE PROGRAM.
  ENDIF.

WHEN '&IC1'.                            "hotspot was clicked
  do nothing if user clicks where no identifiable data value
  IF ls_selfield-VALUE IS INITIAL.
    RETURN.
  ENDIF.
  CASE ls_selfield-fieldname.
    WHEN 'AGENCYNUM'
      OR 'NAME'.                        "display STRAVELAG details
```

Figure 8.40: Save button logic and selfield logic move in zf_user_command (FM)

If the user clicks EXIT, the LEAVE PROGRAM command executes. If the user clicks CONTINUE, the user can continue working in the ALV (Figure 8.41).

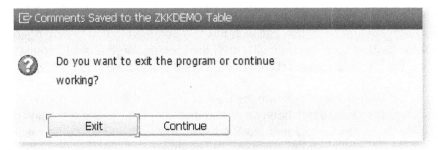

Figure 8.41: User command pop-up for &data_save action (FM)

One last change in ZF_USER_COMMAND (Figure 8.40) is moving the evaluation of SLIS_SELFIELD-VALUE from outside the case statement to inside
the WHEN '&IC1' case statement since it is only relevant to the hotspot
logic.

The ZF_SET_PFSTATUS subroutine is executed before every re-display of
the ALV grid (Figure 8.42). Because the EDIT COMMENT button is being
used only for a one-time switch to edit mode, it could be confusing to
users to retain the button on the toolbar after that has occurred. You can
easily hide the button by checking the GV_EDIT_FLAG variable that was
set in ZF_USER_COMMAND (Figure 8.39) and appending the function code
NOTE to the exclude table.

```
*-------------------------------------------------------------------
FORM zf_set_pfstatus USING lt_exclude TYPE slis_t_extab.
  DATA: ls_exclude TYPE slis_extab.

* add to the exclude table pre-populated by SAP on each pass
  ls_exclude-fcode = '&ABC'.
  APPEND ls_exclude TO lt_exclude.
  ls_exclude-fcode = '&GRAPH'.
  APPEND ls_exclude TO lt_exclude.

  IF gv_edit_flag = 'X'.                   "edit mode
    ls_exclude-fcode = 'NOTE'.
    APPEND ls_exclude TO lt_exclude.
  ENDIF.

  SET PF-STATUS 'ZCUSTOM1' EXCLUDING lt_exclude.

ENDFORM.
```

Figure 8.42: Remove new edit button from toolbar after switch (FM)

The only change needed in ZF_DISPLAY_ALV is the addition of the
GS_GLAY structure to the ALV call (Figure 8.43).

```
*-----------------------------------------------------------------
FORM zf_display_alv.

  CALL FUNCTION 'REUSE_ALV_GRID_DISPLAY'
    EXPORTING
      i_callback_program       = sy-repid
      i_callback_pf_status_set = gc_formname_pf
      is_layout                = gs_layout
      it_fieldcat              = gt_fieldcat[]
      i_grid_settings          = gs_glay
      it_sort                  = gt_sort[]
      i_save                   = gv_save
      is_variant               = gs_variant
      it_events                = gt_events[]
    TABLES
      t_outtab                 = gt_output
    EXCEPTIONS
      program_error            = 1
      OTHERS                   = 2.

  IF sy-subrc <> 0.
    MESSAGE ID '00' TYPE 'I' NUMBER 001
      WITH 'REUSE_ALV_GRID_DISPLAY call error--'(008) sy-subrc.
    RETURN.
  ENDIF.
ENDFORM.
```

Figure 8.43: ALV call with i_grid_settings structure passed (FM)

In edit mode, the ALV grid displays with these changes: SAVE button enabled, REFRESH button added to the ALV application toolbar, EDIT COM-
MENT button removed, row selection column added, and editable field(s)
ready for input (Figure 8.44).

Figure 8.44: Comment column widened and button absent (FM)

8.3.2 ALV control framework

If you have chosen not to create and update the custom table ZKKDEMO for this exercise, you can use CHAR0128 as the type when you add the new field ZCOMMENT at the end of LTY_OUTPUT (Figure 8.45). Other data additions include table type TT_OUTPUT based on type LTY_OUTPUT. This table type will be used in a new DATA_CHANGED method (Figure 8.47). An internal table and structure matching the database table ZKKDEMO are added for retrieval of existing comments. The GV_EDIT_FLAG variable will be used this time to indicate when the EDIT COMMENT button has been clicked so that we stop adding it to the application toolbar on subsequent re-displays.

```
TYPES: BEGIN OF lty_output,
          agencynum TYPE stravelag-agencynum,  "agency number
          name      TYPE stravelag-name,       "agency name
          currency  TYPE stravelag-CURRENCY,   "agency currency
          carrid    TYPE sbook-carrid,         "booked carrier
          connid    TYPE sbook-connid,         "booked connection
          fldate    TYPE sbook-fldate,         "booked date
          bookid    TYPE sbook-bookid,         "booking ID
          forcuram  TYPE sbook-forcuram,       "price in foreign currency
          forcurkey TYPE sbook-forcurkey,      "foreign currency key
          carrname  TYPE scarr-carrname,       "carrier name
          loccuram  TYPE sbook-loccuram,       "price in airline curr
          loccurkey TYPE sbook-loccurkey,      "local currency of airline
          count     TYPE I,                    "for record count
          zcomment  TYPE zkkdemo-zcomment,     "for notes up to 128 chars
       END OF lty_output.

TYPES: tt_output   TYPE STANDARD TABLE OF lty_output.

DATA: gs_layout    TYPE lvc_s_layo,           "layout params
      gs_output    TYPE lty_output,           "local structure (line)
      gt_output    TYPE STANDARD TABLE OF lty_output,
      gt_sort      TYPE lvc_t_sort,
      gt_fieldcat  TYPE lvc_t_fcat,           "table
      gt_exclude   TYPE ui_functions,
      gt_zkkdemo   TYPE STANDARD TABLE OF zkkdemo,
      gs_zkkdemo   TYPE zkkdemo,
      gv_edit_flag TYPE c.
```

Figure 8.45: Data additions for edit exercise (CF)

Five events will be handled in this revised program (Table 8.3), but only DATA_CHANGED is new. The methods for USER_COMMAND and TOOLBAR will be changed, as well. (If you wish to compare to the REUSE_ALV_GRID _DISPLAY exercise, see Table 8.2.)

Event (CF)	Our setup	Activities handled
top_of_page	event_handler	text and logo
hotspot_click	event_handler	hotspot pop-ups
user_command	event_handler	Edit Comment button (new)
toolbar	event_handler	button addition (conditional)
data_changed (new)	event_handler	database table updates

Table 8.3: New event and several event revisions (CF)

Define a new method based on event DATA_CHANGED (Figure 8.46). The DATA_CHANGED event is triggered when the user clicks on the CHECK EN-TRIES button or on the REFRESH button on the application toolbar. Later, you'll see how to register other triggers for this event (Figure 8.57).

```
* * * * * * *
CLASS lcl_event_handler DEFINITION.
  PUBLIC SECTION.
  METHODS:
    data_changed     FOR EVENT data_changed  OF cl_gui_alv_grid
      IMPORTING er_data_changed,
    toolbar_add      FOR EVENT toolbar       OF cl_gui_alv_grid
      IMPORTING e_object
                e_interactive,
    user_command_alv FOR EVENT user_command  OF cl_gui_alv_grid
      IMPORTING e_ucomm,
    top_of_page      FOR EVENT top_of_page   OF cl_gui_alv_grid
      IMPORTING e_dyndoc_id,
    hotspot_click    FOR EVENT hotspot_click OF cl_gui_alv_grid
      IMPORTING e_row_id
                e_column_id.
  ENDCLASS.
```

Figure 8.46: Data_changed method, part 1 (CF)

In the implementation of the new method DATA_CHANGED (Figure 8.47), the FIELD-SYMBOL and ASSIGN statements are used to access the content of modified rows of the ALV. In our program, only single rows are modifi-able so there will only be one row to process, the row whose comment field the user just changed (Figure 8.48). Loop through <FT_OUTPUT> and populate a structure that matches the database table ZKKDEMO. Use the MODIFY command to write the record to the database table ZKKDEMO. (MODIFY will update an existing record or add a record if not found.)

```
********
CLASS lcl_event_handler IMPLEMENTATION.
  METHOD data_changed.
*    triggered by Check Entries, Refresh icons, and user leaving cell
    DATA: ls_output   TYPE lty_output,
          ls_zkkdemo TYPE zkkdemo,
          ls_modif   TYPE lvc_s_modi.

    FIELD-SYMBOLS: <ft_output> TYPE tt_output.

    ASSIGN er_data_changed->mp_mod_rows->* TO <ft_output>.
    LOOP AT <ft_output> INTO ls_output.
      CLEAR ls_zkkdemo.
      ls_zkkdemo-agencynum = ls_output-agencynum.
      ls_zkkdemo-carrid    = ls_output-carrid.
      ls_zkkdemo-connid    = ls_output-connid.
      ls_zkkdemo-fldate    = ls_output-fldate.
      ls_zkkdemo-bookid    = ls_output-bookid.
      ls_zkkdemo-zcomment  = ls_output-zcomment.

      MODIFY zkkdemo FROM ls_zkkdemo.
*      MODIFY will update an existing record or insert a new record
      IF sy-subrc NE 0.
        LOOP AT er_data_changed->mt_mod_cells INTO ls_modif.
          CALL METHOD er_data_changed->add_protocol_entry
          EXPORTING
            i_msgid = '00' i_msgno = '001'  i_msgty = 'W'
        i_msgv1 = 'The comment was not saved to table ZKKDEMO:' (021)
            i_msgv2 = ls_modif-VALUE
            i_fieldname = ls_modif-fieldname.
        ENDLOOP.
        CALL METHOD er_data_changed->display_protocol.
      ENDIF.
    ENDLOOP.
  ENDMETHOD.
```

Figure 8.47: Data_changed method, part 2 (CF)

The record layout of <FT_OUTPUT> matches LTY_OUTPUT with the exception of the first field called ROW (Figure 8.48).

You may recall that we activated column width optimization in the layout structure of this program (Chapter 4.4). When the ALV grid is initially displayed, it is summarized (Figure 8.49). The comment column has no content at a summary level so the narrow display is desirable. Unfortunately, when the user clicks on the EDIT COMMENT button to switch to a detail display, the comment column does not widen. You'll fix that by re-specifying the comment field output length in the USER_COMMAND_ALV method (Figure 8.52).

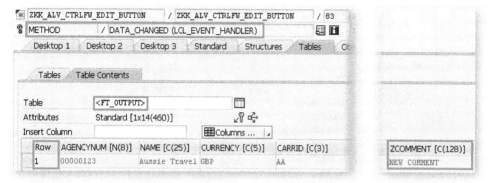

Figure 8.48: User-modified row in debugger (CF)

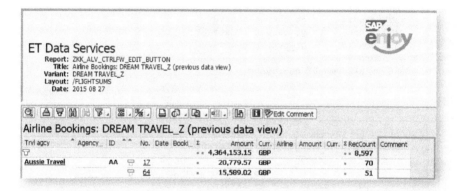

Figure 8.49: Default custom width optimization is not a problem until switched to detail display (CF)

To retrieve any existing comments from the ZKKDEMO table and display them in the ALV grid, you'll need to add logic after the population of GT_OUTPUT (Figure 8.50). The FOR ALL ENTRIES IN syntax can be used because you have first verified that GT_OUTPUT has content by evaluating the result of the DESCRIBE TABLE command.

If relevant records are retrieved into GT_ZKKDEMO, you loop through GT_ZKKDEMO to update GT_OUTPUT (Figure 8.50). (GT_ZKKDEMO is most likely the smaller of the two tables.) If no relevant comments were retrieved from ZKKDEMO, no messaging is required.

Set the GV_EDIT_FLAG to a blank space to signify display mode for initial display (Figure 8.50). The flag will be used in ZF_USER_COMMAND_ALV and ZF_TOOLBAR_ADD to hide the EDIT COMMENT button after its first use.

```
DESCRIBE TABLE gt_output LINES gv_lines.
IF gv_lines NE 0.                        "data was retrieved

  CLEAR gs_output.
  gs_output-COUNT = 1.
  MODIFY gt_output FROM gs_output
    TRANSPORTING COUNT WHERE NOT agencynum IS INITIAL.
  SORT gt_output BY agencynum
                    carrid
                    connid
                    fldate
                    bookid.
```

```
SELECT * FROM zkkdemo
  INTO TABLE gt_zkkdemo
  FOR ALL ENTRIES IN gt_output
  WHERE agencynum = gt_output-agencynum
    AND carrid    = gt_output-carrid
    AND connid    = gt_output-connid
    AND fldate    = gt_output-fldate
    AND bookid    = gt_output-bookid.
IF sy-subrc = 0.                         "comments found
  SORT gt_zkkdemo BY agencynum
                     carrid
                     connid
                     fldate
                     bookid.
  LOOP AT gt_zkkdemo INTO gs_zkkdemo.     "smaller table
    READ TABLE gt_output INTO gs_output
      WITH KEY agencynum = gs_zkkdemo-agencynum
               carrid    = gs_zkkdemo-carrid
               connid    = gs_zkkdemo-connid
               fldate    = gs_zkkdemo-fldate
               bookid    = gs_zkkdemo-bookid.
    IF sy-subrc = 0.
      gs_output-zcomment = gs_zkkdemo-zcomment.
      MODIFY gt_output FROM gs_output INDEX sy-tabix
        TRANSPORTING zcomment.
    ENDIF.
  ENDLOOP.
ENDIF.
gv_edit_flag = ' '.       "indicates display mode for start
```

Figure 8.50: Retrieval of comments from zkkdemo table (CF)

The ALV application toolbar was set as interactive using SET_TOOLBAR _INTERACTIVE in Chapter 6.8.2 so the ZF_TOOLBAR_ADD subroutine is executed on each re-display of the ALV grid (Figure 8.51). Because the EDIT COMMENT button is being used in this exercise for a one-time switch to edit mode, it could be confusing to users to retain the button on the toolbar after that has occurred. You can easily hide the button by check-

248

ing the GV_EDIT_FLAG variable set in ZF_USER_COMMAND_ALV (Figure 8.52).

Sometimes removing means "not adding"

 Use break-points in the ABAP debugger to familiarize yourself with the behavior of your programs. You might think that once you have added a button to the toolbar, you must call a separate method to remove it or must change the exclude table. In the ALV control framework, the standard toolbar is being re-created with the new button on each re-display because we have set it interactive (Figure 8.57). By adding the IF statement (Figure 8.51), you will stop adding the button to the toolbar after the user has clicked it once, as needed in the training scenario. If you prefer, you can change the position of the IF statement so that the button continues to be added, but is grayed out (disabled = 'X').

```
*----------------------------------------------------------------
FORM zf_toolbar_add USING lo_object
                 TYPE REF TO cl_alv_event_toolbar_set.

  DATA: ls_toolbar TYPE stb_button.
  IF gv_edit_flag <> 'X'.       "flag is set once in zf_user_command_alv
*    add button on each re-display UNLESS user has already used it
    CLEAR ls_toolbar.
    ls_toolbar-function  = 'NOTE'.                "own fcode for logic
    ls_toolbar-icon      = icon_annotation.       "from ICON include
    ls_toolbar-quickinfo = 'Add note to record'(022).
    ls_toolbar-butn_type = 0.                     "basic button, not menu
    ls_toolbar-disabled  = ' '.
    ls_toolbar-text      = 'Edit Comment'(023).   "label on button
    APPEND ls_toolbar TO lo_object->mt_toolbar.
  ENDIF.
ENDFORM.
```

Figure 8.51: Stop adding new button after first use (CF)

In Chapter 6.8.2, you inserted a placeholder into a subroutine called ZF_USER_COMMAND_ALV for a new toolbar button (Figure 6.130). Now, you will add the logic that should execute when that button is clicked.

1. Fill a variable to indicate that the button has been clicked.

2. GET the current field catalog and cursor settings.

3. Modify a few of the retrieved settings in order to present detail records with the desired appearance.

4. SET the changes, including the cursor position.

5. Refresh the table display.

Method user_command_alv and zm_user_command_9100

Don't be confused by the two similarly named sections of code in this program. The PAI module called ZM_USER_COMMAND_9100 manages the top row of function keys you configured as BACK, EXIT, and CANCEL in Figure 3.26. The USER_COMMAND event logic coded in ZF_USER_COMMAND_ALV relates to the ALV application toolbar buttons.

Add the local data declarations to the ZF_USER_COMMAND_ALV subroutine (Figure 8.52). The function code of the EDIT COMMENT toolbar button is NOTE (Figure 6.129). In the WHEN 'NOTE' portion of the CASE statement, set the GV_EDIT_FLAG to X to denote that the user has switched to edit mode. (For this exercise, you will code a one-time transition from display to edit mode.)

The methods GET_FRONTEND_FIELDCATALOG and GET_SELECTED_CELLS are used to retrieve the ALV settings of interest to us (Figure 8.52). Other GET/SET methods are available, but these will meet our needs. The returned LT_FIELDCAT table will include any changes that the user may have made after the grid was displayed and will give us a starting point for our modifications. The LT_CELLS table will allow us to re-display the editable grid so that the user can continue from their last position instead of having to scroll to it in the detail list.

ALV FM and ALV control framework are different

Don't assume that code you use in a function module ALV program is also necessary in an ALV control framework program (or vice versa). Test and use the debugger as you write your code, then take appropriate action based on your observations.

Three field catalog table settings will be populated and passed in the set function module: DO_SUM, EDIT, and OUTPUTLEN. To re-display the data at a detail level for editing, clear the field catalog DO_SUM setting on any fields set for summing, not just the ones set by the developer (Figure 8.52). On only the editable field ZCOMMENT, set the EDIT flag to X and the OUTPUTLEN to 128. By passing the output length again, you will fix the too-narrow comment column, a result of optimization done for the initial summarized display (Figure 8.49).

```
*-------------------------------------------------------------------------
FORM zf_user_command_alv USING lv_ucomm TYPE sy-ucomm.
  DATA: lt_fieldcat TYPE lvc_t_fcat,
        ls_fieldcat TYPE lvc_s_fcat,
        ls_stable   TYPE lvc_s_stbl,
        lt_cells    TYPE lvc_t_cell,
        ls_cells    TYPE lvc_s_cell,    "nested structure
        ls_row_id   TYPE lvc_s_row,
        ls_col_id   TYPE lvc_s_col.

  CASE lv_ucomm.
    WHEN 'NOTE'.                   "only executes once, then we omit button
      gv_edit_flag = 'X'.          "flag to prevent button re-add after use

      CALL METHOD grid1->get_frontend_fieldcatalog
        IMPORTING
          et_fieldcatalog = lt_fieldcat.

      CALL METHOD grid1->get_selected_cells
        IMPORTING
          et_cell = lt_cells.
*-------------------------------------------------------------------------
      ls_fieldcat-do_sum   = ' '.
      MODIFY lt_fieldcat FROM ls_fieldcat TRANSPORTING do_sum
        WHERE do_sum = 'X'.                    "any summed field

      ls_fieldcat-edit      = 'X'.
      ls_fieldcat-outputlen = 128.
      MODIFY lt_fieldcat FROM ls_fieldcat TRANSPORTING edit outputlen
        WHERE fieldname = 'ZCOMMENT'.
```

Figure 8.52: User command logic for edit button, part 1 (CF)

Now that the field catalog settings have been retrieved and modified, they are set by calling method SET_FRONTEND_FIELDCATALOG (Figure 8.53).

The user's cursor position in the ALV grid when they clicked on the EDIT COMMENT button was retrieved into LT_CELLS (one row was retrieved) and can now be used to move that detail row to the top of the re-displayed grid using the SET_SCROLL_INFO_VIA_ID method (Figure 8.53). Take care when transferring the index (row number) and fieldname from LS_CELLS (nested structure LVC_S_CELL) to LS_ROW_ID and LS_COL_ID. The syntax to reach the lower level of the nested structure LS_CELLS requires two hyphens: LS_CELLS-ROW_ID-INDEX and LS_CELLS-COL_ID-FIELDNAME.

Finally, signify that this column and row should be retained (by passing XX in LS_STABLE) and refresh/re-display the grid (Figure 8.53).

```
*------------------------------------------------------------
      CALL METHOD grid1->set_frontend_fieldcatalog
        EXPORTING
          it_fieldcatalog = lt_fieldcat.

      READ table lt_cells INTO ls_cells INDEX 1.
      IF sy-subrc = 0.
        ls_row_id-index      = ls_cells-row_id-index.
        ls_col_id-fieldname = ls_cells-col_id-fieldname.
        CALL METHOD grid1->set_scroll_info_via_id
          EXPORTING
            is_row_info = ls_row_id
            is_col_info = ls_col_id.
      ENDIF.
*------------------------------------------------------------
      ls_stable-row = 'X'.
      ls_stable-col = 'X'.
      CALL METHOD grid1->refresh_table_display
        EXPORTING
          is_stable = ls_stable.
  ENDCASE.
ENDFORM.
```

Figure 8.53: User command logic for edit button, part 2 (CF)

The new ZCOMMENT field needs to be added to the end of the field catalog table in ZF_BUILD_FIELDCATALOG (Figure 8.54). To provide a more meaningful label on the ALV column, populate the COLTEXT instead of providing a REF_TABLE value of ZKKDEMO. Provide the EDIT parameter with a blank space value because the ALV grid will not be editable on initial display.

```
  CLEAR ls_fieldcat.
  ls_fieldcat-fieldname = 'ZCOMMENT'.
  ls_fieldcat-outputlen = 128.
  ls_fieldcat-datatype  = 'CHAR'.
  ls_fieldcat-coltext   = 'Comment'.
  ls_fieldcat-edit      = ' '.
  APPEND ls_fieldcat TO lt_fieldcat.
ENDFORM.
```

Figure 8.54: New field added to field catalog with edit parameter set for display (CF)

In edit mode, the ALV grid displays with these changes: row selection column added, editable field(s) ready for input, and new ALV application toolbar buttons visible (Figure 8.55).

- ▶ Check Entries and Refresh buttons
- ▶ Cell-focused buttons: Cut, Copy Text, Insert, and Undo
- ▶ Row-focused buttons: Append Row, Insert Row, Delete Row, and Duplicate Row

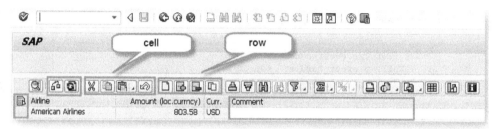

Figure 8.55: Row-focused buttons to be excluded (CF)

Since this program will not be used to remove records from ZKKDEMO or to insert records, the row-focused buttons need to be excluded (Figure 8.58). Exactly as was done in Chapter 6.7.2, add the buttons to be omitted from the ALV application toolbar to an exclusion table (Figure 8.56).

```
*---------------------------------------------------------------
FORM zf_build_exclude_table USING lt_exclude TYPE ui_functions.
  DATA: ls_exclude TYPE ui_func.
* restrict user to changes, no row adds or deletes
  ls_exclude = cl_gui_alv_grid=>MC_FC_LOC_COPY_ROW.
  APPEND ls_exclude TO lt_exclude.
  ls_exclude = cl_gui_alv_grid=>MC_FC_LOC_DELETE_ROW.
  APPEND ls_exclude TO lt_exclude.
  ls_exclude = cl_gui_alv_grid=>MC_FC_LOC_APPEND_ROW.
  APPEND ls_exclude TO lt_exclude.
  ls_exclude = cl_gui_alv_grid=>MC_FC_LOC_INSERT_ROW.
  APPEND ls_exclude TO lt_exclude.
  ls_exclude = cl_gui_alv_grid=>MC_FC_LOC_MOVE_ROW.
  APPEND ls_exclude TO lt_exclude.
  SORT lt_exclude.
  DELETE ADJACENT DUPLICATES FROM lt_exclude COMPARING table_line.
ENDFORM.
```

Figure 8.56: Exclude table for ALV method call (CF)

253

The DATA_CHANGED event is triggered by default when the user clicks on the CHECK ENTRIES button or the REFRESH button in the ALV application toolbar. We can register other triggers, as well (Figure 8.57):

▶ MC_EVT_MODIFIED when cursor is moved from the modified cell

▶ MC_EVT_ENTER for user pressing ⌈Enter⌋ on the keyboard

In the ZM_STATUS_9100 module, we have registered only the modified cell edit event (Figure 8.57). The final change is to set the handler for the new DATA_CHANGED event.

```
    CALL METHOD grid1->register_edit_event
        EXPORTING
            i_event_id = cl_gui_alv_grid=>mc_evt_modified.   "cell leave
*   can repeat/replace previous method call with mc_evt_enter


    CREATE OBJECT g_event_handler.
    SET HANDLER g_event_handler->top_of_page        FOR grid1.
    SET HANDLER g_event_handler->hotspot_click       FOR grid1.
    SET HANDLER g_event_handler->toolbar_add         FOR grid1.
    SET HANDLER g_event_handler->user_command_alv    FOR grid1.
    SET HANDLER g_event_handler->data_changed        FOR grid1.

*   to raise the toolbar event (our method toolbar_add)
    CALL METHOD grid1->set_toolbar_interactive.
```

Figure 8.57: Module zm_status_9100 additions (CF)

After the user clicks on the EDIT COMMENT button, the ALV grid displays as shown (Figure 8.58).

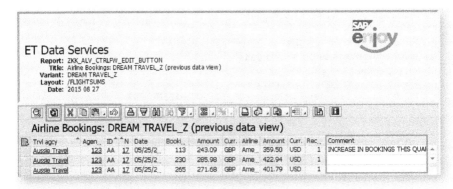

Figure 8.58: Comment column widened and buttons absent (CF)

Enabling the Save button in the ALV control framework programs

 Unlike the function module versions of the programs in this chapter, the SAVE button is not enabled by default when using the ALV control framework technique. If you do wish to enable the SAVE button, use transaction code se80 to edit the GUI status, adding a label to the diskette function key (Figure 3.26), as you did for BACK, CANCEL, and EXIT. After saving and activating, add your custom logic within the CASE statement in the ZM_USER_COMMAND_9100 module (Figure 3.21).

Source code for final ALV control framework program

 The source code of the final example program (ZKK_ALV_CTRLFW_EDIT_BUTTON) is available at https://espresso-tutorials.com/_ABAP_ALV.php

8.4 Summary

Chapter 8 introduced techniques that make an SAP List Viewer editable.

Key points:

▶ Writing cell-level edit logic

▶ Adding logic to insert or modify records in a table based on user input

▶ Retrieving grid configuration information (layout and sort state, for instance) after initial display in order to modify it for re-display

▶ Retaining the user's cursor position

▶ Enabling the edit functionality two different ways: based on selection-screen choice or on toolbar button click

▶ Working with the set_toolbar_interactive method

Table 8.4 provides a comparison.

	Function Module reuse_alv_grid_display	ALV Control Framework set_table_for_first_display
Column editability	edit = 'X' in field catalog	edit = 'X' in field catalog, ready_for_input method (optional, 1 for yes, 0 for no)
Change awareness and values	i_grid_settings parameter (lvc_s_glay-edt_cll_cb), data_changed event	data_changed event, register_edit_event method (optional)
Re-display of toolbar	pf_status_set event	toolbar event, set_toolbar_interactive method
Toolbar exclusions	it_excluding parameter, pf_status_set event	it_toolbar_excluding parameter, toolbar event
Toolbar additions	GUI status copy/modification	toolbar event
Change from summary to detail	do_sum = space in field catalog	do_sum = space in field catalog
Format changes	reuse_alv_grid_layout_info_get, reuse_alv_grid_layout_info_set function modules	get_frontend_* and set_frontend_* methods
Retain cursor position	slis_selfield and is_grid_scroll parameter	get_selected_cells and set_scroll_info_via_id methods
Refresh grid	slis_selfield-col_stable = 'X', slis_selfield-row_stable = 'X', slis_selfield-refresh = 'X' in user_command event	is_stable-row = 'X', is_stable-col = 'X', refresh_table_display method in user_command event

Table 8.4: Editable ALV, comparison

9 Conclusion

Now, with greater awareness of how the SAP List Viewer has evolved over time and with examples of frequently requested features, you can approach assignments with more confidence. When coding a new ALV program, it is important to know how the report will be used. For instance, if it will be used primarily for strategic analysis, you might provide summarized views initially. If it will be used primarily for updating data, you might choose to display detail records initially. Using the examples in this book for guidance, you can accommodate both views with a single program.

When creating new SAP List Viewer programs, use object-oriented techniques rather than function module techniques. This book provides an introduction to object-oriented ALV featuring the ALV control framework technique.

Appendix

Comparison of some report types

The two **bold** report types are covered in this book.

Report Type	Sample Programs	Terminology
ALV with integrated data access (IDA)	SALV_IDA*	In-memory database, ABAP objects, CL_SALV_GUI_TABLE_IDA
ALV object model	SALV_DEMO*	ABAP objects, ALV wrapper, OM, CL_SALV_TABLE, CL_SALV_HIERSEQ_TABLE, CL_SALV_TREE
ALV control framework	**BCALV***	**ABAP objects, grid control, SET_TABLE_FOR_FIRST_DISPLAY, CL_GUI_ALV_GRID, LVC**
ALV grid FMs (not released)	**BALV***	**REUSE_ALV_GRID_DISPLAY, fullscreen grid, SLIS**
ALV list FMs (not released)	BALV*	REUSE_ALV_LIST_DISPLAY, REUSE_ALV_HIERSEQ_LIST _DISPLAY
Standard list	DEMO_LIST_OUTPUT	WRITE
Dialog-oriented	DEMO_DYNPRO-_TABCONT_LOOP_AT*	CONTROLS...TYPE TABLEVIEW/TABSTRIP, table controls, Screen Painter, module pools
Dynamic	DEMO_FREE-_SELECTIONS	field-symbols, CL_SALV_TABLE=>FACTORY, CL_ABAP_TYPEDESCR

Note—ALV is also available for Web Dynpro developers (ABAP and Java).

Resources

SAP Note 551605: ALV FAQ and release status.

259

Demo programs

- ▶ DEMO*
- ▶ BALV*
- ▶ BCALV*
- ▶ SALV_DEMO*

Programs

- ▶ SHOWICON (display symbols and names of icons used on SAP screens)
- ▶ RS_ABAP_SOURCE_SCAN (search programs for a text string)

Transactions

- ▶ ABAPDOCU (ABAP keyword documentation)
- ▶ BIBS (style guide and examples of user interface design elements, branches to "reuse library" and "controls library")
- ▶ DWDM (ABAP workbench demos)

Function modules

- ▶ REUSE_ALV*
- ▶ POPUP*

Sites

- ▶ help.sap.com (SAP Help Portal)
- ▶ scn.sap.com (SAP Community Network)

Acronyms

- ▶ ABAP—Advanced Business Application Programming
- ▶ ALV—ABAP List Viewer, SAP List Viewer
- ▶ CF—Control Framework
- ▶ FM—Function Module
- ▶ GUI—Graphical User Interface
- ▶ HTML—HyperText Markup Language
- ▶ IDA—Integrated Data Access
- ▶ IDES—Internet Demonstration and Evaluation System
- ▶ OM—Object Model
- ▶ SAP—Systems, Applications, and Products in data processing

You have finished the book.

Sign up for our newsletter!

Want to learn more about new e-books?

Get exclusive free downloads and SAP tips.

Sign up for our newsletter!

Please visit us at *newsletter.espresso-tutorials.com* to find out more.

A The Author

Kathi Kones has been working with SAP software since 1995.

After completing her computer science degree at Minnesota State University, Mankato, she was hired by General Mills, Inc., a global corporation that developed in-house talent and encouraged job changes within the company. She gained SAP R/2 and R/3 experience in the roles of functional analyst, ABAP developer, project manager, Finance master data migration specialist, and integration manager. She participated in four SAP implementations and worked in eight countries.

Kathi has most recently worked on SAP master data management projects as a consultant for ThreeBridge Solutions, LLC, Minneapolis, Minnesota.

B Index

▶ **Bold page numbers** for ALV control framework.

▶ *Italicized page numbers* for function module.

▶ Normal page numbers for general references.

C Disclaimer

This publication contains references to the products of SAP SE.

SAP, R/3, SAP NetWeaver, Duet, PartnerEdge, ByDesign, SAP BusinessObjects Explorer, StreamWork, and other SAP products and services mentioned herein as well as their respective logos are trademarks or registered trademarks of SAP SE in Germany and other countries.

Business Objects and the Business Objects logo, BusinessObjects, Crystal Reports, Crystal Decisions, Web Intelligence, Xcelsius, and other Business Objects products and services mentioned herein as well as their respective logos are trademarks or registered trademarks of Business Objects Software Ltd. Business Objects is an SAP company.

Sybase and Adaptive Server, iAnywhere, Sybase 365, SQL Anywhere, and other Sybase products and services mentioned herein as well as their respective logos are trademarks or registered trademarks of Sybase, Inc. Sybase is an SAP company.

SAP SE is neither the author nor the publisher of this publication and is not responsible for its content. SAP Group shall not be liable for errors or omissions with respect to the materials. The only warranties for SAP Group products and services are those that are set forth in the express warranty statements accompanying such products and services, if any. Nothing herein should be construed as constituting an additional warranty.

D   Credits

Vemuru, V. (2010, March 11). How to get the variant name when running the report in background from selection screen [Online forum].

Retrieved from
http://wiki.scn.sap.com/wiki/display/ABAP/How+to+get+the+variant+name+
when+running+the+report+in+background+from+selection+screen

More Espresso Tutorials Books

Boris Rubarth:

First Steps in ABAP®

- ▶ Step-by-Step instructions for beginners
- ▶ Comprehensive descriptions and code examples
- ▶ A guide to create your first ABAP application
- ▶ Tutorials that provide answers to the most commonly asked programming questions

http://5015.espresso-tutorials.com

Antje Kunz:

SAP® Legacy System Migration Workbench (LSMW)

- ▶ Data Migration (No Programming Required)
- ▶ SAP LSMW Explained in Depth
- ▶ Detailed Practical Examples
- ▶ Tips and Tricks for a Successful Data Migration

http://5051.espresso-tutorials.com

Darren Hague:

Universal Worklist with SAP NetWeaver® Portal

- ▶ Learn to easily execute business tasks using Universal Worklist
- ▶ Find in-depth advice on how to mak SAP workflows and alerts available
- ▶ Learn how to Include 3rd party workflows in SAP NetWeaver Portal

http://5076.espresso-tutorials.com

Michal Krawczyk:

SAP® SOA Integration

- ▶ Tools for Monitoring SOA Scenarios
- ▶ Forward Error Handling (FEH) and Error Conflict Handler (ECH)
- ▶ Configuration Tips
- ▶ SAP Application Interface Framework (AIF) Customization Best Practices
- ▶ Detailed Message Monitoring and Reprocessing Examples

http:/5077.espresso-tutorials.com

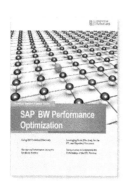

Shreekant Shiralkar & Deepak Sawant:

SAP® BW Performance Optimization

- ▶ Use BW statistics effectively
- ▶ Leverage tools for extraction, loading, modeling and reporting
- ▶ Monitor performance using the Workload Monitor & database statistics
- ▶ Use indexes to understand key elements of performance

http://5102.espresso-tutorials.com

Dominique Alfermann, Stefan Hartmann, Benedikt Engel:

SAP® HANA Advanced Modeling

- ▶ Data modeling guidelines and common test approaches
- ▶ Modular solutions to complex requirements
- ▶ Information view performance optimization
- ▶ Best practices and recommendations

http://4110.espresso-tutorials.com

www.ingramcontent.com/pod-product-compliance
Lightning Source LLC
Chambersburg PA
CBHW071107050326
40690CB00008B/1145